Scanning the Future

20 Eminent Thinkers on the World of Tomorrow

Edited and introduced by Yorick Blumenfeld

Thames & Hudson

A continuation of this copyright page is to be found on page 304 where acknowledgments are listed for the excerpts reprinted in this anthology

© 1999 Thames & Hudson Ltd, London
Introduction and Editor's introductory notes to the excerpts
in this anthology © 1999 Yorick Blumenfeld

First published in the United States of America in 1999 by Thames & Hudson Inc.,
500 Fifth Avenue, New York, New York 10110

Library of Congress Catalog Card Number 98-60037
ISBN 0-500-28045-2

Printed and bound in Slovenia

CONTENTS

PART III CHALLENGING PERSPECTIVES

Yorick Blumenfeld

INTRODUCTION

Prognostication is a speculative art form. It should be regarded as a stimulating challenge to the imagination. The aim of this anthology is to introduce some of the exciting possibilities for a new millennium, to inspire a curiosity about what the twenty-first century has to offer, and to suggest a variety of specific options for mankind. Constructive visions of the future are presented to reveal the abundance of potentialities ahead. This book will be followed by a series of volumes to stir both conscience and imagination, each written to elaborate on one aspect of the future. All are focused on realistic and humanistic possibilities, not on gloom and doom.

We live in a fast-changing world of nanotechnology, the Internet and robot explorations of Mars. Renewable limbs, robotic pets, human hibernation, and artificial intelligence are not that far away. The way we deal with this rapidly expanding and evolving vista will largely determine our success as a society. Thomas Saaty and Larry Boone, paraphrasing Cervantes' great *Don Quixote*, ask, "Who is crazy, the world, because it sees itself as it is, or I, because I see the world as it could be?"

Studying our possible futures can not only enhance our ability to understand what is happening in a wider historical context but can also imbue our consequent acts with a greater awareness and a feeling of participation. Expanding the perceived range of what I call "plausibilities" is enormously challenging because in so doing we can ultimately affect the outcomes. Through these pieces you may participate on many different levels in the creative process of imagining a better world.

The series *Prospects for Tomorrow* was launched because we felt that it was imperative to define what it is we want for the world of tomorrow. We should not be timid about expressing our hopes and desires for our children and grandchildren. Forward planning will not necessarily bind our descendants. Succeeding generations may even reject our attempts, but at least they will acknowledge that we cared, and not only for ourselves.

Collectively we should look clearly at our prospects. Has any politician today even questioned whether we should curb growth? Or cut the number of prisons? Or control the number of robots? Who in our generation is willing to engage in a serious discussion of "acceptable levels of unemployment"?

What are we going to do to reduce the increasing gap between the haves and have-nots? Is capitalism really the economic system we need for the twenty-first century? What role do we truly want community to play in tomorrow's world? The list of dilemmas facing us is long and largely untouched. These issues and many more will be dealt with in the series. It is not possible to depict tomorrow's world with any degree of certainty, but many aspects of it can certainly be anticipated. And such prognostication may itself affect the outcome.

Scanning the Future, the first volume in the series, is different from all the volumes that will follow it. It is a selection from twenty writers who are all in their different ways concerned with the future. Most anthologies dealing with the future tend to look at the potential of a particular field like biology, artificial intelligence or technology. *Scanning the Future* tries to present a broader scope: the humanist aspects of topics covered by future studies. The reader is owed some explanation of what inspired me in making the selection of excerpts. This itself demands some detailed background.

All my life I have been "future focused" out of a basic curiosity to know not only where I might be going but also where my species could be heading. It has always been difficult to try and make sense of the world around me. Growing up in Paris and New York, I often spoke to my parents about "over-population." They could not understand what I was talking about. To them urban civilization was a blessing, the glory of our times. When I complained about the fumes and pollution arising from cars—which affected my breathing—they were puzzled (having been brought up with the stench of horse shit in the streets) how I could complain about such testimonials to progress.

As a child, my world was turned tumultuously upside down by Adolf Hitler. Before the outbreak of World War II my interest had been focused on painting, but after it I began to wonder what I could do to help the world become a more harmonious place. Art did not seem to be the way to accomplish that breakthrough. What, indeed, could stop the barbarian tide? What kind of a world could I look forward to? How could my energy and will do some good? Perhaps because at this early age I was sucked into the nightmare of Hitler's holocaust, the rest of my life has been caught between utopian ideals and pragmatic commitments.

Jules Verne and H.G. Wells were my original favorites in science fiction. Aldous Huxley's *Brave New World* filled me with curiosity when I was in American high school. Edward Bellamy's nineteenth-century novel, *Looking Backward*, was another revelation. The cooperative commonwealth this free and ordered utopia envisioned was one where all worked and shared alike. This stood in sharp contrast to the ruthless face of capitalism I experienced daily on the littered streets of New York.

The first serious paper I ever wrote (in high school) was on the social life of the ants. Did the ordered society of bees and ants not offer some crucially important lessons for humanity? Nature's evolutionary patterns of emergence were almost as little understood then as they are now, but here were insects programmed to live together in cooperation, their roles as workers or queens genetically defined. Theirs was a world of stability. Evolution had not changed their pattern of life for hundreds of millions of years. E.O. Wilson, who is included in this selection, recognized the important lessons to be drawn from studying ants, and he was to gain worldwide recognition for his work on insects. Even in those teenage years I was at once immensely attracted to the organizational structure of the social insects and repulsed by the slavery and sterility of such an existence. Here society was all and the individual worker ant was nothing.

In my late twenties, I tried to imagine a genuine alternative to the stultified society which had flourished in the America of the Eisenhower era. This led me to set up an intentional community in New Zealand. Ant-like communism was out. An anarchical community seemed a plausible experimental alternative. In high pursuit of a more positive resolution to the human predicament, I was determined to consider economic relations different from those which then prevailed in the U.S.A. Like many such community launches, this one failed for a variety of reasons, including a lack of funds. Despite the disillusionment that I suffered about the members who saw the community as a way out of unhappy marriages and the majority who persistently failed to take responsibility for their own actions, my basic interest in community has never waned. My desire for harmony, stability, order, community, continuity and meaning in an anarchical setting seem even more important.

The major subjects I have written about over the past thirty-five years have all dealt with aspects of our common future: television programming, intentional community, the (non) future of communism, the rising tide of global population, the ever-present nuclear threat and the likelihood of genetic engineering. In writing a book about our future direction, *Toward the Millennium* (1997), I spent the better part of a decade reading widely in the areas of community, utopia, economics, socialism, equality, education, progress, Greek philosophy, the Enlightenment, the Industrial Revolution, as well as the biological sciences, artificial intelligence, robotics—several thousand books in all. The exploration, examination, and selection were all my personal choice. My principal problem was how to cull and digest the best and most relevant of what had been written over the past 2500 years.

Rejecting the restricted visions of George Bush and Margaret Thatcher, I felt it was urgent to sketch out a holistic and panoramic vista of what a better

9

world might have to offer. I was not looking for a unified field theory for society and I was highly reluctant to suggest an overall prescription for what might cure the world's ills. Far better to hint at a broad range of ideals from which each reader could pick and choose. Diversity seemed the wave of the future. And, in a sense, in this anthology I have followed that same preferential pattern.

In ancient times the oracles at Delphi and Cumae relied on ambiguity and poetic obscurity—often induced by the inhalation of opium and other drugs. By way of contrast, the authors selected in this anthology are highly focused and disciplined in their approach. They do not engage in prophecy. Only three, De Jouvenel, Wagar, and Lem possibly would admit to being "futurists." Unlike most professionals in the field, the authors articulately express their heuristic outlook. The vast majority of "futurists" wish to be regarded as neutral or detached as they attempt to portray coming trends. But through these essays and the volumes of *Prospects for Tomorrow* the conviction will emerge that we can improve the world through knowledge, that the individual can make a difference and that the future can be faced directly.

There must, of course, be some notes of caution. It is often confusing to weigh and balance the contradictory forces which interact in an increasingly complex world. It is all too easy to let our wishful thinking overshadow both common sense and the laws of probability. There can be no unfolding of a grand plan. If there is a subliminal agenda in this selection, it is my preference for authors who manifest a desire to reexamine our increasingly problematic societal arrangements. All these authors are eloquent advocates of the expansion of education, the safeguarding of the environment, and the reinforcement of both liberty and democracy.

A renewal of idealism grounded in the real world is plausible. I would like to give the reader an insight into what might be termed "utopian realism" (to borrow a phrase coined by the sociologist Anthony Giddens), in which authors pursue their utopianism through realistic proposals. Utopians usually set out a programme for mankind which has little possibility of being fulfilled. Like those Pollyannas who anticipate a happy future in the hope of persuading listeners that a specifically desirable end is around the corner (and should consequently receive all possible support), utopians—while acting out of the loftiest of motives—may fail to keep their feet on the ground. Octavio Paz, the Nobel Prize winning poet and essayist, wrote in his poem "January First", the only poetry included in this volume, that, "Tomorrow, we shall have to invent,/once more,/the reality of this world."

In *Children of the Mire* (The Charles Eliot Norton Lectures at Harvard, 1971–72) Paz wrote with enormous insight: "Modern man is pushed toward the future with the same violence as the Christian was pushed toward heaven or hell." Paz suggested that, "The great revolutionary change was the revolt of the future. In Christian society the future was under sentence of death, for the triumph of the eternal present, following the Last Judgment, was the end of the future." Paz thinks that we have inverted the terms: the future is now the chosen place for perfection and "if perfection is relative in relation to the future and absolute in relation to the past—then the future becomes the center of the temporal triad."

Each generation of historians reinterprets past events. Our understanding of the present tends to be clouded by an overload of information, selective bias, and the copycat fashion among reporters and commentators. And a deep-seated and pervasive conviction holds for some that the future should remain obscure. The study of the future is bedevilled by the fact that there are no iron laws that govern human history or its cultural development. Nevertheless, future change, or so it would appear, is what a great many human beings continue to live for.

For some of us, it would seem, the future has arrived too soon. We feel that the changes of the past three or four decades have been too rapid for us to absorb. The futures that may await us look increasingly complex. The man or woman in the street does not like to contemplate chaos. At school and university, where we learn little enough about the present, we learn nothing at all about what may happen in the next few decades or even how to plan ahead. Small wonder then that so few of us search deep inside ourselves for plausible alternative principles or practices about what might constitute "the good life." In this respect, one might think that our civilization is suffering from a virus of contemplative exhaustion. It is hoped this series may prove to be an antidote, something like a "generic" energizer for the reader.

There is both an art and a science to examining what lies ahead. Such an exploration of future possibilities is integral to our modern consciousness. Any critical look at future projections, however, demands that one knows who is making predictions and what their motives are. Max Dublin points out that there is great scope for the manipulative and destabilizing in prophecy. He is outspoken in his attacks on those prophets who "flutter the banner of endless possibilities" but only "as a hook, as a rhetorical device and as a distraction from the limited choices, from the very narrow road, along which they are encouraging us to follow." He points out that debates about the future are almost always pulled in two directions: what may be and what should be. The first deals with facts, the second with moral matters. That new stars will be born and others will die is a fact; that liberal politicians say that unemployment should fall and investment increase is a moral statement.

Readers often think of themselves as moving in a dynamically linear fashion from a little known past into a totally unknown, but hopefully "improving" tomorrow. The idea of progress holds that mankind has advanced from a past condition of primitiveness or barbarism and is likely to continue such manifest advances. The Enlightenment of the eighteenth century and the scientific and technological revolutions of the nineteenth century which followed it were dominated by the idea of the progress of civilization. The distinguished American historian Robert Nisbet has suggested that, "the idea of progress has done more good over a 2500 year period, led to more creativeness in other spheres, and given more strength of human hope and individual desire for improvement than any other single idea in history."

The twin concepts of progress and technology have been firmly linked in the minds of most Americans and Europeans over the past six generations. The historian of technology Merritt Roe Smith explores the idea of progress in his essay "Technology, Industrialization, and the Idea of Progress in America," by first going back to the early days of the American republic and the vision of Thomas Jefferson. Technology and science were seen by Jefferson as a means towards a positive end, namely human improvements of a material, intellectual, spiritual, and moral kind. Smith argues cogently that the separation of human concerns from the concept of progress has led to a central dilemma for our society. Industry, primarily motivated by profits, has focused on technology at the expense of human values. By failing to consider individual human needs, industry has created considerable worker dissatisfaction even as it has resulted in relatively high pay and material betterment. Smith maintains that because it is patently obvious not everyone benefits from it, we are less optimistic today about technological progress.

Merritt Roe Smith pointed out that the aspirations of Thomas Jefferson, as distinct from those of the technocrats of today, provided tacit limits to, as well as positive ends for, a progressive vision of the future. Today "pure science" and technology are ends in themselves. But there is an undoubted tension between the desire to preserve our values and the need to control run-away technology. We are not clear where we want our new technology to lead us. Of course efficiency, the end of backbreaking labor, safer and better consumer products at decreasing prices are all desirable goals. But is such purely technological advance compatible with social progress? For example, is technology creating the basis for a new class conflict between a managerial class and a working class in our society? Or a gulf between the consumers of the developed countries and exploited labor of underdeveloped countries? These are the kinds of questions few modern futurists would try to answer. Future planning requires more discrimination and judgment about how we design, select and use technology, ranging from city planning to household appliances. Indeed, why should humans conform to machines instead of machines conforming to humans?

There are differing perspectives on what technology means for humanity. The most negative is that it is an evil curse, uncontrollably wrecking our earthly paradise, robbing people of their dignity and often their jobs. The Japanese futurist Yoneji Masuda has developed a vision of the future society he calls "Computopia" that would appear to offer a humanistic environment for computers, but something less of a paradise for human beings. Fundamentalists, on the other hand, most often see technology as destructive of religious beliefs, fostering materialistic values, and bringing about a meritocratic and technocratic society. But there are also many commentators, philosophers, social critics and environmentalists who would endorse a "back to nature" future.

The most positive view is that technology has liberated men and women from unending drudgery, that it is the motor of all progress in the modern world, and that it offers a solution to most of our social problems. The promoters of this positive view believe that technology helps to liberate the individual from the clutches of both the church and dictatorships, that social amateurism will be replaced by the new techniques of "scientific management" and that our human destiny remains firmly in our hands and not in those of robots, machinery or computers.

Merritt Roe Smith shows how complex the interaction of society and technology actually is: it creates new opportunities for workers and society at the same time as it generates new problems. The automobile, for example, created vast alterations in employment, the physical landscape, our mobility and ways of life, and the very structure of our cities, all of which deeply affected our capacity to cope with the subsequent auto-induced chain reactions. Nobody was in the business to anticipate these changes or to plan or prepare for the vast dislocations. No futurologist was there to draw attention to the possible results of all the decisions regarding the introduction of the automobile for either the individual or for society. Indeed, if anyone had done so in 1900, who would have listened to their prophecies? More likely, they would have been sent to a lunatic asylum.

Owen Paepke's approach in his book *The Evolution of Progress* (1993) is highly positive. His belief is that in terms of the prospect of freeing ourselves from toil and hunger—thanks to nanotechnology, abundant energy through fusion, and leaps of progress in biotechnology—humanity can entertain hopes of vast improvement. "Within a generation, machine intelligence will be making significant, independent contributions to several fields," predicts Paepke. It is not that tomorrow's machines will be so markedly different from today's, however, it is that human beings themselves will be revolutionized. "Indeed, even using the word 'people' to denote these beings is an anachronism. Within a century or two, genetic engineering will likely have changed our descendants so fundamentally as to prevent them from mating with humans in their present form, making them biologically a separate species." Such prognostications can be as frightening as any prospective robot takeover of the world. The ongoing revolution in genetic research promises to change the way we look at life itself, but futurists do not generally believe that tomorrow's humans can be entirely retooled. Technology may be the answer to some of our material problems but fails to ameliorate our spiritual or moral condition. Pharmacology could induce a more optimistic attitude towards life or help us to get along with one another, but it is unlikely to increase our sense of social, environmental and ultimately political responsibility.

Our tendency as humans has been to define what *is* as both necessary and inevitable. It is neither. Grandiose claims can be heard about the "ultimate triumph of capitalism," the "death of socialism," and the globalization of the market. What exists right now, who is in power, does not present an irreversible trend. It merely represents current fashions of preference. Writers like Francis Fukuyama (and Hegel some two centuries before him) have written about the "end of history." Such finality seems somewhat premature. Although Fukuyama's "After the End of Social Engineering" and "The Spiritualization of Economic Life" are included in this book, I believe that his predictions are too facile and far too fashionable. One must not confuse a serious examination of the future with a dubious ideological programme (which sees capitalism and "the market" as the only plausible framework for the economic organization of a modern society.) I do not think that we are anywhere near the culmination of human historical evolution which Fukuyama describes as "the ultimate end of human activity." Such oversimplifications seem rather characteristic of an economic fundamentalism inherent in the current range of American approaches towards the future.

How we predict, why we predict, and who does the predicting are dependent on the nature of the society in which we live. Involved are a set of cultural assumptions about the relationship of the past to the present as well as to the future. Perhaps that is why more than half of the authors included here are American. As a society, the United States has been "at the cutting edge" of global change. Whereas one society, such as the American, welcomes experiments, structural modifications and opportunities for development, another, such as Iran or Burma, may view all change as inimical. As Wagar points out in his *The Next Three Futures*, we study the future in the hope of learning how to control it, avoid past mistakes, and to make the world a better place than it might have been without our intervention. The problem universally arises: who is to define what is "better"?

Most of the authors included in this book are searching for alternative sets of practices and principles about what constitutes the "good life," but their approaches embrace a whole range of attitudes. There are the ecological optimists, such as Murray Gell-Mann, the "cornucopians" such as Rosabeth Kanter (who sees no limits to any kind of growth), and the "environmental alarmists," such as Tom Athanasiou, who believe the earth has the capacity to take care of only a limited number of people. "Visions of a better world come hard these days," writes Athanasiou. "Apocalyptic fear has long dogged rationalist optimism and this inevitably colors attempts to tell the whole grim ecological tale." Athanasiou suggests that "environmentalists live double lives." As activists they must demonstrate their conviction that they can win, and yet as Greens they are lost if they do not hold dark suspicions.

In the twentieth century the principal architect of this universal popularization of the future was H.G. Wells. It is significant that he was born at a time of great optimism for Britain, a moment in history when its empire was at an apogee. Wells was obsessed with the prospect of things to come both in fiction and his other voluminous writings. In a series of articles called *Anticipations* (1901) he outlined the first comprehensive survey of predictive writing. This was followed by a lecture at the Royal Institution in London in 1902 titled "The Discovery of the Future." Wells said the time was soon coming when a "systematic exploration of the future" would look at the development of mankind. He told his audience that such a science, much like geology, would not provide us with ultimate truths but "a working knowledge of things in the future." Wells's most comprehensive portrait of the future was completed in 1933 with *The Shape of Things to Come*. His ultimate prediction was that our future history would be a race between education and catastrophe.

Modern "think-tanks," the engines of so much of current thinking about the future, started just at the end of World War II when the U.S. Air Force funded Project RAND (Research And Development, which soon came to be known by the trade as Research And No Development) as a department of the Douglas Aircraft Company. Its first major work was most appropriately titled "Preliminary Design of an Experimental World Circling Spaceship." The study laid the groundwork for unmanned ventures into space by the U.S.A., and RAND's remarkably prophetic appraisal later brought considerable prestige to the company. At first RAND was staffed by engineers and scientists but within a year it began to add economists, psychologists, sociologists, anthropologists, and political scientists so that its outlook and corporate clients could be broadened. It began to offer long-range options on a wide variety of issues to government departments whose staffs were geared to coping with day to day emergencies rather than long-term thinking. Within fifteen years RAND had grown to a staff of about a thousand and was receiving twenty-five million dollars a year to think ahead for a broad range of sponsors.

RAND developed new methods, such as the Delphi technique, in which experts in different fields are polled for their intuitive "guesses." A Delphi panel would typically look at:

- A list of developments arranged by the respondents to highlight those they feel are most important
- Evaluations of the desirability of these developments and their possible consequences
- Estimates of when such developments are likely to happen
- Guestimates of the probability that such developments could occur
- Policy alternatives that might increase the likelihood of those events coming about
- Policy alternatives likely to decrease the chances of undesirable events happening
- The evaluation of extreme opinions at every stage of this process

The embroidery of long-term "scenarios," which became popular at that time, was turned into a fine art by Herman Kahn in his first book *On Thermonuclear War* (1960). In building grisly scenarios, Kahn followed a single set of premises to a plausible conclusion. The problem was that each scenario only envisaged one future. Kahn often extrapolated the present to its logical end and thus reduced the creative and highly imaginative dimensions of predictions as projected by Jules Verne or H.G. Wells. Kahn who left RAND to found his own think-tank, the Hudson Institute (1961) described himself as "an ex-physicist and half an economist." Kahn (the model for Dr. Strangelove) soon became something of a nuclear bogeyman and his institute coined such words as "doomsday machine," "megacorpse," and "wargasm" (defined by one of the fellows as "when all the buttons are pushed"). Kahn's *Thinking about the Unthinkable* (1962) considered probable casualties in a thermo-nuclear confrontation with numerical specificity.

The Hudson Institute staff was composed of "expert amateurs" who could develop strategies in a vast number of fields. Sometimes these scenarios were helpful in getting people to foresee difficult decisions that they might otherwise miss or even deny. However, there were also pitfalls with these *Alice in Wonderland* fantasies. For example, Kahn failed to foresee the pervasive use of the personal computer. His kind of over-dramatized extrapolations were to lead to Heidi and Alvin Toffler's *Future Shock* (1970) in which they tried to anticipate a whole range of forthcoming developments. The Tofflers wrote that "a well-oiled machinery for the creation and diffusion of fads is now an entrenched part of the modern economy." The Tofflers offered "pop sociology", glibness, clichés and jargon such as "massive adaptational breakdown" and "social future assemblies."

A generation later we have yet to recognize that mere projections of current trends are rarely successful. Foresight and intuition, especially when combined with probability studies and quantitative analysis, are far more effective as deliberate processes in expanding our understanding of tomorrow. George Orwell had already pointed out in the 1940s the intellectual fallacy of predicting a continuation of a thing that is happening. And Francis Galton, that most extraordinary Victorian statistician, had long ago discovered "regression to the mean" as a modification of the notion of probability. Whether it be in genetics or in astronomy, the impulse toward the average is constant, inevitable, and predictable.

The gap between Bertrand de Jouvenel and Kahn was both symbolic of Franco-American differences and pronounced. Kahn's was the language of scenarios, megatrends, options, projections, extrapolations. The quaint and often wistful De Jouvenel would have been quite at home among the eighteenth-century Encyclopédistes, such as the Marquis de Condorcet. De Jouvenel suggested that studying the future was an art because it is an expression and a creation of the human mind. It was not a question of knowledge or facts but of conjecture. His essay, which opens this volume, was based on three assumptions: the future is not predictable, it is not predetermined, and it can be affected by individual choices and decisions. "It would be naive to think that over-all progress automatically leads to progress in our knowledge of the future," he wrote. De Jouvenel did fervently believe that the future was deserving of our most disciplined and creative thinking and for this he has gained my sympathy.

Thomas Saaty and Larry Bone in *Embracing the Future* (1990) point out that futurists come in different kinds of packages. *Futurists of the possible* tend to be mavericks, visionaries, geniuses and madmen. *Futurists of the probable* tend to be statisticians, mathematicians, or systems analysts who are generally preoccupied with short-range forecasting. *Futurists of the preferable* tend to be political scientists, and are often focused on specific long-range problems such as global pollution. Environmentally conscious futurism, which has become so prominent in recent years, was launched in the 1970s by such serious researchers as Barry Commoner, Lester Brown, Paul Ehrlich, and Donella and Dennis Meadows.

Aurelio Peccei's Club of Rome (founded in 1968) made extensive use of computerized data on interlinked global factors such as population, energy, raw materials, agricultural production and manufacturing output. One of the resulting books, *Limits to Growth*, by Donella Meadows and Dennis Meadows, terrified readers with its predictions of drastic shortages of food and raw materials. The impact of their study was all the more powerful because the input was computer-based and thus thought to be less biased. Herman Kahn's response was a book, *The Next 200 Years* (1976), in which he wrote that, "No obvious limits are apparent . . . energy abundance is probably the world's best insurance that the entire human population [even of 20 billion people] can be well cared for, at least physically, for many years to come." There the two opposing viewpoints parted course.

Max Dublin, who launched a frontal attack on what he calls futurologist boosterism, cautioned against the tyranny of prophecy in his book *Futurehype* (1989 and 1991). Dublin warns that prediction has been coopted by trend-setters. "From railroads in our transportation system, to the humanities in our education system, to innumerable viable industries, we hasten to dissociate ourselves from worthwhile endeavors that enrich our lives in large part because their demise has been predicted and we do not want to be 'left behind.'" Dublin's scathing analysis of the prediction business must give us pause.

I did not include those writers who predict dire futures merely because frightening readers is an effective way to get across their agenda for political action. I believe reasoned argument is usually the better way. For example, I admire the deeply humanist approach of The Commission on Population and Quality of Life. The authors advertised their outstanding report, *Caring for the Future* (1996), as "a radical agenda for positive change." The Commission defined four major challenges for a world in transition: population, poverty, the environment, and production/consumption in the globalized economy. While warning that population was not something that could be left to "market forces" the authors collectively avoided any specific prophecies of gloom and doom. However, they regarded abandoning tens of millions of people in modern societies to unemployment and abject poverty as a much worse abasement of humanity than polluting the atmosphere. The gap between technology and needs in the developing world is wide and growing wider. It doesn't take a futurologist to suggest the dangers this presents.

Many of the gloomiest prognosticators have been the writers of science fiction. William Gibson in *Neuromancer* (1984), for example, has pushed forward the frontiers of tomorrow by describing a wholly technologized society, amoral in its outlook and hedonistically materialist in its ethics. Ray Bradbury, another acclaimed writer of science fiction, has remarked: "I don't try to predict the future, I try to prevent it." (As in his best-selling novel of 1953, *Fahrenheit 451*.) Arthur C. Clarke, who, with Stanley Kubrick, wrote the screenplay of his story 2001: A Space Odyssey (1968), said that science fiction writers very seldom attempted prophecy, but he himself predicted: "The finite velocity of light will, inevitably, divide the human race once more into scattered communities, sundered by barriers of space and time. We will be one with our remote ancestors, who lived in a world of immense and often insuperable distances, for we are moving out into a universe vaster than all their dreams." Clarke is representative of a much more humanist kind of futurology. As early as the 1960s he was concerned whether the world was headed for *full unemployment* because of the rapid expansion of both computers and robotics. "In the long run," he said in 1972, "the gathering and handling of knowledge is the only growth industry—as it should be."

Many of the most startling predictions have come from imaginative writers, going back to Jonathan Swift in the eighteenth century whose hero, Gulliver, visits the Grand Academy of Lagado on the Isle of Balnibari. I don't believe think-tanks come any better than that. The nineteenth-century novels of Jules Verne are full of predictions about submarines and space travel that continue to charm us. Even the novelist E.M. Forster, who usually wrote of his own time, described in "*The Machine Stops*" (*c.* 1914) a world of three-dimensional projections and computer communications where most people preferred not to leave their individual apartment cells.

It is rare that one reads a book or an article that makes one look at familiar phenomena in an entirely new way. I found J.D. Bernal's prophecies in *The World, the Flesh and the Devil* (1929) one of the most insightful pieces of scientific prophecy of the twentieth century. Bernal, who was both a noted crystallographer and an outspoken socialist, wanted to explore how we could defeat "the three enemies of the rational soul": the forces of nature (that is, the World), man's own physical limitations (the Flesh), and the ignorance and stupidity which beset the human spirit (the Devil).

Freeman Dyson, another brilliant scientist, writing *Imagined Worlds* (1997), exerted a similarly profound impact on me with his predictions. Dyson suggested that mankind will succeed in leaving the Earth and spread slowly into the universe. Ahead lies a golden age of exploration. In the next millennium we may well see deviant colonies established in outer space where half-human and half-machine creatures will be exiled much as criminals were exiled to Australia and Georgia two hundred years ago. Freeman Dyson believes that we are also headed for a golden age of mental exploration which could well see incredible breakthroughs in neurophysiology. For example, as our understanding of the brain grows, humans will become empowered to practice radiotelepathy. He believes this will cause severe problems if left unregulated: "Laws regulating radiotelepathy must begin with a guarantee of privacy." This will require reliable means for both turning on and switching off transmitters and receivers in the brain. Such a guarantee, he writes "would go some way to protecting the individual from telepathic eavesdropping and coercion." The idea of radiotelepathy is not a new one. It first appeared in Olaf Stapledon's novel, *Last and First Men* (1931). Symbolically, the only work of fiction I have included in this selection is by that extraordinarily fecund Polish writer, Stanislaw Lem, who wickedly satirized the profession of futurism itself in his novel, *The Futurological Congress* (1974).

Our knowledge of the way things work—the economy for instance—is much clouded by ignorance. What we do know is that vast ills usually result from a belief in economic certainties. In dealing with the world economy, both Joel Kurtzman and George Brockway are convinced that in the twenty-first century a complex blend of role models may be preferable to the kind of free-market capitalism which became so prominent in the 1980s. Kurtzman gives the reader an inkling of the high stakes being played by the casino economies of the advanced industrial nations. He believes the 1987 stock-market crash was merely a foretaste of what is to come and predicts that the world's economy will be far more volatile and chaotic than anything which preceded it. Brockway in *The End of Economic Man* (1996 edition) regards the present inhumanity of the economic system as "intolerable." He suggests that the economics of tomorrow will have to have "a clearer and more obvious relevance to our daily lives . . . ."

The challenge in anticipating, imagining and possibly even initiating some of the potential economic transformations is at the core of futurism. It goes without saying that such improvisations are filled with uncertainty. The economist Peter L. Bernstein in his book *Against the Gods* (1996) suggests: "The revolutionary idea that defines the boundary between modern times and the past is the mastery of risk: the notion that the future is more than a whim of the gods and that men and women are not passive before nature." G.K. Chesterton (1874–1936) had suggested that the problem with prediction is that life is nearly reasonable and logical, but not quite: "It looks just a little more mathematical and regular than it is." As a consequence we must take maximum advantage of those factors and areas where we have some control over the outcome while minimizing those where we have absolutely no control and where we don't understand the links between cause and effect. Like Prometheus, we must probe the darkness in search of the light that will liberate us from our servitude to ignorance.

"Money and power are necessary as means, but they are not the proper measures of a good society and a good world," write Bellah and his associates in the piece "Democracy Means Paying Attention." The authors of *The Good Society* (1991), from which this excerpt is taken, are convinced both of the manifest frailty of democracy and its dependence on social trust. Freedom, they suggest in paraphrasing Albert Camus, is nothing more than a chance to be better.

Rosabeth Kanter is now a professor at the Harvard Business School and is much sought after as an advocate of positive business practice. When she wrote her brilliant work on community back in the late 1960s, an extract from which is included in this book, her aspirations were far more universal. She declared a generation ago, "communal ventures represent not only alternatives to life in the dominant culture, but also attempts to realize unique ideals, dreams and aspirations." Today Kanter believes the best way to further societal advancement is through the encouragement of "better practice" in the cut-throat world of free-market capitalism. Failure to grasp the opportunities created by a new technology, such as computers or robotics, means that one will fall behind one's neighbors and this ultimately implies that a society can make less efficient use of its members.

The Media Lab at the Massachusetts Institute of Technology (MIT) is conducting wide-ranging studies on the interaction between computers installed in everyday appliances, like electric irons and coffee makers, and their users. Nicholas Negroponte, the visionary director of the Media Lab, stresses that the world of tomorrow means connectivity, or immediate access in communications. He is very much aware that futurologists can be led astray when they rely too heavily on technology and not enough on human values.

The interplay between the two is crucial. Harth, Wilson, Weinberg, Gell-Mann, and Saaty and Boone, all of whom are included in this volume, suggest that the methodology of science can offer a more reasoned way to the future. "Science began when humans had the audacity to pit their brain power against every mystery with which nature confronted them. One after another, the mysteries have yielded to our supreme self-confidence and steady pursuit," writes Harth. He cautions that the salt, sugar and fat, which caveman needed for survival, now kill us prematurely. The anger and aggressiveness which once were essential for survival are now highly counterproductive to creating a more civil society. "We have become p ,werful beyond all expectations, only to find ourselves threatened by our toys of war, as well as by our instruments of peace."

Professor Edward O. Wilson, the noted biologist and founder oi sociobiology, in his essay "Scientific Humanism and Religion," originally written for a church conference, provocatively suggests that the entire notion of the future was once the almost exclusive domain of the church. Natural evolution was an idea that the Catholic hierarchy strenuously opposed. Wilson cautions: "Which position—scientific materialism or religious transcendentalism—proves correct will eventually make a very great difference in how humanity views itself and plans its future." At the same time, today's think-tanks often use the cloak of scientific method to strengthen and legitimate their predictions while masking the ideological content.

Murray Gell-Mann's chapter on "Transitions to a More Sustainable World" suggests we must not attribute more validity to such policy studies about a sustainable world "than they are likely to possess." This Nobel Prize winner in theoretical Physics is in no doubt that it is "hardest to get people to think about the long term vision of a more sustainable world." Gell-Mann helped to establish the Santa Fe Institute in New Mexico which looks at the various manifestations of complexity ranging from quantum mechanics to the human immune system, and even to the evolution of language as a complex evolving form. Running through the text of his book *The Quark and the Jaguar* (1994), from which this chapter is taken, is the interplay between the operation of chance and the fundamental laws of nature: "The images of the quark and the jaguar seem to me to convey perfectly the two aspects of nature that I call the simple and the complex. . . . Just as the quark is a symbol of the physical laws that, once discovered, come into view before the mind's analytical eye, so the jaguar is, for me at least, a possible metaphor for the elusive."

Looking at the broadest of all perspectives, Nobel Prize winning physicist Steven Weinberg concludes this anthology with an imaginative but scientifically based projection of our understanding of the universe. Ultimately, humanity (or even its artificial successors) will have to come to terms with the limitations imposed by the inexorable laws of physics on our very existence.

The first half of this book is generally more concerned about the varying possible approaches, or methodologies of forecasting, involved in anticipating tomorrow's world. The second half is focused on the scope of what we must consider when looking at the twenty-first century. While the principal driving forces in society today are free-market economics, the rapid expansion of technology and the increasing domination of science, all the writers recognize that none of these forces touch on the spreading moral void. The manifest appeal of some of these authors is that their promises as well as their warnings touch the strings of conscience deep within us.

Readers, in general, no longer believe in a predictable future because prices, values, technological developments, and even politics remain so haphazard. At the same time, predictions have power. The field of futurist studies is, as I have tried to make clear, both compelling and heady, full of promises and pitfalls. If I were to claim that Newcastle upon Tyne or Albuquerque, New Mexico, are up-and-coming cities, this might exert considerable influence on people's assessments. Businessmen will consider investing in a new and promising locale, hamburger chains will apply for extra franchises, and something may be made to happen. Futurism is therefore difficult to separate from propaganda—especially when it involves political propaganda. Every politician proclaims he is going to win and, while such predictions are recognized as a propagandistic or rhetorical device, they are also prescriptive and thus may become powerful tools. Suggesting a dark outcome if the opponent is victorious is also a common predictive technique and one of which the public has become wary.

Fortunately, even in the field of futurology fashions change. A decade ago think-tanks had trouble getting clients such as banks and oil companies interested in anything but short-range futures, that is under five years. Now, near the turn of the millennium, manufacturers and others are more interested in an intermediate-range future—that is ten years or more. In this period I can predict that anti-aging pills will become popular, that half the world will be using polluted water, the reproduction of children will become increasingly restricted, a boom in artificial pets will be under way and some computers will be based on DNA-type sequencing. One can see why "prospective history" (to use a phrase coined by Daniel Bell) is becoming one of the world's top industries. At the same time, we must also make sure that we avoid imposing today's aspirations on future generations. Today's goals, values and outlook may not be what the next generation desires. Imposing our dreams of the future on others may lead to—and may even foster— entirely unwanted consequences.

The goal of forecasts and predictions should not be to form an accurate picture of tomorrow, but to help us to make better decisions now. Our visions and reality are fast catching up. It is no longer merely a dream to reanimate vanished species from bone, hair or nail fragments. The benefits of fusion power loom before us, as do euphoria-producing drugs, enhanced intellects, Artificial Intelligence machines, and disease-free lives. . . . All that and much more beckons. "The future, the promised land of history is an inaccessible realm," suggested Paz. "Perhaps we'll open the day's doors and then we shall enter the unknown."

PART I

METHODOLOGIES AND APPROACHES

BERTRAND DE JOUVENEL

MAX DUBLIN

MURRAY GELL-MANN

MERRITT ROE SMITH

ERIC HARTH

THOMAS L. SAATY AND LARRY W. BOONE

W. WARREN WAGAR

THE INDEPENDENT COMMISSION ON
POPULATION AND QUALITY OF LIFE

BERTRAND DE JOUVENEL's The Art of Conjecture *established him as France's leading futurologist and led to the foundation of his think-tank, Futuribles. "The intellectual construction of a likely future is a work of art, in the fullest sense of the term, and this is what 'conjecture' means here," he wrote by way of explanation of the title. The book was first published in France in 1961, and this excerpt is a chapter from the 1967 English translation by Nikita Lary. De Jouvenel was more interested in a genealogy of the present than in prophecy or prediction or the extrapolative techniques being used by his American contemporaries. Although some aspects of this piece may seem slightly out of tune or almost quaint when compared to contemporary views, the questions De Jouvenel raises are as relevant today as they were in the 1960s. One might say he represents what one could call "the old school" of futurism.*

BERTRAND DE JOUVENEL

THE POLITICAL ORDER
AND FORESEEABILITY

Society and economics determine one another. Economic forecasting and social forecasting provide each other mutual help, and in certain respects, it seems, merge into one. Political forecasting is quite another matter. Men think it is easy insofar as they think political change follows of necessity from social change, particularly since the latter, a slow and heavy process, lends itself to forecasting. Is it here perhaps that the way of overcoming the difficulty men have always encountered in political forecasting is to be found? Not according to Hume:

> It affords a violent prejudice against every science, that no prudent man, however sure of his principles, dares prophesy concerning any event, or *foretell* the remote consequences of things. A physician will not venture to pronounce concerning the condition of his patient a fortnight or a month after. And still less dares a politician foretell the structure of political affairs a few years hence. HARRINGTON thought himself so sure of his general principle, *that the balance of power depends on that of property*, that he ventured to pronounce it impossible ever to re-establish monarchy in ENGLAND: but his book [*Oceana*] was scarcely published when the king was restored. . . .
>
> [*Essays and Treatises on Several Subjects*, 1767]

A hundred years later, at the time of the Second Empire, Prévost-Paradol asserted that the democratization of society was an ineluctable, irreversible process, however it might unfold. But for a society to be or become democratic was one thing, and for its government to be or become democratic was another. A democratic society with an undemocratic government was perfectly possible, and the irreversible course observed in social transformation was by no means observed in political transformation:

> But whether the transformation of an aristocratic into a democratic society be slow or prompt, violent or peaceful, this transformation is nonetheless inevitable and, once accomplished, irrevocable. More than once a society may pass through all the extremes of anarchy and servitude, abolish thrones then raise them up only to abolish them again, effect abrupt revolutions in dress and language, affect in turn

republican austerity or the servile flabbiness of the Eastern Roman Empire; but a river would sooner flow back to its source than a democratic society revert to aristocracy.

[*La France Nouvelle*, 1868]

Throughout his book, Prévost-Paradol linked the idea of continuity in the social system with the idea of unstable equilibrium in the political regime.

I would not, of course, claim to adequately treat an important subject simply by quoting two authors, but wish only to stress that a political forecast is not given to us as a bonus once we have completed an economic and social forecast to the best of our ability . . . .

In 1932 the United States and Germany, two great industrial powers, were affected in like measure by an economic crisis so acute that nearly one worker in three was jobless, the youngest being particularly hard hit. The governments, powerless to remedy these intolerable social situations, were clearly condemned, and great political changes were called for. These political changes were, largely, foreseeable, given the social necessity, which was identical in both countries. Men had to be put back to work, and for this a policy actively pursued by the state was urgently required. The obstacles in 1932 were neither ill-will nor vested interests (which, on the contrary, were endangered by the situation) but convictions nurtured by academic orthodoxy and honestly held by political and economic leaders as well as by men in high administrative positions. In this state of paralysis by conviction, there could be no energetic action without a new and heretical personnel, animated by determination if not by doctrine. In taking bold measures, this personnel would come into conflict with existing institutions and would be unable to carry through their measures without strengthened executive powers. It was easy to foresee that in these two countries—both possessed of federal constitutions—the federal government, the source of effort, would acquire powers to the detriment of the rights of the individual states.

This much of the political order was foreseeable from the social order. In a word, what could be foreseen was what Rooseveltism and Hitlerism had *in common.* Surely nobody would regard the difference between the two as insignificant. In relation to social economy, Hitlerism bore an initial similarity to Roosevelt's New Deal, and were it not for Hitler's passion-ruled policies, clearly the history of the world would be far different and far better. Why did Germany not have a German Roosevelt in 1933 instead of Hitler? I very much doubt that even an *ex post* social forecast can answer this question.

Think of the social characteristics of the two men in relation to the social characteristics of their respective countries at that particular time. One of the men belonged to a patrician and consular family of wealth and renown whose forebears were founders of the nation. The other, a nobody (*Homo novissimus*), was not even native-born. The former had received an excellent education, the latter was virtually self-taught.

I know I have already given this example [in a previous chapter] but I have no hesitation in using it again, for it shows how imprudent it is to derive a political prediction from social vision alone. Had we predicted a "Roosevelt-like" government when in fact a Hitler came to power, we would have little grounds for satisfaction with our prediction.

Such an intellectual procedure is dangerous, for it is imbued with systematic optimism. It leads us into thinking that events in the political order fit the needs of the social economy, and since these needs can be grasped by rational analysis, we end up assuming that politics is the rational adjuvant of social change—an assumption which unfortunately is without foundation. Anti-Semitism in no way corresponded to the social needs of Germany, was irrelevant to its economic crisis, and with regard to diplomatic and military relations with foreign powers, was harmful to the national interests of the Reich and the special interests of the Nazi regime. Without this frenzied policy, it is not certain Germany would have been at war with the United States, and it is possible Germany would have been the first power to possess the atom bomb.

Nor is it necessary to refer to the past in order to see political passions causing a diversion from the course of things that might be foreseen from social economy alone. The Arab countries of the Middle East have a great lack of scientific and technical experts, of whom there is a great abundance in the neighboring state of Israel. By using these available talents, the Arab countries would save several years of economic growth, but for political reasons such a move is unthinkable.

"Politics has its own reasons which do not pertain to social economy." To ignore them or weigh them insufficiently is to condemn oneself to grave errors of judgment and forecasting. Hence it seems that political forecasting demands a large degree of intellectual autonomy: political history is not pre-formed in the material transformations of society. The proliferation of Caesarism in a multitude of states with very different social situations serves to confirm this impression.

I fear that what is said here may be misconstrued, for the terms "political" and "social" are ambiguous. The "social forecasting" discussed here is the forecasting of big, slow changes in society, connected with economic and technological changes. I am warning against a simple deduction of political regimes or policies from these structural changes. This is not to say that such changes do not affect politics, but that our knowledge or forecasts of such changes do not entail necessary political forecasts. Our forecasts based on the growth and exploitation of technology do not lead to certainty about the political domain and do not entitle us to treat political change as an epiphenomenon.

I do not propose to tackle here the subject of political forecasting as such but rather to turn it upside down: instead of discussing the forecasting of political change, I will stress that it is a main function of the political order to afford conditions favorable to the making of nonpolitical forecasts. Any sort of forecasting relies upon a presumed foreknowledge of some aspects of the future—the public authorities provide us with such foreknowledge in that their control of society aims at securing certain aspects of the future; thereby the public authorities serve us as guarantors of foreseeability.

There are many traits of the future for which the authorities stand surety, whether by implicit underwriting (the old way) or by explicit promise (the new way). The enumeration of these traits for a given government at a given time is as good a way as any of describing its character; one will find very different mixtures of traits to be preserved and traits to be achieved (targets). Now consider forward speculation on behalf of any discrete part of society, be it a family, a firm, or a social group. Every guaranteed trait of the future affords a support for intellectual speculation, but also constitutes a constraint upon the group's prospects. It follows that while a foreknown always has positive value, as information, it may, in the eyes of a given group, have such negative value as a constraint that the group is willing to trade that item of information against more hope. A prudent government will be responsive to pressures arising on that score, and this will induce the authorities not to multiply the foreknowns it guarantees beyond necessity.

But it may also happen that pressure develops against a guaranteed trait of the future which the rulers believe plays a key role in the whole structure of information they provide, in which case the pressure may result in a conflict whose first consequence is to topple the whole set of assurances. A brutal political discontinuity brings a period of utter uncertainty. These summary remarks may suggest that this view of government as an aid to forecasting by members of society could lead us back to the means of forecasting the fate of a particular government. But this is not our present concern.

Men would dispense with political power if they could, because of the harm it is capable of wreaking. But they can do so only in small and primitive societies. Authority must become greater as society grows in size and complexity. There is a reason for this, and it is relevant to our subject: in a small, traditional society, a man meets no one he does not know; men are linked to one another by familiar customs. This is not so in a large, mixed society. The more the society is mixed, the more a man needs to know what to expect of the unlike-seeming stranger. He needs a security for and against the behavior of "another." The more the society is changing, the greater is the number of innovations in men's behavior, and the more definitions of legitimate expectations are needed. The government assumes responsibility; this is why we may call it a "guarantor for foreseeability"—a role which in our age we have seen extended into new domains (social security and full employment).

We have no need to base the whole order on authority, in the manner of Hobbes, in order to recognize that authority is conservative. Conservative of what?—of an order which is changing and into which authority introduces changes. The nature of the "social guarantee" given by the state for our legitimate expectations continues in principle unchanged, while the content of these expectations changes. And since we know that their content will change, without knowing the how or when of it, uncertainty prevails. In other words, the state, which is the guarantor of certainties, is also the instigator of uncertainty. Generally speaking, if it seems likely the future will differ from the past, we think it is desirable that this future should be a foreknown of which we are warned, rather than an unknown "something or other." Accordingly, we are that much more inclined to grant the state powers of dominating this future; but these powers can only be powers over us, and the greater these powers, the more public decisions matter to us. A public decision projects uncertainty until it is known. And this uncertainty is, in a sense, drained from society and gathered up in the state, attaching to all its decisions.

Let us put things somewhat differently. Any power is a power over the future, a capacity for action affecting the future. In consequence, compelled as we are to conjecture the future so that we may make deliberate use of the minute power belonging to us individually, we must foresee the use that will be made of other powers, and pay particular attention to concentrated and weighty powers, rather than to powers on our own scale of action. An unpredictable authority is therefore worse than no authority at all.

A Regular Political System

For the above reasons, a regular state may be defined by this characteristic: its decisions are known a long time in advance. This condition obtains if, between their proposition and their promulgation, decisions pass slowly and openly through a long process of public discussion. Suddenly announced decisions are the infallible mark of an arbitrary state. The only occasion for a sudden decision in a regular state is peril from abroad. Except in such an event, decisions must never be published unexpectedly, and must be formed ostensibly rather than occultly. Where declarations of a head of state or leader of the government are awaited as revelations, there—indubitably—the system is despotic rather than regular.

This criterion for distinguishing between a regular system and an arbitrary one presents two advantages: it is easy to apply; and it gives an empirical justification for why our preference ought to go to a regular rather than an arbitrary system. If authority—the guarantor of foreseeability—is itself unforeseeable, it is the author of an evil that it should be preventing.

Political uncertainty is uncertainty about public decisions, and about the use authority will make of the ways and means at its disposal. Political uncertainty is small in England, where most of what there is of mystery attaches to one object—the red dispatch box the Chancellor of the Exchequer carries with him into Commons on the day of the Budget Speech. It is worth noting that in this speech the Chancellor speaks in the first person singular: and indeed, on this occasion, he has taken his decisions in secret, as in a system of personal power. But his decisions—kept secret for financial reasons—produce nothing more than marginal changes. If the Chancellor wished to make a radical change, as for instance, the introduction of a tax on wealth, he would prepare public opinion for it (as the last "Shadow Chancellor" started to do while still of the Opposition party) and would set up a Royal Commission, which after examining the pros and cons would eventually publish a Blue Book containing a majority report and possibly a minority report as well.

There is only one important uncertainty in the British political order, and that is a systematic uncertainty to do with general elections. But consider how small that uncertainty is. It concerns a simple alternative: either this same party will remain in power, or it will be the turn of that party sitting in the benches on the opposite side of the House. The Opposition is almost as well known as the government: its program is public, the changes it has promised are known. Nor is the alternative to the present government all that is known, since by studying opinion polls and the results of by-elections and local elections psephologists can predict the results of general elections with good chances of success.

The Conditions of Political Foreseeability

Let us try to single out some definitive characteristics of the British system. First, *procedures are sacred*—whether in the exercise of justice, or in judiciary appointments, or in the making and execution of decisions. As more rules are observed, so is the system better defined and the guarantees it affords more numerous. It is a great and dangerous madness to think that an abstract principle can define a system and afford guarantees. Sovereignty of the people assorts with sauces of all kinds, as Benjamin Constant noted long ago, and his observation is still true today.

Secondly, there is an *intention common to all active participants in political life* to faithfully maintain the accepted procedures. There can be no question of acceding to power by illegal means, nor of exercising power by other than known procedures. People often talk about "observing the rules of the game": this long-familiar expression has acquired added force now that we are acquainted with game theory . . . . Game theory presupposes a universe in which possible actions are well defined, but ordinary life does not satisfy this condition. In a regular system, men deliberately enclose themselves in a universe with restricted possibilities. And this entails a greatly improved foreseeability.

Thirdly, *the stakes are limited.* The participants accept from the very start that they will not make all the changes they would like, even if they can make them by regular procedures. This "minimalism" is an indispensable condition for preservation of the system, because if one party was to set about doing everything it wanted by the regular ways and means, it would drive the other into reacting by irregular means. In pushing one's opponent to the limit, one motivates his acts of despair and so becomes partly responsible for them.

Under conditions of a maximalist use of power, rules might nonetheless remain inviolate, and parties might succeed one another in regular alternation. But in such a situation there would be great swing-abouts of policy, reflected, in the long run, in the tottering course of affairs of state.

The little I have said suffices to show how very "artificial" a regular system is—which is in fact a tribute to the system. "Natural" politics consists of doing just what one likes to the full extent of one's capacity. In other words, "natural" politics is arbitrariness unlimited save by the world of fact. An "artificial" system is fragile: always present is the danger of a conquering band of maximalists brutally simplifying the system. By way of analogy, we may think of two (or more) tribes which are accustomed to jockey with one another for the positions of command, displaying neither violence nor spite, when, suddenly, they are swept away by a warlike tribe, which to gain its ends has contracted alliances with various peaceful tribes and then treats its allies no better than the others.

Men Have Always Sought Political Foreseeability

"But your model is simply the British system once again. For the past two hundred years you and your likes seem to have been unable to dish up anything better." The reason for this is that for two centuries and more England has offered a system better regulated, more resistant, and more flexible than any other.

Before the British system there was another model of a regular system— the French monarchy. Foreseeability was assured by the principle of legitimacy, which comes down to this idea: "Long ours, and hence rightfully ours."

Long-standing possession of power constituted a right to power, transmitted through the male line according to the system of primogeniture. It would be wrong to underrate the guarantee of civil peace afforded by this regular succession, which spared France from internal wars such as divided England, and from subjugation—the fate of the elective monarchies of Hungary, Bohemia, and Poland. But the principle of legitimacy was of far wider application: it governed the whole social order. If one could show that a piece of land or an office had long been in one's possession, it could not be taken away. The generalized principle of legitimacy I am describing will seem familiar to the welfare economist of today, for it embodies one of his main concerns—that change should bring improvements to some and harm to none, or, at any rate, adequate compensation where harm is done. It is obvious that such a principle rigorously applied acts as a brake on change—sometimes too much so. But it is also clear that by this principle subjects enjoy the same rights in their order as the sovereign in his. According to a very telling story, the miller of Sans-Souci once refused to sell his mill to Frederick II, saying he had the same right to his mill as the king to his crown. Yes, the same right! The rights, more or less extensive and exalted, are of like solidity, and the sovereign right cannot break the private right. The picture of the *ancien régime* sketched in revolutionary legends gives no inkling of this. Men have been mistaken about the vices of the *ancien régime:* the major failing was not arbitrariness, but the incapacity to promote necessary change.

The ancient French monarchy was guilty of acts as frightful as the massacre of St. Bartholomew's Day and the revocation of the Edict of Nantes, but only when confronted with utterly disconcerting situations, since its system of thought had no place for the Protestant phenomenon. It was undone not by these acts, but by the powerlessness of "New Deal" officials to drive necessary reforms through the parliament—the custodian of acquired rights. The parliament conceived its charge as that of reminding the king he was the guarantor of foreseeability, and of acting, itself, as such a guarantor. This can be seen in a careful reading of the remonstrances of the parliament of Paris upon Turgot's edicts suppressing the *corvées* [days of unpaid labour due to the state] and the *jurandes* [guild supervisors].

These remonstrances are of great interest because their substance is shocking. The reforms proposed by Turgot were quite necessary and mild enough. Their rejection by parliament served nothing but established interests, and that for a short time: these were soon to be swept brutally away. The instance therefore illustrates the proposition that attention to the preservation of known rights, while in principle functional to the purpose of foreseeability, may easily become dysfunctional. To my mind, it is only by looking forward that we can judge which of the established assurances deserve to be maintained.

The ambiguous attitude of the ancient monarchic government toward change was manifested conspicuously and most disastrously in the decisions relating to the representation of the Third Estate at the States-General of 1789. The increased importance of the Third Estate in the life of the nation had to be recognized; and so its representation was doubled. But established positions had to be protected; and so each of the Estates was to deliberate and vote separately. Thus the Third Estate would not weigh in proportion to its just recognized importance. The latter decision could not be accepted by the Third Estate, and this was the beginning of conflict. Mirabeau warned the queen that the throne was now opposing a transformation the king had once supported—a transformation in the king's own interest. All in vain. The king was bound to the idea of maintaining acquired rights, taking this to be an essential duty of his office.

This glimpse at the past—cursory and therefore necessarily simplified—is justified by the need for emphasizing two points: foreseeability has always been the responsibility of the sovereign; and this responsibility can be so interpreted as to make for conflict with inevitable or desirable changes.

Major political crises are characterized by the sudden loss of many or most social certainties. As is well known, these are often brought on by reluctance, or powerlessness, to liquidate outworn certainties, and this not only in the realm of private rights but also of political institutions, without exception of the most hallowed. It behoves us to recognize that we live in an age of precipitate change in processes, a tempo productive of rapid obsolescence for material equipment. Obsolescence is communicated to institutions themselves. Therefore we can far less than at other periods guarantee that what is established shall endure. This involves for members of Society a loss of information which must somehow be recouped.

Information about the Future

Information about the future, as I see it, has the social and moral function of overcoming the contradiction between change and foreknowledge. It is wrong not to recognize that conservatism expresses a fundamental human need; we would be lost and helpless without the many landmarks we have memorized, and therefore we cling to the maintenance of the familiar to the eventual detriment of what might be. This conservative propensity is not specific to the most favored, some of whom indeed are emboldened by their good fortune; anxiety is most natural in those who are aware of holding their own only thanks to a daily effort, and nothing is more understandable than workers' fear of automation and attachment to work rules. In all walks of life, men have cause to defend present certainties failing alternative assurances. To such defensiveness, it is at least a necessary answer—not always a sufficient one—to offer reasonable prospects.

The term "reasonable" is stressed; nothing is more dangerous for psychological equilibrium than the launching of heady promises incapable of implementation. It is one of the tasks of those who envisage the future to zone off the unattainable. Many pleasing prospects are irreconcilable with likely human behavior; the sociologists and the political scientist must here weed out the improbable, just as the economist must cut down, in view of their investment costs, some of the technological forecasters' visions.

The second and even more important duty of the social forecaster and strategist is to combat the general feeling of uncertainty which the rapidity of change sheds indistinctly over all institutions. The more change there is, the more valuable are some fixed points; which structural certainties should be tied down and placed beyond doubt? This is no small or easy subject, but it forms an essential contribution to foreseeability.

In between the unachievable and the unchanging stands the ample zone of feasible futures. It is the social strategist's concern to recommend plausible procedures for moving ahead in that zone, procedures favoring change and procuring some sufficient degree of foreknowledge.

The social scientist cannot hesitate to reject both as a nightmare and as a myth the supposed combination of maximum change with perfect foreseeability by means of total Government control; firstly such complete control is effectively impossible, secondly however far it be carried the fruits announced cannot be guaranteed; thirdly it is for the exercise of our liberty that we require foreseeability, and therefore the model is absurd. This is not to say that we can afford to be heedless of its seduction.

Turning to more acceptable prospects, how can we devise the reconciliation sought between freedom and foreknowledge? To set forth the means thereto is easy, but to execute them is not. Suppose all agents are required to declare their intentions as to future actions. It will then be possible to discuss what mutual accommodations will be required if their intentions are to be coapted to one another. Men's intentions must be inflected. It is obvious that to operate on actions by issuing commands is of far less moral worth than to operate on intentions by rational persuasion. In the liberal regime of the future, an important position should be allotted to anticipatory discussion of intentions, and a reduced position to authoritarian prescriptions. This will be possible only if men honestly state their intentions and are open to persuasion on the need of modifying their declared intentions. Although such a system can never be perfect—for no perfection is ever attained in reality—we

36

can strive to approach it. Discussions of the kind held for the French Plan and at the Conseil Economique et Social are a prefiguring of what is to come.

Declarations of intent coming from powerful sources are particularly interesting. Large public agencies, large companies, large trade unions must be induced to speak. The discussions of intentions must be based on the representation of real forces. And since intentions must be adapted to one another, it is clear that the task of calculation and persuasion must devolve upon men of recognized prudence, who do not represent particular sectional interests. Thus in practice the discussion will lie between the *mighty* and the *prudent*.

Only a raving optimist would suppose that the prudent will succeed in conciliating all of the mighty. There will be passionate divisions over certain questions—and these residual questions will have to be treated as subjects of political contention.

Nothing should be settled by a simple weighing of wishes if it can be settled by rational argument. Cournot said that the science (I would say the art) of social economy is mainly concerned with sectional interests, whereas politics deals for the most part with human passions [in *L'Enchaînement des idées fondamentales*, 1911]. He went on to explain that in practice the two are intermingled because "interest engenders passion." But if we were to succeed in using reason to settle everything that is justiciable, the realm of the political would shrink to that remnant which is not justiciable, and conflict would be dulled because men will want to safeguard the harmony established in other domains.

I am not so great an optimist as to think that passionate divisions of opinion will cease once good solutions are found for all material problems. But it is evident that such divisions thrive where material problems are left untended or are only partially solved.

MAX DUBLIN *is a poet and writer now based in Canada. While researching* Futurehype, *published in 1989 (these excerpts are from the Epilogue, from the 1991 edition), he became highly concerned about "the techniques and rhetoric that make our prophets credible and persuasive, and also about how prophecy shapes our world." Highly derisive of futurological trend chasers, Dublin sought to expose "the extent to which prophecy in our time, though often claiming on the basis of science to be an objective business which transcends any system of values or ethics, nevertheless still plays a highly value-ridden part in our political and economic debates." He writes that, "There is no rhetorical or propaganda device more powerful than prophecy." He explains that, "Predictions do not simply describe the world—they act on it." While purporting "to be objective and scientific, modern-day prophecy merely uses the mantle of science to strengthen and legitimize itself while masking its ideological content."*

MAX DUBLIN

EROS AND PLANNING: THE ANT AND THE GRASSHOPPER RETOLD

It is often said that we are living in the age of information, but, insofar as this is true, it follows that we must also be living in the midst of a great deal of bad information, that is, misinformation, propaganda, nonsense and hype. In our time prophecy, in its various forms of prediction, forecasting, futurology and scenario writing, has become a major source of bad information—bad in the sense that it misleads us by distorting our regard for both the present and the future. It thereby brings out the worst in us, encouraging us to behave in narrow, selfish and self-defeating ways.

Because it so often works this way, notwithstanding the good that may sometimes come from trying to be mindful of the future, the role of prophecy today has become rather malign. Although our prophets like to tout themselves as being escorts along the avenues of salvation and exploration, all too often they act as legitimators of questionable schemes and programs that unleash the forces of abandonment, neglect, irresponsibility, destabilization and exploitation. But this is not surprising when you consider how simple-minded, self-serving and childishly impressionable most of our prophets are.

Yet the problem with modern prophecy cannot entirely be attributed to the fecklessness of our prophets; they are, after all, a product of our times and . . . reflect the pathologies of their willing audiences. They exploit only that which is eminently exploitable. The problem with prophecy today and the source of our sometimes pathological obsession with the future is much the same as what Ivan Illich has said is the problem with medicine, that is, prophecy and medicine both represent major interventions in our lives that often cause harm. They do not, of course, always cause harm, and if we wish to give them the benefit of the doubt we should say that they usually intend to do good. But they cause harm often enough and decisively enough so that we should be seriously concerned about the role they play in our lives, both unbidden and at our behest. And we should be particularly concerned because their malign side is not aberrant or accidental but part of their very nature, characteristic of the role these enterprises play today.

Illich's book *Limits to Medicine* [1977] is subtitled *Medical Nemesis: The Expropriation of Health,* and a large part of his argument is that, aside from any other harms the modern practice of medicine may entail, it also expropriates from individuals, with their consent, responsibility for their own health. Therefore, on the positive side, he argues that we should reappropriate the responsibility for our health, which we have both relinquished and had taken away from us, by learning to take better care of ourselves and relying less on health professionals. Modern prophecy, again with our consent, has also developed in such a way that it has come to rob us of an essentially human right and responsibility: the right to dream our own dreams and set our own goals; the right, ultimately, to exercise the freedom, individually and collectively, to make the decisions that will shape our destinies.

It is no accident that prophecy and medicine have both come to work this way; the same could be said of a great deal of present human endeavor. There are many areas in which we abdicate responsibility for our growth and development and for our regular duties and pass it on to professionals, to experts, thereby empowering them and at the same time rendering ourselves ever more irresponsible and helpless. On this level, prophecy today can be regarded as being no more than an attempt by self-appointed experts to rationalize the future. Rationalization today has become little more than an attempt to order and control just about everything by pressing it into the mold of formal logic, and into the paltry calculus of formal means geared towards the achievement of what usually turn out to be extremely narrow ends. In the process of trying to fit everything into this mold, we are constantly deluding ourselves about what can or cannot be done. We are ignoring a great deal of substance in life that cannot easily be fit into this mold, that cannot easily be defined as a problem to which an expert can apply a formal bag of tricks. In this way, we often avoid or ignore vast areas of human endeavor which rationalization cannot easily capture. Our tendency to ignore in the present that which cannot be easily defined and managed as a problem is the intellectual and spiritual precursor to the all-too-common habit of our prophets of trivializing the problems of the future.

The persistent themes of modern prophecy—including its penchant to trivialize and depersonalize all problems, its concomitant obsession with automated decision-making, its "gaming" of life situations, its anti-individualism and its view of the human population as being basically anonymous and homogeneous—are all extremely mechanistic ideas. They necessarily follow from our obsession with the mechanized world view represented by rationalization and the type of control that is supposed to come from it. However, individuality, diversity and heterogeneity are too difficult to capture and predict and therefore defy control. Notwithstanding their power and utility, all machines are a caricature of nature, and the mechanistic future is no more than a caricature of the present, that is, of life.

Yet the way we live is not in the nature of things. Our culture is of our own making, and the beginning of trying to ameliorate its faults is to try to become conscious of them. There are certainly alternative ways to look at the world and think about it than those suggested by our futurologists who, in addition to adopting a mechanistic view of the universe, often lack the imagination to envision a future world that is other than a mere extrapolation of the present, no matter how questionable some parts of that present may be, and who, as George Orwell rightly observed, so often appeal to our fears and our craving for power.

As a point of departure for exploring these alternative views, I will begin by trying to deal with a little unfinished business relating to the panic that so many people feel about the future, and which makes them turn to futurologists for guidance. Early in this book I made the observation that futurologists frequently justify their enterprise by making the claim that, because things are changing so rapidly, we need to be able to predict the future in order to be able, by anticipatory action, to adapt to it. To support this claim they usually refer to familiar slogans such as, "There are far more scientists and technologists alive and working to change the world today than in all the previous history of civilization," and, "The amount of information in the world is doubling every few years and increasing at a far more rapid rate than was previously imaginable." These commonplaces are said to be indisputable facts, and are supposed to portend revolutionary futures for everyone on earth.

However, if you scrutinize them closely, all such statements are questionable, if not simply false. For one thing, we should not mistake the hectic pace of modern life, which includes a great deal of wasted and duplicated effort, for rapid change, or even for forward motion. But even assuming, for the sake of argument, that all change is for the better, what does it mean, after all, to say that the rate of change is accelerating, and why should we assume that an accelerating—or even merely rapid—rate of change can and will be sustained indefinitely? There have been other bursts of scientific and technological activity followed by long or short lulls; is there any basis for assuming that our age will be different? Any number of developments can slow down or even halt the rate of technological innovation and the social and economic transformations that are said to follow it. These include: war; declining prosperity; a turning away of the human spirit from outer, materialistic matters towards inner, spiritual ones; and even a failure of intelligence and/or imagination. Given the importance of mathematics, it is worth bearing in mind that in every age there are unsolved mathematical problems around. That most or even all of these will eventually be solved is highly probable; but exactly when any particular problem will be solved—no matter how important it may be to do so—is unpredictable. The serious decline during the Reagan administration in patent applications in the United States, a nation which prides itself on its innovative ability, is in and of itself evidence enough that these changes can happen to any nation, even during our age, which often likes to think of itself as being above the greater forces of history.

Furthermore, although social change is related to technological development, far less personal change is actually necessitated by such development than our prophets, who are typically so enamored with it, would like us to assume. This means, quite simply, that if we are only willing to exercise it, we can have much more control over our lives than is commonly supposed. To cite a crude example, just because televisions exist, and most of us are likely to bring them into our homes, does not mean that they have to be used as the centerpiece for social life in the family. Just because jet planes make traveling fast and relatively easy does not mean that any given married couple must keep houses in two cities at once in order to develop their individual careers, simply because it is possible to do so. There are perhaps difficult choices involved when a technological development makes a decision in personal life-style possible—many opportunities present precisely these kinds of difficult choices—but they are real choices nevertheless, choices which we can make to shape our own futures.

Now let me return again to the original question: How fast are things really changing? The only way to answer this question is to compare our time with previous eras. Because we take electricity and mechanical power for granted, we have lost perspective on how dramatic was the introduction of these things in the world of the nineteenth century—dramatic not simply because the world at that time was technically naive, as our prophetic hucksters flatter us into assuming, but because these innovations were truly astounding. Perhaps what one considers to be earth-shaking is a matter of personal judgment, values and taste, but I know of no development in the twentieth century, including the computer and biotechnology, which has had and continues to have as dramatic and far-reaching an effect on our lives as the invention and development in the eighteenth and nineteenth centuries of the different kinds of mechanical engine and the electric generator.

In fact, it can be argued that, from the perspective of the power of its impact on our lives, technical innovation has been steadily slowing down during the entire course of this century. To understand what I mean by this statement, ask yourself which of the following innovations have had the greatest impact on your life: the refrigerator, which started making its appearance in the homes of the industrialized nations in the 1940s, or the microwave oven, which started becoming common in the 1970s? The automobile, which became common starting in the 1920s, or the home computer, which started to make its presence felt only in the 1980s? To assess the importance of these appliances, ask yourself the following questions: in each set, which would you sooner give up, the earlier or the later innovation? Which has made the greatest difference in your life?

As we press towards the end of this century, most innovations are no more than refinements of existing technologies: they enable us to do things faster or more neatly, in a glitzier fashion, or more precisely, but not *differently*. Furthermore, the existing technologies, upon whose development so much innovation depends, may themselves find their limits or be exhausted before they perform the miracles that our prophets tell us they will perform in the future. This has often happened in the past. For example, in the Middle Ages many communities in Europe competed with one another to see who could build the biggest and highest cathedral. Many of their accomplishments stand to this day as monuments to their ingenuity. Who has not heard of the cathedrals of Notre Dame, at Chartres, at Amiens and Rheims? But the biggest cathedral that was ever planned and erected was the cathedral at Beauvais. Sound familiar? It shouldn't, because this greatest of all cathedrals is no longer standing. Begun in 1247 and completed by 1557, this marvelous structure collapsed on Ascension Day of 1573. Its ambitious builders had pushed the technology of gothic architecture to the breaking point—and then beyond. This and similar lessons from history should teach us that we should not make predictions simply on the basis of extending present technologies; there is no basis for assuming that any technology is infinitely extensible.

Of course today, using the technologies of reinforced concrete and structural steel, we can build structures even higher and grander than the Beauvais cathedral. But when one technology reaches its limits, it is impossible to predict when a new one will be developed to replace it and push its logic forward. For example, the digital computer of today is based on the "analytic engine" which was invented by the Englishman Charles Babbage in the early nineteenth century. (The "analytic engine" was itself based on the Jacquard loom, the complete development of which, it should be noted, had to be delayed because of the advent of the French Revolution.) The theory of the modern digital computing machine is exactly the same as that of this early predecessor, so why wasn't the nineteenth century the computer age? The answer to this question is very simple: Babbage's "analytic engine" was completely mechanical and the mechanics, that is, the *practice* of the machine, simply could not do justice to its *theory*. There were no alloys in those days that were both light enough and strong enough to sustain the extremely rapid mechanical activity that computing with these machines required. The earliest computers used vacuum tubes and did present some problems with overheating, but the modern computer is basically electronic and therefore has very few mechanical parts so the problem of wear and tear caused by the extremely rapid movement of parts is no longer an issue, although other maintenance problems do remain.

Yet even the development of the modern computer has been limited by the development of software. . . . Software development problems . . . have now for a quarter of a century seriously limited the scope and effectiveness of the computerization of our education system. Admittedly, education is one of the most complex fields in existence for which one might try to develop software, but it is by no means unique. Similar problems are being experienced, for example, in the fields of meteorology and weapons systems.

These apparent limitations on innovation are not a pessimist's list of past and recent failures. Undoubtedly, with persistence, we will eventually be able to solve some, if not all, of the technical problems that now seem intractable. However problem solving, especially the way we practice it today, is not everything: not all of life's difficulties are reducible to these neat little things we call problems, and wishful thinking, intellectual dishonesty and half-baked answers solve nothing. Therefore we should not be basing human existence, including, especially, the existence of future generations, on premises and promises based on false predictions which stem from untried theories and claims of future mastery which may never exist.

It is much more effective, healthy and honest to recognize the complex nature of development as it occurs in this world and, as far as this pertains to definable problems, not to assume that anything can be solved until it has been solved—especially when there is an element of danger involved in failing to do so. It is, of course, morally questionable to create and bequeath any problems for future generations to solve when this is avoidable. But if we do convince ourselves that our development does indeed depend on this type of decision-making, we should ensure that problems that are created in the present will be solvable at some time in the future, and that we know how far in the future this will be likely to happen. The legacy of present problems that stem from the decisions of past actors who either did not care about the future—that is, *our present*—or assumed, conveniently, that we would be clever enough to deal with what, by disdain or neglect, they were preparing for us, is evidence of the importance of this care for the future. From crushing debt burdens—not only in the Third World but now also in the West—to exhausted and eroded soil, to unmanageable nuclear waste: there is ample evidence of this around us. The irony is that it was our prophets, who make the greatest claim to be mindful of the future, who encouraged us to get into these predicaments with their foolish, self-serving, dishonest and irresponsible predictions, and their assurance that if we pursued these paths to the future everything would turn out all right. It is all very well for a futurologist like Jerrold Maxmen to praise the virtue of making bold, optimistic predictions, but it is precisely these kinds of predictions that are likely to put us in greatest jeopardy if proven false.

Now let us look again at the premise that it is necessary to try to predict the future in order to adapt to it by anticipatory action. . . . This kind of adaptation often has a bandwagon effect which can lead to making the prophecies in question self-fulfilling. On the other hand, why does one have to arrive in the future with, as it were, ready-made answers? Why does one have to predict to adapt? Do you have to know there will be a road in your future to be able to cross it? After all, it is not the prediction of the road but your eyes and legs, your intelligence and ability, that get you across. Likewise it is mastery of the present, which "living in the future" often makes us neglect, that will get us through the real future when it finally arrives.

Henry Kissinger has been the prophet of our time who, more than any other, has been enamored of the ready-made answer which can be persistently carried forward to the future. Characteristically, he likes to call this ready-made answer *doctrine*. Not surprisingly, therefore, he has had a strong aversion to, and very little patience with, real, that is, open-ended discussion. So he has written: "If there is no doctrine at all and a society operates pragmatically, solving problems 'on their merits' as the saying goes, every event becomes a special case. More energy is spent deciding where one is than where one is going." ["American Strategic Doctrine and Diplomacy" in M. Howard, ed., *The Theory and Practice of War*, 1965.] And so obsessed has he been with where we are going that he has expressed great impatience with the sticky business of taking stock of where we presently are and where we are coming from. It is surprising that this kind of statement has been so appealing for so long in a country like America which prides itself on its pragmatism, which of course always entails dealing with issues "on their merits" and in context. Probably its sway and the closed-minded abstraction it entails have been major factors in America's decline, because in nations, as in individuals, there are few things that retard growth more than ready-made answers.

One cannot help but contrast Kissinger's penchant for ready-made answers with the views of Edmund Burke, the great English conservative statesman of the late eighteenth century. Burke once wrote: "In my course I have known and, according to my measure, have cooperated with great men; and I have never yet seen any plan which has not been mended by the observations of those who were much inferior in understanding to the person who took the lead in the business." It is worth noting that, because of his willingness to consider all cases on their merits, and because he did not believe in approaching developments with ready-made answers, Burke was able in his time both to oppose the French Revolution on the one hand and to support the American Revolution on the other. Kissinger's statement may be appealing to foreign policy makers, but it would never appeal to airline pilots: they know the importance of knowing exactly where one is coming from and all of the other conditions of one's departure in order to be able to both depart and arrive safely. During the post-war years we have all been witness to how doctrine, precisely because of this aversion to open-ended discussion and the pragmatism that can flow from it, has degenerated to dogma; and we have all seen how this degeneration on both ideological fronts has prolonged and exacerbated the arms race.

The greatest development successes of this century have been based not on abstract goals or grand schemes, but on mastery of the concrete details relating to the situation at hand. This has often meant mastery of received technology, not of innovation. This was as true of the United States in the first half of this century as it has been of Japan in the second. No part of the automobile, except for the electric ignition system, was invented in the United States. But Ford and other pioneers in this industry were foremost at mastering quality control and efficiently producing mechanical systems that were invented in Europe, and thus they created the auto-industrial age. Similarly, Japan is not known to be an innovative country, but a masterful one. It is the high-level mastery of manufacturing technique and not innovation that has earned Japan her reputation for quality. By now it is a well-known fact that many of the things that Japan manufactures, from silicon chips to printed circuit boards, were invented in the United States and other countries; in fact even the much touted Japanese management techniques were invented in the United States.

For years after World War II, Japanese industry kept churning out the same dull and unimaginative models of everything from cars to transistor radios while they were mastering their production and quality-control techniques. In a sense, innovation would simply have been a distraction and an unnecessary luxury at that point. The Japanese were not concentrating on the model of the future, but on the one in front of their noses. Once they had complete control of the production process and were able to manufacture things exactly the way they wanted to, they began to introduce variety and to innovate on their own. By then their innovation was grounded in what they had already really mastered and could therefore do exceedingly well . . . .

There are many races to the future going on now, cheered on by our prophets, and we are already beginning to see some of the consequences of the whole world chasing after the same goals. With more and more people and nations setting their sights on the same targets, the future is becoming like the small end of a funnel. One consequence of so many nations choosing the same developmental goals is that, with everyone heading for the same place, the way is very crowded and it is hard to find any standing room when one arrives. That is why it is said that we are living in such a competitive world. It is not because we are so masterful—too many of our goods, in spite of their glitz, are actually rather uninteresting and shoddy—but because there are too few goals being pursued by too many comers. Another consequence of the whole world chasing the same goals is that the globe is actually becoming increasingly homogeneous and losing some of its rich diversity. This has resulted, of course, in the boredom of finding the same sorts of goods and services all over the world; but it has also led to the loss of some invaluable cultural forms, from literacy to railways, that have been or are being abandoned in the process.

However, in the short run, just as bad as the sometimes harmful homogeneity that chasing after a narrow number of goals is imposing upon the world is the fact that the constant innovation upon which a great deal of futurology is based—and which it encourages—undermines our ability to act effectively in the present. Thinking about the past in moderation is a good thing and can enhance the present. That is why Goethe said that he who knows no history lives in darkness. But thinking about the past excessively, which is commonly referred to as "living in the past," is harmful because it undermines the present by halting human growth and development. The same can be said about thinking about the future: in moderation, it should enhance the present. But the modern obsession with the future is the same as "living in the future," and is simply the other side of the coin to "living in the past." It does not inhibit growth by fixing it at some stage in the past, as living in the past does; it inhibits it by limiting choice and paralyzing the capacity of individuals, communities and nations to maximize the discovery and creation which belong to the present. And it encourages us to live dishonestly and irresponsibly in the present in expectations of future redemption. Finally, living in the future undermines our ability to act effectively in the present because it forces us to constantly learn the "up-and-coming thing" regardless of its merits—sometimes even before the old one has been mastered.

Because of our obsession with the future, many of us have become innovation junkies, but this lust for innovation, often for its own sake, needlessly puts everyone, especially adults, who are often slow learners, into situations where they are periodically, sometimes permanently, being put off balance and rendered incompetent. And it puts children, who are fast learners, in the position of having to invest great amounts of energy in mastering ephemeral things, like rapidly obsolescing computer languages, while neglecting the proven and still necessary skills that would serve them in better stead in the long run. And the institutionalized lust for innovation often leads to institutionalized incompetence in all sorts of public and private organizations. When presented with proposals that are said to be our future salvation, we should always bear these problems in mind, and also bear in mind that today innovation is often no more than a racket. One student of this phenomenon, the educator Michael Fullan, has observed that, although few of the innovations in the education system have made any positive difference in the lives of students or teachers, they have made a great deal of difference in the lives of the innovators themselves; they help them develop their own careers. Just to get an idea of the magnitude of intervention which is here in question, one should bear in mind that in New York City alone there were no fewer than 781 innovative programs introduced into the education system between 1979 and 1981. [Michael Fullan, *The Meaning of Education Change*, 1982.]

Perhaps the best way to understand our obsession with the future and the lust for innovation which it engenders is to think of it as a trap in our culture into which our prophets have been able to lure us because of our fear. But there are other ways of understanding our susceptibility to being lured into this trap. In an illuminating study called *The Myth of the Eternal Return* [1954], Mircea Eliade, the distinguished professor of comparative religion, discusses a phenomenon which he calls "the terror of history." The terror of history is an existential critique of the linear progress of modern history, and a way of comprehending why so many of its steps have been so horrifying. Eliade credits Hegel with formulating the existential position that accepts all historical developments, no matter how terrifying they may be, as being *necessary*. He writes:

> From Hegel on, every effort is directed toward saving and conferring value on the historical event as such, the event in itself and for itself. In his study of the German Constitution, Hegel wrote that if we recognize that things are necessarily as they are, that is, that they are not arbitrary and not the result of chance, we shall at the same time recognize that they *must* be as they are. A century later, the concept of historical necessity will enjoy a more and more triumphant practical application: in fact, all the cruelties, aberrations, and tragedies of history have been, and still are, justified by the necessities of the "historical moment." (emphasis in original)

Hegel's sense of historical necessity should sound familiar because the "necessary past" is basically just the other side of the coin of the "inevitable future" with which so many of our prophets are smitten. Both of these views are born of a linear view of the passage of time; they both act as a rationale for narrowing choice, for narrowing the scope of human endeavor; and ultimately they both act also as an apology for the loss of human freedom this entails. Therefore, Eliade concludes this part of his argument with the following painfully ironic observation: "How could Hegel know what was *necessary* in history, what, consequently, must occur exactly as it had occurred? Hegel believed that he knew what the Universal Spirit wanted. We shall not insist on the audacity of this thesis, which, after all, abolishes precisely what Hegel wanted to save in history—human freedom." (emphasis in original)

The attack on human freedom by modern prophecy is perhaps the most disturbing aspect of futurology. Squeezed between the "terror of history" and the "tyranny of prophecy" people today—in spite of the freedom that is much vaunted, especially in the West—find that they have little room to maneuver. No wonder our prophets appeal, as Orwell observed, to our fear and our craving for power: these are precisely the drives that dominate those who feel trapped. . . .

Of course we cannot, and should not, try to reconstruct the world view and ethos of the so-called archaic societies, but it would be foolish not to recognize the fact that there is more scope for cycles and repetition in modern life, and more virtue in this than our modern prophets would allow.

The cyclical view of time is basically feminine, whereas the linear view, which appeals to virtually all of our prophets, is masculine. The cyclical view therefore sheds a very different light on human development than that which comes from our prophets. Nothing illustrates this better than Aesop's fable about the ant and the grasshopper. Though he lived in the sixth century B.C., morally Aesop had a great deal in common with our modern day futurologists—the seeds of their thinking have always been with us. This fable, is very short so here is the whole thing:

> One fine day in winter some Ants were busy drying their store of corn, which had got rather damp during a spell of rain. Presently up came a Grasshopper and begged them to spare her a few grains, "For," she said, "I'm simply starving." The Ants stopped work for a moment, though this was against their principles. "May we ask," said they, "what you were doing with yourself all last summer? Why didn't you collect a store of food for the winter?" "The fact is," replied the Grasshopper, "I was so busy singing that I hadn't the time." "If you spent the summer singing," replied the Ants, "you can't do better than spend the winter dancing." And they chuckled and went on with their work.

Aesop's fable, which is told in the familiar retrospective mode of the fore-caster writing the history of future time, speaks volumes about the world view of the typical futurologist. The ants, to be sure, had a prophetic vision: they foresaw a grim and cruel future in the coming of winter and, in anticipation, planned for it by stocking provisions. They grasshopper, however, who lived only in the present, failed to see this vision, failed to take the necessary adaptive measures and therefore, from the ants' perspective, was destined to "deservedly" perish. But when you think of it, these ants were not really that insightful; they were, after all, preparing not for an unprecedented future catastrophe, but for the change of the seasons, for the winter which they had seen before and were to see time and again as it was to recur during their life-times. They were only your typical extrapolating futurologists, feeling clever about pointing to the obvious. That is the key: they were motivated not so much by insight as by anxiety, and even when they had a full storehouse that only needed ordinary maintenance based on received wisdom about preventing spoilage, their fear and grim vision drove them on to create a very narrow little world, to cultivate a narrow little niche and live a spiritually impoverished life-style.

This is the most charitable interpretation that one can give to Aesop's fable, but by neglecting other issues it gives him, as a moralist, far more credit than he deserves. Bear in mind how nasty these clever little ant-prophets were when confronted by someone whose world view was different from their own. They were reluctant to stop work even to consider her plight. They did not merely tell the grasshopper to go her own way, they mocked her about her life-style and on account of her profession. They were the prophetic ones; they had vision; they knew the world of the future would be cruel to such as she; they had anticipated it, had made their plans and preparations, and were ready for it. But when you consider the matter more closely, were they not purposive and logical to an extreme? They consulted their heads in all things, including the plight of a fellow creature, but not their hearts. Finally, they denigrated her work, her profession, which was singing; there was not room for it in their world, not in the present and certainly not in the future, where it is represented as being no more than mere folly.

To see how typical they are of modern prophets one has only to recall Feigenbaum's similar tirade: "These intellectuals who persist in their indifference, not to say snobbery, will find themselves stranded in a quaint museum of the intellect, forced to live petulantly, and rather irrelevantly, on the charity of those who understand the real dimensions of the revolution and can deal with the new world it will bring about." [*The Fifth Generation*, 1984.] By now this vision should also sound familiar from other prophetic sources. The reader will recall that Plato, who was one of Aesop's spiritual heirs, took a similar view. In the *Republic* we also have an idealization of narrowly purposive behavior, but there, instead of tilling the soil, an activity which is denigrated, we have the single-minded pursuit of philosophy and athletics relating to military skills. Plato also . . . had no room in his vision for the arts, especially the so-called imitative ones. Similarly Richardson, in his City of Health [*Hygeia*, 1876], where the single purpose was to gear all life to the promotion and sustenance of health, also had no room in his vision for the aesthetic side of life and so he promptly banished all decorations from its households.

There is something very troubling about these visions and the plans and schemes they legitimate and promote—aside from their prissy and uncharitable views, and aside also from the fact that they leave no room for aesthetics. It is not just that they are purposive and spell out future goals, but that their purposes are so very narrow, and their goals are to the exclusion of so many other worthwhile ones. Aesop, falsely but characteristically, makes this single-minded purposiveness a matter of life-and-death necessity; this kind of falseness, at bottom, is what the tyranny of prophecy is all about. More than this, these visions that claim to be very wise seem very foolish when one considers how the world really does develop. The arts, for example, are not a matter of mere luxury, but of necessity, and by saying this I mean more than that music and poetry and fine arts and theatre are good for you—even the meanest agricultural laborer knows the value of a barn dance. Not all of the drive for development comes from science. From the arts come also the creative forces in life, some of which have had profound practical impacts on even our technological and economic development. . . .

The research that is going on now at the Media Lab at MIT and in a similar vein in many of our research and development establishments all over the world is all based on a paradigm of planning that is itself largely based on the paradigm of war. These research endeavors are generally parts of grim campaigns to be the first to occupy a rather unimaginative and narrow future industrial-technological niche: the clever telephone, the artless but glitzy robot secretary, mechanized graphics, and so on. The alternative paradigm of development, which is based on the artist's methods of cultivation and of play do not, because they cannot, have a prophetic quality and therefore are treated with indifference.

War is a seductive paradigm because, in a sense, it is the ultimate act of subjugating substance to form. And it is surely the intellectual basis of a great deal of modern planning, especially the grandest and most ambitious schemes. It is therefore no mere coincidence that many futurologists of our time—perhaps Herman Kahn is most prominent among these—started their careers in military planning. Nor is it accidental that those "think tanks" that have specialized in military research, like the Rand Corporation and the Hudson Institute, have also been major centers for work in futurology. If there is a god of warfare, he undoubtedly serves double time as the god of modern prophecy. And, since influence works in both directions, a great deal of modern futurology is rife with the "campaign" mentality, and the paradigm of war has in turn even invaded the thinking of other areas of futurology, like economics and health.

Planning today is based all too often on the war paradigm. It depends on prior destruction, on the obliteration of a great deal, if not all, present context and detail in order to achieve its ends. Planning, which usually relies heavily on forecasting, has become something of a fetish in social and economic thinking since the end of World War II. In recent years it has been argued, particularly by economic theorists like Professor Lester Thurow of MIT, that the main advantage that Japan and Germany have over the United States is that the former countries have national industrial plans whereas the American economy is developed on an ad hoc basis [*Zero-sum Solution*, 1987]. But there is no magic in planning. Whatever merit there may be in planning per se, its meaning and effectiveness will vary greatly from time to time and from place to place. More than goals, materials or objectives, and far more than any elaborate or simple concepts, planning, to be effective, requires *context*.

This fact is well illustrated by an examination of the outcome of the Marshall Plan and its descendants, some of the grandest economic plans of this or any century. Although the Marshall Plan was devised by the United States to assist all of the nations of Europe that had been devastated by World War II in their effort to build themselves economically, it is well known that it was not equally effective everywhere it was applied. Jane Jacobs, an economist who has a rare understanding of both the uses and the limits of planning, has summarized the different effects of the Marshall Plan in Europe in this way:

> Some of the aided economies, such as those of the Netherlands, West Germany, parts of France and parts of Italy, did proceed to expand and develop—as San Francisco did after its [1906 earthquake] disaster. But others did nothing of the kind. Britain received Marshall Plan equipment, as West Germany did, but this bounty did not make Britain's economy behave like West Germany's. Southern Italy received Marshall Plan aid, just as northern Italy did, but the sequels were strikingly different. Northern Italy, already the most prosperous and economically creative part of the country, proceeded to prosper, develop and expand further. Southern Italy, which had previously been persistently backward, poor and economically passive, stayed so. Insofar as Marshall Plan aid (or the much larger

aid given later from the north of Italy) changed southern Italy, the changes did not transcend the gifts themselves, for southern Italy's economy did not take to expanding and developing on its own account or under its own steam . . . .

[*Cities and the Wealth of Nations*, 1985]

The gist of Jacobs's argument is that, in the different countries that were targeted by the Marshall Plan and by the subsequent Marshall-type plans that were aimed at Third World countries, these plans, in the form of economic and material aid, took hold only where there was context, where there were already enough people who had the necessary types of knowledge and skills to implement them, and in the context of networks and interactive systems in which this infusion of economic and material aid could take hold. In other places, like southern Italy, the Marshall Plan worked as effectively as sprinkling seed on rock or barren ground—in spite of the predictions.

My argument, of course, is not against planning per se any more than it is, in the final analysis, against being mindful of the future. Our experience with the Marshall Plan and similar enterprises has long demonstrated that, in spite of our fetishistic attachment to it, planning in and of itself is inherently neither good nor bad. Like regulation (a related process), planning can be either good or bad. The question is not whether or not one is to make plans. The question is, on what shall these plans be based? If plans are to be based on mere predictions then one must always ask: one what are these predictions really based? And whose interests will their fulfilment or self-fulfilment serve? But we should not delude ourselves into thinking that planning, per se, is always a good, always a virtuous thing to do. On the contrary, a significant part of planning is not only sterile, as was Marshall Plan aid to southern Italy, but often also debilitating, and even destructive.

Good planning should never unnecessarily limit choices; it should expand them. Ideally, good planning will not consist of that which is borrowed, but that which is bred. It will be a natural, concomitant activity, a by-product, if you will, of living as well as possible *in the present*; it will never be a substitute for it, which is often precisely what bad planning is about.

It is worth bearing in mind that the most effective method of combating the spread of AIDS has not been based on the war paradigm, so dear to the futurist. Even five years ago, the war paradigm dominated our thinking on how to deal with this challenge. Great cures were predicted. The disease would be knocked out by a heroic international research effort. But these predictions have so far come to naught. Meanwhile, the most effective means for coping with this disease have come from cultivation, which has led to changes in day-to-day habits of relationship. It is unfortunate that it has taken desperation for us to change in the present instead of continuing to wait for some future miracle to save us, but at least our experience with AIDS is teaching us that we can work effectively with present means, and that the present is the appropriate time in which to combat this or any future catastrophe. Unfortunately, in most other seemingly less desperate situations, we continue to wait for future miracles because we are told by our prophets that they will come.

The paradigm of war, which so many modern prophets invite us to worship, is also the ultimate depersonalizer of life, and therefore cares very little about relationships. It depersonalizes and trivializes all human relationships, all acts of nurturance and love that precede it and many that follow. That is why it is the ideal metaphor for our modern prophets—it fits perfectly into their psychology.

It is impossible to imagine a worse paradigm for thinking of the future, for growth and development, than the paradigm of war. One can say much against it, but basically it entails two main problems. The lesser of these is that it encourages us to put vast amounts of energy not only into preparation, but into overpreparation, to the point where our resources for other endeavors are sapped and we are never at ease to enjoy the fruits of our labor and the repose which should be the gift of everyday life. Those of us who think this is virtuous will stagger through life constantly pressed under the weight of their weapons; those who do not will simply retreat from life and try not to get trampled. No one has described this condition better than E.M. Forster in his novel *Howard's End* [1910], where he writes: "Actual life is full of false clues and sign-posts that lead nowhere. With infinite effort we nerve ourselves for a crisis that never comes. The most successful career must show a waste of strength that might have removed mountains, and the most unsuccessful is not that of the man who is taken unprepared, but of him who has prepared and is never taken. On a tragedy of that kind our national morality is duly silent. It assumes that preparation against danger is in itself good, and that men, like nations, are the better for staggering through life fully armed." Too many of us have completely forgotten the virtues of traveling light through life, relying on our character and inner resources rather than on externalities, on weapons.

The second problem with this mentality is, of course, that in any war there will be winners and there will be losers. In this context I have already mentioned the deadly dullness and homogeneity that results when all nations pursue the same goals; the world as a whole becomes the loser. The war paradigm, which has been a favorite among false prophets from Aesop on down, is not sometimes, but always, a recipe for disaster, if not your own then that of someone else.

The god of war has many attributes that have much to do with how we are today encouraged to regard the future. The god of war, the god of kill, is also the god of overkill, not only because fear of reprisal is a great motivator, but because relentless, blind pursuit is his nature. Even when the battle is going the wrong way, when the plan and the premises on which the plan were based are proving themselves to be useless, or worse than useless, the pursuit is relentless. Soldiers are told to ignore feedback that might distract them from their relentless course, and also to ignore details and context. Very rapidly, and increasingly, everyone becomes the enemy.

The alternative to the paradigm of war which has come to play such a great part in our contemplation of the future is Eros, who is commonly regarded as the god of love, but in this context can more generally be thought of as the god of connectedness. I will describe some of his attributes because they also belong to the alternative paradigm for thinking of the future. I have already mentioned two: repetition and the cyclical mode of living.

The uses of repetition are many in a world which strives for connectedness rather than merely for extension. It is used for gaining mastery and creating meaning, and repeated cycles serve the invaluable purpose of grounding life in the familiar rather than leaving it constantly subjected to the inherent strangeness of the novel. Open-endedness is another of this god's main attributes. Openness means that one never plans on arriving at a future encounter with the false prophet's ready-made answer, but alternatively on discovering the answer in the richness of exploring the new experience. But perhaps the most important attribute of this god which we must understand if we are to change our war-like mentality with regard to the future is cultivation.

Cultivation as an alternative paradigm to war for facing the future is different not only because it is ever constructive, but also because it is constructive by means of being respectful of context and paying close attention to detail. It is not like a moonshot, which is essentially an exercise in decontextualization through the creation of a self-contained environment. Few things in life are like moonshots. Most things are not like that, cannot be made like that because they are too complex, too dependent for their success on paying attention to and interacting with context, to the external environment— including the needs of other people—rather than subduing it by blasting through it. Because it examines context, cultivation requires attention to detail and interaction with that which is being cultivated, be it a school, a child, a tree, a car, a factory.

There is much talk today of competitiveness, of excellence, and much of this talk is patently war talk. It is talk about grimly purposive actions, about heroic acts of will geared towards the achievement of some future goal. But most goals are not achieved by single acts of will, even heroic ones. They are achieved by *sustained acts of will*, that is, by a change of habit, of custom and of culture. That is why all failures in achieving goals, that is, in mastery, be they in our ability to build cars or to make love, are based on failures in cultivation, in nurturance.

Cultivation takes time. Its effect or its failure are cumulative, even though sometimes expressions of the success that comes from it may be dramatic, as when you make a breakthrough in your piano-playing technique, or a tree that has for years been carefully pruned one year bursts forth in blossom and fruit. Sustained acts are necessary because nature is generally forgiving in the short run but not in the long. An occasional inappropriate response to the needs of a child will not permanently damage him or her, but persistent abuse or neglect will. The failures of nurturance, of cultivation, are persistent failures; they are failures which result from persistent neglect of the present.

Neglect and abandonment of the present are symptoms and necessary results of our obsession with the future, and with the relentless pursuit of narrow goals that we think will make the future for us. The heart of all prediction is a correlation of means and ends, but one of the pathologies of modern futurology is to think that means *are* ends. That is why every little innovation—which is usually no more than a disembodied means—gets extrapolated and lionized by our prophets. The tendency to think this way is deadly because it entails the subjugation of ends to means, of questions to answers. The search for applications for the latest innovation becomes not an associative but an exploitative search. Means masquerading as goals, means looking for ends, answers looking for questions, are all agents of exploitation. On the contrary, between ends and means should be continual dialogue. A good answer always changes the question which elicited it, and the changed question requires then a different good answer, until answer and question, means and ends, are entirely different from what they started as.

Tadao Umesao, a Japanese cultural anthropologist, considers narrow goal orientation to be the deadliest form of cultural habit we can develop. He writes: "To say that a goal is clear is to say that it is functional. To say that it is functional is to say that it is 'unifunctional.' What I believe is that at some point our world became filled exclusively with such unifunctional things, and it is this that has led to our present state of confusion." He then goes on to ask: "Is it really so absurd to envisage a plan which does not take a single goal as its final end, a plan in which each successive goal emerges and grows from the process of planning itself—i.e., a process which is rather like a succession of makeshift expedients?" ["Soul and Material Things," keynote address to International Council of Societies of Industrial Design, 1973.] Those who understand Japanese culture on the basis only of the caricature that is presented to the West may find Umesao's contention puzzling, because Japan is usually portrayed in the West as being single-minded. This is true to a point, but it is only a recent development born of the desperation that arose in the aftermath of World War II. Japan has been successful in part because of its single-minded goal orientation, but in larger part because of its ability, like Sweden, to act concertedly as a nation. Umesao argues, however, that in the process of overplanning, Japan has worked itself into a very narrow niche, and he thinks that this will be deadly in the long run.

Context is the enemy of our prophets who like to oversimplify and trivialize everything. The rich, sticky and stubborn nature of reality is their bane. That is why so many of them are so enamored with systems and mechanical precision—yet one must never underestimate how close the precise can be to the petty. So in thinking about future wars Nitze worried not only about controlling the situation with precise language, but also about how atom bombs could be dropped precisely enough to avoid civilian casualties [Paul Nitze, "Atoms, Strategy and Policy," *Foreign Affairs*, January 1956]. It is certainly a high-minded goal if you accept the premise of such a war itself and allow for the vanity in such thinking. Similarly Papert wants to decontextualize the future [Seymour Papert, *Mindstorms*, 1982]. Not only does he want to introduce his LOGO system into the schools, but he has predicted the abolition of the school system itself—and even our system of knowledge which took thousands of years to cultivate—in the process. That would certainly be a great exercise in decontextualization.

If we continue to follow the lead of prophets who trivialize and depersonalize future life in order to make it manageable, imaginable, then our goals will become simpleminded and we will continue to abandon the richness and complexity that works, albeit with difficulties, for a narrow future at best and an impoverished fantasy at worst. We will be sacrificing reality to fantasy. Present reality must be sacrificed, will be sacrificed sooner or later, but then this should be to a new reality, equally rich or richer—not to the impoverished visions of our prophets. There is room for any amount of innovation in this world, but in introducing it we should where possible follow the lead of our most sophisticated cultivators who are now practicing the art and science of intersowing. We should make our gardens richer and more diverse rather than always wanting to start with scorched earth and the new unknown crop.

When those who have power avoid responsibility for making the present work, those who are helpless suffer. The best years of the lives of a large part of the population are frittered away waiting for that miraculous time in the ever receding future when the economy will be ready to let them be a part of it; when society will be less alienating; the world will be safe; the education system will work; a cure will be discovered for the latest disease. There is an enormous amount that can be done with present knowledge, techniques and technology to significantly alleviate these types of problems *now*. Not to act now as best we can to deal with present problems is simply irresponsible. We do not know, cannot know, what will work to solve our problems in the future, but we can find out what will solve them in the present by working to solve them now, with proven means that are already at hand.

By being so enthralled by the future we have made a perversion out of what, when tempered with prudence, can be a virtue, that is, the postponement of gratification. Even on the level of the individual, decisions in which the importance of timing is fairly self-evident are very often indefinitely deferred for the sake of waiting for the "perfect moment," which is always at some time in the future. Countless numbers of people delay marriage and having children to the point where it becomes improbable, if not impossible, to make these decisions sanely and soberly—let alone on the basis of love. Greater numbers refuse to enjoy the daily gifts that life has to offer them for the sake of first completing the dieting or fitness regimen which they have persuaded themselves will make them more worthy people at some point in the future. This kind of thinking has become so prevalent in our society that for many it has become an almost lethal sort of second nature. By adopting this kind of thinking we deny not only our bodies, but our very souls; we postpone not only gratification, but the quest for meaning and fulfilment that should be part of our daily lives.

Furthermore, when it comes to thinking about the future—largely due to the way it is incessantly hyped by some of the most influential leaders in government, business and the media—we have become like impressionable children at a carnival, wildly dashing from one huckster to the next, never finishing a thing before dropping it and running off to grab at the next marvel or treat that is dangled before our eyes. With children, such mad dashing about usually leads to exhaustion and sore stomachs. Is this really the way we want to develop our lives and culture?

This last question is a paraphrase of Tolstoy, who asked not, What does the future hold in store for us? but, What shall we do and how shall we live? If the futurologists who tell us that the future has endless possibilities are really right, we need not wait to hear from them what the future ought to be like. This, as Tolstoy suggests, is a question we should pose to ourselves. Unless we do so, unless we exercise the real freedom we have *at present* to shape our destinies according to the way we want to live, rather than acting on the basis of our prophets' versions of the good and the "inevitable," the less freedom in the long run we will have to exercise. Talk of the inevitable is cheap, but it is also insidious. When we hear it we would do well to ask ourselves: What does the promoter of a particular inevitable scenario have at stake in having it realized? What do they have to gain? And, perhaps more important, because there is no such thing as a neutral future, what do other, undoubtedly more helpless members of our society, have to lose?

In the Jewish tradition, waiting for the Messiah, that is, for the salvation of the future, is now considered to be morally corrupt. One must make the most of the present, not only because it is the given, but in order even to be worthy of the Messiah's coming. There are also similar precepts in Christianity (even though that religion believes the Messiah has already come), and in the other major religions of the world. These religions consider true prophecy to be the highest calling because they recognize that all questions surrounding the uses of prophecy are ultimately moral questions, questions that are concerned with what we want to become. In this sense prophecy that is not grounded in morality is always false. Far from being foresightful, it is myopic and evasive to forget that most questions that can be posed about the future can more meaningfully and forcefully be posed about the present. It is only at our peril that we forget that if we used only the knowledge we now have, and used it only for the good, we could have heaven on earth, without one further innovation or discovery, and thereby create a better world than any of our false prophets are capable of envisioning. This may be a truism but cannot successfully be evaded. It is a matter not of ingenuity but of character, and it is the key to any and all possible good futures.

MURRAY GELL-MANN *was awarded the Nobel Prize in Physics in 1969 for work leading to his discovery of the quark—the basic building block of all atomic nuclei. In this excerpt from* The Quark and the Jaguar: Adventures in the Simple and the Complex, *(1994), he brings the outlook of a physicist (and promoter of the science of complexity) to bear on our human predicament. Gell-Mann, who is Millikan Professor Emeritus of Theoretical Physics at the California Institute of Technology, Professor and Co-Chairman of the Science Board of the Santa Fe Institute, as well as Chairman of the President's Council of Advisers on Science and Technology, makes mental leaps between chimpanzee behavior, superstring theory, and Shakespeare's verse into a unifying vision of the natural world. He focuses his vaulting interests into a complex, but comprehensible vision of a more sustainable world. "It is worthwhile to try to construct models of the future—not as blueprints but as aids to the imagination—and see if the paths can be sketched out that may lead to such a sustainable and desirable world late in the next century . . . ."*

Murray Gell-Mann

Transitions to a More Sustainable World

Concern for the preservation of biological diversity is inseparable from concern about the future of the biosphere as a whole, but the fate of the biosphere is in turn closely linked with virtually every aspect of the human future. I intend to describe here a kind of research agenda on the future of the human race and the rest of the biosphere. That agenda does not call, however, for open-ended forecasting. Instead, it calls for people from a great many institutions and a wide variety of disciplines to think together about whether there may be evolutionary scenarios that lead from the present situation toward a more nearly sustainable world during the twenty-first century. Such an approach is more focused than simple speculation about what might happen in the future.

Why should anyone try to think on such a grand scale? Shouldn't one plan a more manageable project that concentrates on a particular aspect of the world situation?

We live in an age of increasing specialization, and for good reason. Humanity keeps learning more about each field of study; and as every specialty grows, it tends to split into subspecialties. That process happens over and over again, and it is necessary and desirable. However, there is also a growing need for specialization to be supplemented by integration. The reason is that no complex, nonlinear system can be adequately described by dividing it up into subsystems or into various aspects, defined beforehand. If those subsystems or those aspects, all in strong interaction with one another, are studied separately, even with great care, the results, when put together, do not give a useful picture of the whole. In that sense, there is profound truth in the old adage, "The whole is more than the sum of its parts."

People must therefore get away from the idea that serious work is restricted to beating to death a well-defined problem in a narrow discipline, while broadly integrative thinking is relegated to cocktail parties. In academic life, in bureaucracies, and elsewhere, the task of integration is insufficiently respected. Yet anyone at the top of an organization, a president or a prime minister or a CEO [Chief Executive Officer], has to make decisions *as if* all aspects of a situation, along with the interaction among those aspects, were being taken into account. Is it reasonable for the leader, reaching down into the organization for help, to encounter only specialists and for integrative thinking to take place only when he or she makes the final intuitive judgments?

At the Santa Fe Institute, where scientists, scholars, and other thinkers from all over the world, representing virtually all disciplines, meet to do research on complex systems and on how complexity arises from simple underlying laws, people are found who have the courage to take a *crude look at the whole* in addition to studying the behavior of parts of a system in the traditional way. Perhaps the Institute can help to spark collaborative research, by institutions from around the globe dedicated to the study of particular aspects of the world situation, on potential paths toward a more nearly sustainable world. The aspects in question will have to include political, military, diplomatic, economic, social, ideological, demographic, and environmental issues. A comparatively modest effort has already begun, under the name of Project 2050, under the leadership of the World Resources Institute, the Brookings Institution, and the Santa Fe Institute, with participation of people and institutions from many parts of the world.

Now what is meant here by sustainable? In *Through the Looking Glass*, Humpty Dumpty explains to Alice how he uses words to mean anything he wants, paying them for the privilege each Saturday night (the end of the nineteenth-century work week). These days a great many people must be paying wages to the word "sustainable." For example, if the World Bank finances some old-fashioned massive development project destructive of the environment, that project may well be labeled "sustainable development" in the hope of making it more acceptable.

This practice reminds me of the Monty Python routine in which a man enters an office to get a license for his fish, Eric. Told that there is no such thing as a fish license, he points out that he had received the same reply when he asked about cat licenses, but that he has one anyway. Producing it, he is told, "That's not a cat license. That's a dog license with the word 'dog' crossed out and the word 'cat' written in with a pencil."

Today many people are busy writing in the word "sustainable" in pencil. The definition is not always clear. Thus it is not unreasonable to try to *assign* a meaning here. The literal signification of the word is evidently not adequate. The complete absence of life on Earth might be sustainable for hundreds of millions of years, but that is not what is meant. Universal tyranny might be sustainable for generations, but we do not mean that either. Imagine a very crowded and highly regimented, perhaps extremely violent world with only a few species of plants and animals surviving (those with intimate connections with human society). Even if such conditions could somehow be kept going, they would not correspond to what is meant here by a sustainable world.

Clearly, what we are after embraces a modicum of desirability along with sustainability. Remarkably, there is a certain measure of theoretical agreement today on what is desirable, on the aspirations of the human race, as embodied, for example, in declarations of the United Nations.

What kind of future, then, are we envisaging for our planet and our species when we speak of sustainability, tempering our desires with some dose of realism? Surely we do not mean stagnation, with no hope of improvement in the lives of hungry or oppressed human beings. But neither do we mean continued and growing abuse of the environment as population increases, as the poor try to raise their standard of living, and as the wealthy exert an enormous per capita environmental impact. Moreover, sustainability does not refer to environmental and economic concerns alone.

In negative terms, the human race needs to avoid catastrophic war, widespread tyranny, and the continued prevalence of extreme poverty, as well as disastrous degradation of the biosphere and destruction of biological and ecological diversity. The key concept is the achievement of quality of human life and of the state of the biosphere that is not purchased mainly at the expense of the future. It encompasses survival of a measure of human cultural diversity and also of many of the organisms with which we share the planet, as well as the ecological communities that they form.

Some people may be technological optimists, believing that we humans do not need to change course very much in order to avoid a disastrous future, that we can achieve approximate sustainability without special effort, merely through an endless series of technological fixes. Some may not believe in the goal of sustainability at all. Nevertheless, we can all think about it. Even those of us who do not accept sustainability as a goal can still ask whether there are ways to approach it during the next fifty to a hundred years and if so, what those ways might be and what the world might look like as a result. Discussion of the questions does not require sharing the values of those who posed them.

Historians tend to be impatient with people who say, "This is a unique period in history," because that claim has been made about so many eras. Still, our time is special in two well-defined and closely related ways.

First, the human race has attained the technical capability to alter the biosphere through effects of order one [of magnitude]. War is old, but the scale on which it can now be fought is entirely new. It is notorious that a full-scale thermonuclear war could wipe out a significant fraction of life on the planet, not to mention the trouble that could be caused by biological or chemical warfare. Moreover, through population growth and certain economic activities, humans are altering the global climate and exterminating significant numbers of plant and animal species. Actually, human beings caused more destruction in the past than is usually admitted. Deforestation by the axe and by goats and sheep, followed by erosion and desiccation, is thousands of years old and was remarked, for example, by Pliny the Elder. Even the tiny numbers of people living in North America ten thousand years ago may have contributed to the extinction of the North American ice-age megafauna, such as mammoths and giant sloths, dire wolves, sabre-toothed cats, and species of camels and horses. (One theory blames some of the extinctions at least partially on the habit of driving whole herds of animals over cliffs in order to use the meat and skins of just a few.) Nevertheless, today the potential for damage to the entire biosphere is much greater than ever before. Human activity has already created a multiplicity of environmental problems, including climate change, ocean pollution, diminishing quality of fresh water, deforestation, soil erosion, and so on, with strong interactions among them. As with conflict, many of the environmental ills are old ones, but their scale is unprecedented.

Second, the rising curves of world population and natural resource depletion cannot go on rising steeply forever; they must soon pass through inflection points (when the rate of increase starts to decrease). The twenty-first century is a crucial time (in the original sense of a crossroad) for the human race and the planet. For many centuries, total human population as a function of time hewed closely to a simple hyperbolic curve that reaches infinity in about the year 2025. Ours is obviously the generation in which world population must start to peel away from that hyperbola, and it has already begun to do so. But will the population curve flatten out as a result of human foresight and progress toward a sustainable world, or will it turn over and fluctuate as a result of the traditional scourges of war, famine, and pestilence? If the curves of population and resource depletion do flatten out, will they do so at levels that permit a reasonable quality of human life, including a measure of freedom, and the persistence of a large amount of biological diversity, or at levels that correspond to a gray world of scarcity, pollution, and regimentation, with plants and animals restricted to a few species that co-exist easily with mankind?

A similar question can be posed about the progressive development of the means and scale of military competition. Will people allow large-scale, thoroughly destructive wars to break out, or will they use intelligence and foresight to limit and redirect competition, to damp down conflict, and to balance competition with cooperation? Will we learn, or have we perhaps already learned, to manage our differences in ways short of catastrophic war? And what of smaller conflicts arising from political disintegration?

Gus Speth, who was the first president of the World Resources Institute (which I am proud to have played a role in founding), has suggested that the challenge to the human race over the next few decades is to accomplish a set of interlinked transitions. I propose to amplify slightly his conception of those transitions so as to incorporate more political, military, and diplomatic considerations in addition to the social, economic, and environmental ones that he emphasizes. With those modifications, the rest of this chapter is organized around that crude but useful notion of a set of transitions.

The Demographic Transition

We have seen that the coming decades must witness a historic change in the curve of world population versus time. Most authorities estimate that world population will level off during the next century, but at a figure something like twice the present number of 5.5 billion or so. Today, high rates of population growth (associated particularly with improvements in medicine and public health without corresponding declines in fertility) still prevail in many parts of the world. That is especially true of tropical, less developed regions, including countries, such as Kenya, that can least afford it ecologically or economically. Meanwhile, the developed countries have generally achieved rather stable populations, except for the effects of migration, which will certainly be a major issue in the coming decades.

Scholars have engaged in much discussion of the factors thought to be responsible for the decline in net fertility that has taken place in most of the developed countries. They now suggest measures that may help to produce similar declines in various parts of the tropical world. Those measures include improved provisions for women's health, literacy, further education, and opportunities to participate in the work force, as well as other advancements in the position of women; reduced infant mortality (which initially works in the opposite direction, of course, but may later prevent couples from compensating for expected deaths by producing more children than they really want); and social insurance for the elderly, still a distant goal in many developing countries.

Naturally the availability of safe and effective contraception is crucial, but so is the erosion of traditional incentives for having large families. In some parts of the world the average couple (and especially the average male) still wants to have many children. What kinds of rewards can be offered to one- and two-child families? How can people be persuaded, in culturally appropriate ways, that in the modern world such families are in the common interest, with higher levels of health, education, prosperity, and quality of life than would be possible for families with many children? With swings of fashion having such importance in human affairs, what can be done to help the idea of small families to become popular? These questions are still sadly neglected in many places, even by organizations that claim to be helping to solve the world population problem.

If human population is really going through an inflection point and will level off, globally and in most places, in a few decades, not only is that a historical process of the greatest significance, but its timing and the resulting numbers are likely to be of critical importance as well. The exact character and magnitude of the effect of population growth on environmental quality depend on many variables, such as patterns of land tenure, and are worth careful study in various different areas. Nevertheless it already seems overwhelmingly probable that, on the whole, population growth encourages environmental degradation, whether through the huge consumption rates of the wealthy or through the desperate struggle of the poor to survive at whatever cost to the future.

The environmental consequences are likely to be much more serious if the world simply waits for improved economic conditions among impoverished populations to effect reductions in net fertility, as opposed to trying to encourage such reductions in parallel with economic development. The total environmental impact per person is likely to be considerably greater after economic improvement than before, and the fewer the numbers when relative prosperity is finally achieved, the better for the people and for the rest of the biosphere.

The Technological Transition

Decades ago some of us (particularly Paul Ehrlich and John Holdren) pointed out the fairly obvious fact that environmental impact, say in a given geographical area, can be usefully factored into three numbers multiplied together: population, conventionally measured prosperity per person, and environmental impact per person per unit of conventional prosperity. The last factor is the one that particularly depends on technology. It is technological change that has permitted today's giant human population to exist at all, and while billions of people are desperately poor, quite a few others manage to live in reasonable comfort as a consequence of advances in science and technology, including medicine. The environmental costs have been huge, but nowhere near as great as they may be in the future if the human race does not exercise some foresight.

Technology, if properly harnessed, can work to make the third factor as small as can be practically arranged, given the laws of nature. How much the prosperity factor can be improved, especially for the very poor, depends to a considerable extent on how much is squandered on the first factor, mere numbers of people.

Evidence of the beginning of the technological transition is starting to show up in many places, even though the bulk of it is yet to occur. Even apparently simply technological fixes, however, can end up posing extremely complex problems.

Consider the example of eradicating malaria in human populations. Not too long ago, the draining of swamps was still the principal method of control. But now it is understood that the destruction of wetlands is to be avoided whenever possible. Meanwhile, science has identified the plasmodia responsible for malaria and the mosquito vectors that carry them. Spraying with chemical pesticides like DDT to eliminate the mosquitos seemed to be a step forward, but turned out to have serious environmental consequences. For one thing, birds at the top of the aquatic food chain got very concentrated doses of the metabolic product DDE, which caused thinning of egg shells and reproductive failure in many species, including the American national bird, the bald eagle. Twenty years ago, DDT was phased out in the developed world, and the threatened bird populations started to recover. It is still used elsewhere, although resistant strains of the mosquito vectors are starting to appear.

It then turned out that some of the immediately available replacements for DDT were fairly dangerous to humans. Nowadays, however, much more sophisticated methods are available for reducing the populations of the vectors, including the use of chemicals that specifically target them, as well as the release of sterile mating partners and other "bio-environmental controls." Such measures can be coordinated in what is called "integrated pest management." So far, they are still fairly expensive, if deployed on a large scale. In the future, cheaper and equally gentle techniques may be developed. Insect repellents are also available, of course, but they are expensive too and cause problems of their own.

Meanwhile, a simple, behavioral approach that is effective in many places is to use mosquito netting and stay under it for half an hour at dawn and half an hour at dusk, when the vector mosquitoes are biting. Unfortunately, in many tropical countries, the rural poor are very busy outdoors at those times and cannot stay under netting.

Some day antimalarial vaccines will probably be developed, which may even wipe out the various forms of the disease entirely, but then another difficulty will arise: important wild areas that had been protected by the dangers of malaria will be exposed to unwise development.

I have no doubt spent too long on this apparently simple example, in order to expose some of its complexities. Analogous complexities can be expected to crop up anywhere in the technological transition to lower environmental impact, whether in industrial production, the extraction of minerals, food production, or energy generation.

Like the conversion from defense industries to civilian production, the technological transition requires financial assistance and retraining for workers as opportunities close down in one kind of employment and develop in another. Policy makers may be well advised to consider these different types of conversion as posing related challenges. Thus, ceasing to manufacture chemical warfare agents would be regarded as similar to phasing out logging in the old growth forests of the Pacific Northwest of the United States. Moreover, such policy issues come up again when society tries to reduce the consumption of products injurious to human health, whether legal, like tobacco, or illegal, like crack cocaine.

However, on the demand side the three kinds of conversion present somewhat different problems. In the case of chemical weapons, the principal challenge was to persuade governments not to order them any more and to ferret out and destroy the stocks that exist. In the case of drugs, the issues are matters of angry dispute. In the case of the technological transition to lower environmental impact, the question is what the incentives are to develop gentler technologies and to use them. That brings us to the economic transition.

The Economic Transition

If the air or water is treated as a free good in economic transactions, then polluting it, using up its quality, costs nothing; the associated economic activity is carried on by stealing from the environment and from the future. Authorities have attempted for centuries to deal with such problems by means of prohibitions and fines, but those were often ineffective. Today regulation is being attempted on a massive scale in some places, and some successes have been achieved. However, it seems that the most efficient way for governments to deal with such issues is to charge, more or less, for the cost of restoring quality. That is what economists call internalizing externalities. Regulation, with its fines and other punishments, is itself a form of charging. Regulators, however, usually require specific actions by polluters, whereas internalizing costs encourages restoring quality, or avoiding its degradation in the first place, by whatever means is cheapest. The engineers and accountants of the industry concerned are the ones who prescribe the measures to be taken. Micromanagement by bureaucrats is unnecessary.

Attempting to charge real costs is a principal element of the required economic transition from living in large part on nature's capital to living mainly on nature's income. While charging is usually better than regulation, it is certainly much better than mere exhortation. For one thing, it reduces ambiguities.

Suppose you are engaged in awarding green medallions to products with low environmental impact. Soon you encounter a problem. A particular detergent may be lower in phosphates than another and thus produce less eutrophication (growth of algae) in lakes, but it may require greater energy use because it needs hotter water in the wash. As you go on you find more such tradeoffs. How do you balance one consideration against another? If at least a crude attempt is made to charge producers for eutrophication caused by their detergents and if the cost of the energy needed for a wash is clearly marked on the package, a consumer can just use total expenditure to make decisions, and the market will work out the prices. The green medallion may become unnecessary.

The great difficulty in charging true costs, of course, is estimating them. We discussed earlier how economics has never really succeeded in coming to grips with subtle problems of quality and irreversibility, issues analogous to those that arise in connection with the second law of thermodynamics in natural science. Such problems can, of course, be shoved over into the political arena and treated as matters of public opinion only, but surely in the long run science will have something to say about them too. Meanwhile, the simplest approach is to estimate the cost of restoring whatever is lost. In the case of the irreplaceable, some form of strictly enforced prohibition may be necessary, but otherwise the sustainability of quality is closely tied to the idea of paying to restore it, and the definition of quality will be dealt with by science and public opinion in interaction with each other.

A critical part of any program to charge true costs is the elimination of subsidies for destructive economic activity, much of which would not be economic at all were it not for those subsidies. In the work of the World Commission on Environment and Development (the Brundtland Commission), composed of distinguished statesmen from many parts of the world, it took the brilliant Secretary-General of the Commission, Jim MacNeill of Canada, to point out that in order to see what is happening to the environment, one must look not so much at the activities of the Environment Ministry as at the Ministry of Finance and the budget. It is there that the destructive subsidies can be hunted down and sometimes, albeit with great political difficulties, killed.

Discussion of budgets leads directly to the question of whether national accounting procedures include the depletion of nature's capital. Usually they do not. If the president of a tropical country contracts with a foreign lumber company to have a large chunk of the nation's forests cut down for a low price and a bribe, the national accounts show the price as part of the national income, and maybe even the bribe as well if it is spent at home and not sent to a Swiss bank, but the disappearance of the forest, with all its benefits and potential, does not appear as a corresponding loss. Nor is it only tropical countries that sell their forests too cheaply, as attested by the fate of the temperate rain forests of the U.S. Pacific Northwest, British Columbia, and Alaska. Clearly the reform of national accounting systems is a major need in all countries. Fortunately, efforts to accomplish that reform are already being undertaken in some places. Our example also makes clear that the struggle against major corruption is a key element in achieving the economic transition.

Another indicator of the level of concern over living on nature's capital is the discount rate. I understand that the World Bank, in financing projects with large environmental impacts, still applies a discount rate of 10 percent per year to the future. If that is true, it means that the loss of some great natural asset thirty years in the future is discounted by a factor of 20. The natural heritage of the next generation is valued at 5 percent of its assigned value today, if indeed it is counted at all.

The discount rate, used in this way, is a measure of what is called intergenerational equity, which is crucial to the notion of sustainable quality. Discounting the future too steeply amounts to robbing the future. If the notion of discount rate is generalized somewhat, it can be used to encapsulate much of what is meant by sustainability.

The Social Transition

Some economists make much of possible tradeoffs between inter-generational equity and intragenerational equity, that is, between concern for the future and concern for today's poor, who need to exploit some resources in order to survive. Although some of the degradation of the biosphere today is caused by the very poor scrabbling for a living, much of it can be attributed to the wealthy squandering resources on frills. A great deal of it, however, is connected with massive projects that are supposed to help, for example, the rural poor of a developing country, but often do so, if at all, rather inefficiently and destructively. In contrast, the same people can often be aided very effectively through large numbers of small efforts, applied locally, as for example in the practice known as microlending.

In microlending, a financial institution is established to provide very small loans to local entrepreneurs, many of them women, to start small enterprises that provide a living locally to a number of people. Frequently such businesses provide comparatively nondestructive employment and contribute to intergenerational as well as intragenerational equity. Fortunately, microlending to support sustainable economic activity is becoming more widespread.

It is hard to see how quality of life can be sustainable in the long run if it is very inequitably shared, if there are large numbers of people starving, lacking shelter, or dying young of disease when they can see a more comfortable existence attained by billions of other people. Clearly, large-scale moves in the direction of intragenerational equity are needed for sustainability. As in the case of microlending for sustainable development, there is often more synergy than conflict between intergenerational and intragenerational equity. Policies that really help the rural poor in developing countries are much more compatible with those that preserve nature than is often claimed. Policies that truly benefit the urban poor certainly include provisions for avoiding urban environmental catastrophes. Such policies also include measures to resolve the problems in the countryside that are producing large-scale migrations to the cities, many of which are already swollen to such proportions as to be almost unmanageable. In fact, the social transition clearly must include the alleviation of some of the worst problems of the megacities.

Today, even more than in the past, no nation can deal with problems affecting either urban or rural economic activity without taking account of international issues. The emergence of the global economy is a dominant feature of the contemporary scene, and the desire to participate more actively in that economy is a major force affecting the policies of governments and businesses around the world. Together with rapid transport, global communications, and global environmental effects, the prominence of global economic issues means that a greater degree of worldwide cooperation is essential to deal with the serious and interlocking issues that face the whole human race. That brings us to the institutional or governance transition.

The Institutional Transition

The need for regional and global cooperation is hardly restricted to environmental matters, or even environmental and economic matters. The maintenance of peace, so-called international security, is at least as important.

Recently, with the dissolution of the Soviet Union and the "Soviet bloc" of nations, and with a greater degree of cooperation on the part of China, it has become possible for world institutions, including organs of the United Nations, to function more effectively than in the past. For the U.N. to organize the monitoring of elections or to sponsor negotiations for ending a civil war is now a matter of routine. "Peacekeeping" activities are in progress in many parts of the world. The outcomes are by no means always satisfactory, but at least the processes are becoming established.

Meanwhile, transnational cooperation is taking place in many other ways, and indeed the role of the national state is necessarily weakened in a world where so many important phenomena increasingly transcend national boundaries. In many spheres of human activity, transnational and even universal (or nearly universal) institutions, formal or informal, have been functioning for a long time. Now there are many more. Typically, they channel competition into sustainable patterns and temper it with cooperation. Some are more important or more effective than others, but they are all of some significance. A few diverse examples are the air travel system; the International Postal Union; the Convention on Broadcasting Frequencies; Interpol; migratory bird treaties; CITES (the Convention on International Trade in Endangered Species); the Convention on Chemical Weapons; The International Union of Pure and Applied Physics, The International Council of Scientific Unions, etc.; World Congresses of Mathematics, Astronomy, Anthropology, Psychiatry, etc.; PEN, the international writers' organization; financial institutions such as the World Bank and the International Monetary Fund; multinational corporations, including McDonald's as well as IBM; U.N. Agencies such as WHO, UNEP, UNDP, UNFPA, UNICEF, and UNESCO; and the Red Cross, Red Crescent, Red Shield of David, and Red Sun and Lion. Moreover, the increasing importance of English as an international language should not be ignored.

Gradually, bit by bit, the human race is beginning to come to grips, on a global or highly transnational basis, with some of the problems of managing the biosphere and human activities in it. Here the effect of the changed situation in the former Soviet Union and in Eastern Europe is extremely encouraging. It results in the probability of near-universality for numerous activities for which there was little hope of anything like universality before.

Also, negotiations are going forward on issues of the global commons—those aspects of the environment that are not recognized as belonging to anyone and therefore belong to all, where selfish exploitation without cooperation can only lead to results bad for all parties. Obvious examples are the oceans, space, and Antarctica.

Agreements between more and less developed countries can follow the pattern of the planetary bargain, which we encountered earlier in connection with the conservation of nature. Here it assumes a more general significance: resource transfers from wealthier countries to poorer ones carry an obligation for the poorer ones to take measures that advance sustainability in the broad sense, so that avoiding nuclear proliferation is included along with activities such as protecting wilderness areas. (Another manifestation of the planetary bargain is that electric utilities in temperate countries offset their emissions of carbon dioxide by paying to preserve forests in tropical countries.)

However, the problem of destructive particularism—the sharp and often violent competition among peoples of different language, religion, race, nation, or whatever—has come into even sharper focus than usual in the last few years, especially with the lifting of some of the lids that had been put on these competitions by authoritarian regimes. Dozens of violent ethnic or religious struggles are under way in different parts of the globe. Many different brands of fundamentalism are on the march. The world is experiencing simultaneous trends toward unity and toward fragmentation within that unity.

We have mentioned that seemingly no difference is so small that it cannot be used to divide people into harshly antagonistic groups. Look, for example, at the bitter struggle going on in Somalia. Language difference? No, all speak Somali. Religious difference? Virtually all Muslims. Different sects within Islam? No. Clan differences? Yes, but they are not causing so much trouble. It is mainly *subclans* that are at war with each other, under rival war lords, as legal order has collapsed.

The Ideological Transition

What will happen to these trends? If our long-outdated proclivities toward destructive particularism are excessively indulged, we will have military competitions, breeding competitions, and competitions for resources at levels that will make the sustainability of quality difficult or impossible to achieve. Seemingly a dramatic ideological transition is needed, comprising the transformation of our ways of thinking, our schemata, our paradigms, if we humans are to approach sustainability in our relations with one another, to say nothing of our interactions with the rest of the biosphere.

Scientific research has not yet made clear to what extent human attitudes toward other people who are perceived as different (and toward other organisms) are governed by inherited, hard-wired tendencies developed long ago in the course of biological evolution. It may be that to some degree our propensities to form groups that don't get along with one another and to wreak unnecessary destruction on the environment have such origins. They may be biologically evolved tendencies that were perhaps once adaptive but are so no longer, in a world of interdependence, destructive weapons, and greatly increased capacity to degrade the biosphere. Biological evolution is too slow to keep up with such changes. Still, we know that cultural evolution, which is much more rapid, can modify biological propensities.

Sociobiologists emphasize that we humans, like other animals, inherit a tendency to protect ourselves and our close relatives so that we and they can survive to procreate and pass on some of our genetic patterns. But in human beings that instinct to promote inclusive fitness is profoundly transformed by culture. A sociobiologist, invoking the image of someone jumping into a river to save another person from a crocodile, would argue that such "altruistic" behavior is more likely if the other person is a close relative. A cultural anthropologist might point out that in many tribes certain relatives, including fairly distant relatives, are "classificatory" siblings or parents or off-spring, who are treated in many respects as if they really were those close relatives. Perhaps members of such a tribe are just as willing to risk their lives to save their classificatory brothers and sisters as their real ones. In any event, sociobiologists now agree that patterns of altruistic behavior in humans are greatly affected by culture. A certain willingness to risk one's life for another human being can easily extend to all the members of one's tribe.

Such behavior occurs at higher levels of organization as well. On the scale of a nation state, it is known as patriotism. As people have aggregated into larger and larger societies, the concept of "us" has tended to grow in scope. (Unfortunately, stress can reveal lines of weakness in the social fabric that cause it to tear apart again into smaller units. That is what has happened, for example, in the vicinity of Sarajevo, where one resident was quoted as saying: "We have lived next door to those people for forty years, and we have inter-married with them, but now we realize that they are not fully human.") Despite such setbacks, the undeniable trend is toward a more and more inclusive sense of solidarity.

The greatest ideological question is whether, on a short time scale, that sense of solidarity can come to encompass the whole of humanity and also, in some measure, the other organisms of the biosphere and the ecological systems to which we all belong. Can parochial and short-term concerns be accompanied increasingly by concerns that are global and long-term? Can family consciousness undergo a rapid enough cultural evolution to planetary consciousness?

When political unity has been achieved in the past, it has often come about through conquest, sometimes followed by attempts to suppress cultural diversity, because cultural diversity and ethnic competition are two sides of the same coin. To meet the requirement of sustainable quality, however, evolution toward planetary consciousness must accommodate cultural diversity. The human race needs unity in diversity, with the diverse traditions evolving so as to permit cooperation and the accomplishment of the many interlinked transitions to sustainability. Community is essential to human activity, but only communities motivated to work together are likely to be adaptive in the world of the future.

Meanwhile, human cultural diversity has given rise to a multiplicity of ideologies or paradigms, schemata that characterize ways of thinking across the globe. Some of those ways of looking at the world, including particular views of what is the good life, may be especially conducive to sustainable quality. It is desirable that such attitudes become more widespread, even though cultural diversity would suffer through the decline of other attitudes with more destructive consequences. As usual, the preservation of cultural diversity can engender not only paradoxes but conflict with other goals as well.

A few years ago I attended a remarkable lecture given at UCLA by Václav Havel, then president of the soon-to-be-divided Czech and Slovak Federated Republic and now president of the Czech Republic. His topic was the environmental damage to his country during the last decades, with serious effects on human health. He blamed the damage on anthropocentrism, especially the notion that we humans own the planet and have enough wisdom to know what to do with it. He complained that neither greedy capitalists nor dogmatic communists have sufficient respect for the larger system of which we are merely a part. Havel, of course, is a writer and a fighter for human rights as well as a politician. Most ordinary politicians refrain from attacking anthropocentrism, since the voters are all human. But it may indeed be healthy for our species to attribute intrinsic worth to nature and not only perceived utility for a particularly kind of primate that calls itself *sapiens*.

The Informational Transition

Coping on local, national, and transnational levels with environmental and demographic issues, social and economic problems, and questions of international security, as well as the strong interactions among all of them, requires a transition in knowledge and understanding and in the dissemination of that knowledge and understanding. We can call it the informational transition. Here natural science, technology, behavioral science, and professions such as law, medicine, teaching, and diplomacy must all contribute, as, of course, must business and government as well. Only if there is a higher degree of comprehension, among ordinary people as well as elite groups, of the complex issues facing humanity is there any hope of achieving sustainable quality.

It is not sufficient for that knowledge and understanding to be specialized. Of course, specialization is necessary today. But so is the integration of specialized understanding to make a coherent whole, as we discussed earlier. It is essential, therefore, that society assign a higher value than heretofore to integrative studies, necessarily crude, that try to encompass at once all the important features of a comprehensive situation, along with their interactions, by a kind of rough modeling or simulation. Some early examples of such attempts to take a crude look at the whole have been discredited, partly because the results were released too soon and because too much was made of them. That should not deter people from trying again, but with appropriately modest claims for what will necessarily be very tentative and approximate results.

An additional defect of those early studies, such as *Limits to Growth*, the first report to the Club of Rome, was that many of the critical assumptions and quantities that determined the outcome were not varied parametrically in such a way that a reader could see the consequences of altered assumptions and altered numbers. Nowadays, with the ready availability of powerful computers, the consequences of varying parameters can be much more easily explored. The sensitivity of the results to different assumptions can be checked, and the structure of the study can thus be made more transparent. Moreover, part of the study can take the form of games, such as *SimCity* or *SimEarth*, which are commercial products developed by the Maxis Corporation under the leadership of Will Wright. Games permit a critic to revamp the assumptions to suit his or her own taste and see what results.

Peter Schwartz, in his book *The Art of the Long View* [1991], relates how the planning team of the Royal Dutch Shell Corporation concluded some years ago that the price of oil would soon decline sharply and recommended that the company act accordingly. The directors were skeptical, and some of them said they were unimpressed with the assumptions made by the planners. Schwartz says that the analysis was then presented in the form of a game and that the directors were handed the controls, so to speak, allowing them to alter, within reason, inputs they thought were misguided. According to his account, the main result kept coming out the same, whereupon the directors gave in and started planning for an era of lower oil prices. Some participants have a different recollection of what happened at Royal Dutch Shell, but in any case the story beautifully illustrates the importance of transparency in the construction of models. As models incorporate more and more features of the real world and become correspondingly more complex, the task of making them transparent, of exhibiting the assumptions and showing how they might be varied, becomes at once more challenging and more critical.

Those of us participating in a study such as Project 2050, aimed at sketching out paths that may lead toward a more sustainable world in the middle of the next century, face difficult questions. How can these transitions toward sustainable quality be accomplished, if at all, during the next fifty to one hundred years? Can we hope to understand, even crudely, the complex interactions among the transitions and especially the issues that arise from their delicate relative and absolute timing? Is there any hope of taking sufficient account of the wide variations in conditions around the world? Are there other transitions, or other ways of looking at the whole set of issues, that are more important? These questions concern the period, around the middle of the twenty-first century, when the various transitions may be partly accomplished or at least well under way. Thinking usefully about that era is difficult, but not necessarily impossible. As Eilert Lövborg said, in Ibsen's *Hedda Gabler*, when surprise was expressed that his history book had a continuation describing the future, "there is a thing or two to be said about it just the same."

As to the more distant future, what kind of global conditions might prevail, after the middle of the next century, that would really approach the sustainability of quality? What are our visions of such a situation? What would we see and hear and feel if we were there? We should really try to envision it, especially a world with growth in quality finally predominating over growth in quantity. We should imagine a world in which, Utopian as it sounds, the *State of the World Report* and the *World Resources Report* do not look worse every year, population is stabilizing in most places, extreme poverty is disappearing, prosperity is more equitably shared, serious attempts are made to charge true costs, global and other transnational institutions (as well as national and local ones) are beginning to cope with the complex interlocking issues of human society and the rest of the biosphere, and ideologies favoring sustainability and planetary consciousness are gaining adherents, while ethnic hatreds and fundamentalisms of all kinds are losing out as divisive forces even though a great deal of cultural diversity remains. We can scarcely hope to attain anything approaching such a world if we cannot even imagine what it would look like or estimate on a quantitative basis how it might function.

Of the three ranges of time, it is naturally hardest to get people to think about the long-term vision of a more sustainable world, but it is vital that we overcome our reluctance to make concrete images of such a world. Only then can our imagination escape from the confines of the practices and attitudes that are now causing or threatening to cause so much trouble, and invent improved ways to manage our relations with one another and with the rest of the biosphere.

As we try to envision a sustainable future, we must also ask what kinds of surprises, technological or psychological or social, could make that fairly distant future totally different from what we might anticipate today. A special team of imaginative challengers is required to keep posing that question.

The same team could also ponder the question of what new serious problems might arise in a world where many of today's worst fears are somewhat allayed. Just a few years ago, most pundits were not predicting that the Cold War era would soon turn into a new age with different problems, but even those few that were predicting it were not speculating seriously on which concerns would replace the familiar ones that were no longer dominant.

What of the short term, the next few decades? What kinds of policies and activities in the immediate future can contribute to the possibility of approaching sustainable quality later on? It is not at all difficult to get discussions going about the near future, and some of the problems we face in the short run are becoming clear to many observers. Perhaps the chief lesson to be learned from contemporary experience is one that we touched on when we mentioned microlending. It is the importance of bottom-up as opposed to top-down initiatives. If local people are deeply involved in a process, if they help to organize it, and if they have a perceived stake, especially an economic stake, in the outcome, then the process often has a better chance of success than if it is imposed by a distant bureaucracy or a powerful exploiter. In helping tropical areas to achieve objectives in the preservation of nature along with at least partially sustainable economic development, conservationists have found that what pays off the most is investment in local groups and local leadership, and particularly in training for local leaders.

Although it is fairly easy to persuade people to discuss the middle range of time—the era during which the interlinked transitions must be largely accomplished if anything like sustainability is to be achieved—the extraordinary complexity of the challenge may be daunting. All those transitions must be considered, each with character and timing to be determined, perhaps different in different parts of the world, and all strongly coupled to one another. Still, that very complexity may lead to a kind of simplicity. Certainly it is true in physical science (which is much less difficult to analyze, to be sure, but may still have some lessons to teach) that in the neighborhood of a transition, say from a gas to a liquid, near a mathematical singularity, there are only a few crucial parameters on which the nature of the transition depends. Those parameters cannot always be characterized in advance, however; they must emerge from a careful study of the whole problem. It is true in general that the behavior of highly complex nonlinear systems may exhibit simplicity, but simplicity that is typically emergent and not obvious at the outset.

Integrated policy studies of possible paths toward a more nearly sustainable world can be exceedingly valuable. But we must be careful to treat all such studies as "prostheses for the imagination," and not to attribute to them more validity than they are likely to possess. Trying to fit human behavior, and especially problems of society, into the Procrustean bed of some necessarily limited mathematical framework has already brought much grief to the world. For instance, the science of economics has often been used in that way with unfortunate consequences. Besides, ideologies destructive of human freedom or welfare have often been justified by arguments loosely based on science, and especially on analogies between sciences. The social Darwinism preached by some political philosophers of the nineteenth century is one of many examples, and by no means the worst.

Nevertheless, taken in the proper spirit, a multiplicity of crude but integrative policy studies, involving not just linear projection but evolution and highly nonlinear simulation and gaming, may provide some modest help in generating a collective foresight function for the human race. An early Project 2050 document puts it this way: We are all in a situation that resembles driving a fast vehicle at night over unknown terrain that is rough, full of gullies, with precipices not far off. Some kind of headlight, even a feeble and flickering one, may help to avoid some of the worst disasters.

If humanity does equip itself somehow with a measure of collective foresight—some degree of understanding of the branching histories of the future—a highly adaptive change will have taken place, but not yet a gateway event. The accomplishment of the interlinked transitions to greater sustainability, however, would be such an event. In particular, the ideological transition implies a major step for humanity toward planetary consciousness, perhaps with the aid of widely managed technical advances now only dimly foreseeable. After the transitions, humanity as a whole—together with the other organisms inhabiting the planet—would function, much more than now, as a composite, richly diverse complex adaptive system.

MERRITT ROE SMITH *is Professor of the History of Technology at the Massachusetts Institute of Technology. He contributed the paper selected for this anthology at the twenty-first Nobel Conference in 1985 at Gustavus Adolphus College in Minnesota (published in* Responsible Science: The Impact of Technology on Society, *edited by Kevin B. Byrne, in 1986). Smith examines how the concept of progress itself has evolved since the days of Thomas Jefferson. He also looks intensively at the processes of technology and industrialization as they affect our future. Keeping in mind nineteenth-century attitudes, Smith asks what kind of progress society longs for and what price it is willing to pay for it. In terms of the twenty-first century, he suggests that progress does not entail any unfolding of a grand plan.*

MERRITT ROE SMITH

TECHNOLOGY, INDUSTRIALIZATION, AND THE IDEA OF PROGRESS IN AMERICA

"*Science finds—industry applies—man conforms.*" Though little noticed at the time, these bold words epitomized the main theme of Chicago's Century of Progress International Exposition in 1933. Everywhere—in artwork, architecture, exhibits, lighting, and overall symbolism—the fair's promoters underscored the idea that progress rests on technology. Reflecting on the same theme in a book written to commemorate the Chicago fair [*The Idea of Progress*], historian Charles A. Beard observed that "technology is the fundamental basis of modern civilization," "the supreme instrument of modern progress." "Of all the ideas pertinent to the concept of progress," he emphasized, "none is more relevant than technology."

But that was more than fifty years ago. In view of recent events like the accidents at Bhopal, Love Canal, and Three Mile Island, as well as the continuing nuclear arms race, today's audience is likely to consider such pronouncements overstated, even naive. Have public attitudes changed or does the Promethean ethos manifest at Chicago continue to hold sway in our society? How have Americans viewed technology historically? What popular technological legacies live on in the American mind and how have these experiences shaped our present perceptions of technological change? What is the relationship between technology and the idea of progress in America? Obviously, these questions have no easy answers. This essay addresses the promises and pitfalls of viewing technology as the primary vehicle of social progress.

Changing Perceptions of Progress: The Erosion of the Jeffersonian View

The idea of progress is deeply rooted in American culture. Briefly defined, it consists of the belief that things are getting better and better and that eventually the good life will be achieved "across the entire range of human endeavor" primarily through advances in science and technology [Leo Marx in *Science, Technology and Human Values* 8, Fall 1983]. Although the concept can be traced back to classical times, its modern phase dates to the seventeenth century (the age of the Scientific Revolution) and is associated with thinkers like Sir Francis Bacon and René Descartes. In its American form, the idea of progress initially drew more vitality from evangelical religion and the frontier experience than from science or technology, though that relation-

81

ship changed appreciably as the United States achieved independence and entered a period of sustained economic growth. That the frontier experience fostered an aggressive "go-ahead" mentality among Americans, while evangelical Protestantism encouraged a strain of millennial optimism that melded nicely with earlier Calvinistic beliefs about individual predestination and national destiny, is often remarked. Clearly, the idea of progress and the idea of destiny are closely intertwined in American history. Together they form our culture's dominant conception of history—much of which is mythological, to be sure, but which nonetheless permeates our perspective both as individuals and as a nation. The quasi-religious character of the idea of progress needs to be underscored in this context because it helps us to understand why the concept is so deeply rooted in American culture and why, as Leo Marx so aptly puts it, "a causal nexus exists between progress *within* science and technology and the general progress of humanity."

What constitutes progress? Intellectual, material, moral, political improvement? Given the definition just provided, these categories seem adequate. However, complications arise because meanings shift and emphases vary over time. What we mean by progress today is markedly different from what was meant in the eighteenth century. Take, for example, Thomas Jefferson's views about the subject. No one of his generation held science and technology in greater esteem. Yet, as much as he revered discovery and invention, he always kept them in perspective and considered them *means* to achieving a larger social end. For Jefferson, progress ultimately meant the realization of a republican polity (with its emphases on liberty and virtue) in a predominantly agrarian society. "The manners and spirit of a people" counted most to him because they helped to "preserve a republic in vigour." As for factory cities and large-scale manufacturing enterprises, he feared that their unconstrained growth would eat like a cancer into the social fabric and destroy the laws and constitution of the United States. "Let our workshops remain in Europe," he admonished in 1787. "While we have land to labour then, let us never wish to see our citizens occupied at a workbench, or twirling a distaff." [*Notes on the State of Virginia.*]

Although Jefferson held these views throughout his life, his actions as president and public policy maker ironically helped launch the United States into the Industrial Revolution. To him credit is due, for example, for first calling attention to interchangeable manufacturing methods in European armories and urging their adoption in the United States—a development that subsequently became one of the primary sources of mass production in America. Later in life, he even admitted in correspondence with friends the need for a factory system of production. What deserves special emphasis here is that his reservations about large-scale manufacturing reflected a more general concern about the implications of progress. Like many of his compatriots, Jefferson worried that progress in some areas could mean back-sliding in others. As one of the primary architects of the American governmental system, he well recognized how precarious the equilibrium between liberty, power, and virtue really was and how easily republics could be corrupted. In the minds of late eighteenth-century Americans, thin lines separated virtue from vice, prosperity from decadence, and civilization from savagery. If carried to extremes, the civilizing process of technology and industrialization could easily be corrupted and bring down the moral and political economy he and his contemporaries had worked so hard to erect. Given the seriousness of this threat, Jeffersonians (as well as many other Americans) could never completely shed their misgivings about the factory system, even though they allowed it and, in many cases, actively participated in it. When they spoke of progress, as they often did, they consequently gave human betterment (intellectual, moral, spiritual) equal weight with material prosperity. Without betterment, prosperity was meaningless. The pursuit of science and the development of technology doubtless occupied an important place in this scheme of things. But as means to larger social ends, they assumed a lesser order of magnitude in the Jeffersonian scale of values.

When Thomas Jefferson died in 1826, the United States had already joined the Industrial Revolution. By that time, the Boston Manufacturing Company's famous "integrated" textile mill at Waltham, Massachusetts, had been in operation well over a decade and scores of mechanized factories dotted the eastern landscape of America. In the same year, a little-known Yankee mechanic named John H. Hall unveiled a complete set of wood- and metal-working machinery capable of manufacturing firearms with interchangeable parts and actually demonstrated the practicality of the concept before an astonished group of government officials. Only a year earlier, the Erie Canal had successfully linked the Great Lakes with the Hudson River, thus opening an enormous hinterland market to New York City and inaugurating a transportation revolution that would culminate decades later with the completion of a transcontinental railroad system. Clearly, a new era had dawned and with it emerged a different set of attitudes about progress in general and the role technology would play in it. Slowly but perceptibly, the belief in progress began to shift away from the moral and spiritual anchors of the revolutionary era toward a more utilitarian and hardheaded business-oriented emphasis on profit, order, and prosperity.

Specifying exactly when and where these new attitudes first appeared is difficult. No doubt they had resided in the culture all along, only to become more manifest as the pace of technological change quickened during the early national period (c. 1787–1825). In any case, one finds ample evidence of the new viewpoint among Jefferson's contemporaries, particularly those merchants and politicians who supported Alexander Hamilton's controversial programs for national economic development during the 1790s.

A case in point is Tench Coxe (1755–1824). A prickly Philadelphia aristocrat who eventually ended up as a middle-level civil servant (Purveyor of Public Supplies), Coxe emerged as the new nation's foremost political economist and exponent of industrial development during the years that spanned the administrations of five presidents from the 1780s to the 1820s. Like many of his contemporaries, he believed that America's political independence hinged on the establishment of economic independence. Given the country's lowly economic status, he emphasized the need for machine-based manufactures as the prime solution to its political problems. Indeed, he told an audience of sympathetic listeners in the summer of 1787 that manufacturing represented "the means of our POLITICAL SALVATION."

> It will consume our native productions . . . it will improve our agriculture . . . it will accelerate the improvement of our internal navigation . . . it will lead us once more into the paths of virtue by restoring frugality and industry, those potent antidotes to the vices of mankind and will give us real independence by rescuing us from the tyranny of foreign fashions, and the destructive torrent of luxury.
>
> [reprinted in Folsom and Lubar, *The Philosophy of Manufactures*]

Contrary to those who viewed manufacturing as a threat to America's agrarian way of life. Coxe (a Jeffersonian in politics) held that mechanized industry would stimulate agriculture by consuming its products and creating even larger markets for agricultural goods. Throughout his writings, he tactfully subordinated manufactures to agriculture, referring to the latter as America's "great leading interest." Yet Coxe's priorities clearly contrast with Jefferson's. For Jefferson, progress meant the pursuit of science and technology in the interest of spiritual and material needs of people, and maintaining a proper balance between them. For Coxe, the emphasis shifted away from individual human needs to more impersonal societal ends, particularly the establishment of law and order. Coxe's anxiety about the nation's shaky economy clearly reflected an even deeper concern about the state of society. In his papers and addresses of the period, he repeatedly expressed his fear that "extreme poverty and idleness in the citizens of a free government will ever produce vicious habits and disobedience to the laws, and must render the people fit instruments for the dangerous purposes of ambitious men." Convinced that such behavior would ultimately destroy the country's liberty, he thus supported the establishment of a strong central government as well as policy measures aimed at shoring up the republic against the excesses of democracy. In effect, he sought to substitute institutional for ideological constraints.

One measure, surely the one dearest to his heart, aimed at putting people to work in factories. "A man oppressed by extreme want is prepared for all evil and the idler is ever prone to wickedness," Coxe declared, "while the habits of industry, filling the mind with honest thoughts . . . do not leave leisure for meditating or executing mischief." The factory promised to employ the poor and indigent (particularly women and children) and "deliver them from the curse of idleness." In a word, it would be more than a place of employment; it would be a moral gymnasium where "correct habits" of discipline, hard work, obedience, and punctuality could be inculcated. Every establishment of any size had work rules that enjoined employees from drinking, gambling, swearing, and loitering during working hours and prodded them to attend church on Sunday as well. But in the process of fostering a tightly controlled, paternalistic environment, factory masters established a wall between themselves and their employees that eventually led to bitter confrontations over wages, working hours, and general control over the shop floor. As industrialization proceeded apace, class distinctions became more pronounced as the face-to-face relationships of the traditional craft shop gave way to the bureaucratized rule of the factory. By the 1830s, considerable tension seethed beneath the surface of industrial achievement. What had begun as an honest effort to improve and stabilize society ended up fraught with ideological and class differences.

In the midst of this strife, popular orators and journalists hailed "the progress of the age," reassuring their audiences that technological innovation not only exemplified but actually guaranteed progress. The evidence seemed incontrovertible. Decade by decade the pace of technological change quickened—railroads, steamships, machine tools, telegraphy, structures of iron and steel, electricity—and with each decade popular enthusiasm grew for inventors—these "Men of Progress"—and their inventions. Owing to their efforts, Ralph Waldo Emerson exclaimed, "life seems almost made over new." "Are not our inventors," asked another enthusiastic writer, "absolutely ushering in the very dawn of the millennium?" It certainly seemed so to Horace Greeley, the editor of the New York Tribune. Upon visiting that city's Crystal Palace Exhibition in 1853, he pronounced: "We have universalized all the beautiful and glorious results of industry and skill. We have made them a common possession of the people. . . . We have democratized the means and appliances of a higher life." In Greeley's opinion, technology had become democracy's greatest ally.

Not everyone saw things the same way, however. Members of America's intellectual community—artists such as Thomas Cole; writers such as Nathaniel Hawthorne, Herman Melville, and Henry David Thoreau expressed serious misgivings about the new technology and its social consequences. One thinks, for example, of Hawthorne's ingenious short story, "The Celestial Railroad" (1843), in which the steam locomotive and its cars are depicted as a satanic implement following a path straight to hell. Others, such as Emerson, felt more ambivalent about the changes taking place, at times hailing the "mechanic arts" as a great liberating force for humanity and on other occasions expressing concern about their implications. The sage of Concord seemed to grow more pessimistic with the passage of time. "What have these arts done for the character, for the worth of mankind?" he asked an audience in 1857. "Are men better?" The answer, unfortunately, seemed clear to Emerson. " 'Tis too plain," he concluded, "that with the material power the moral progress has not kept pace. It appears that we have not made a judicious investment. Works and days were offered us, and we took works."

Emerson came closer than perhaps any other writer of his time to capturing the tensions that confronted working people in nineteenth-century America. Reflecting the powerful influence Protestant theology and republican ideology exercised on the popular imagination, this tension consisted of a bifurcated view of industrial progress. On the one hand, workers (like other Americans) were fascinated with the age's technical creativity as well as the ingenious products that issued from it. On the other hand, they frequently became apprehensive when new techniques actually entered their workplaces and threatened to upset and rearrange accustomed methods of doing things. No one knows whether large numbers of workers actually read Emerson's writings about technology, let alone appreciated his complex double-edged message. I suspect they did not. Emerson the philosopher and the common factory hand lived in different social worlds and operated on different planes of perception and understanding. Emerson sought to extrapolate to the highest level of human experience; workers had to cope with their own immediate experiences. While Emerson blamed the "mechanic arts" for the country's materialistic emphases and threatened spiritual bankruptcy, workers worried about more mundane issues such as the design, deployment, and management of new machines and the effect they might have on wages, hours, and working conditions.

American working people seem to have been ambivalent about innovations that impinged on their work ways. While they seldom completely repudiated the new technology, they did not fully embrace it either. Instead they vacillated between the old and the new, curious—even admiring—but always apprehensive. As citizens and consumers, however, their attitude toward technology often took a different twist. Here, owing partly to patriotic pride and partly to personal predispositions, working-class Americans seemed to embrace the idea of progress as fervently as members of other classes. This is amply attested to by their eager acquisition of industrial products, their admiration of others, and their strong support for public education. Without question, one's view of progress depended, among other things, on whether one was at home or at work, at the store or in the mill. Recognizing the existence of this double-sided attitude toward technology helps us grasp more clearly the complexities as well as the paradoxes inherent in the idea of progress and how perceptions of it varied among different segments of the population. Progress not only meant different things to different social classes, but also different things to the same person.

Was Emerson correct? Had the country—its people and its institutions—sacrificed moral progress for material power? Had the critical balance between spiritual growth and worldly prosperity, a concern so central to Americans of Jefferson's era, been lost? The answer, I believe, is yes, although some qualification is needed. With rapid industrial growth, the population gradually drifted away from its revolutionary republican moorings toward a more secular and materialistic frame of belief. It did so more by default than by conscious choice. To be sure, the old republican creed could still be heard occasionally in Fourth of July speeches and on other celebratory occasions, but its purpose was primarily rhetorical, its effect nostalgic. In its place had emerged a new creed that glorified the "march of invention" and the material "progress of the age." Henry Adams, one of the most astute observers of nineteenth-century America, witnessed these changes and wrote movingly about them in his famous autobiography. At the outset, he recognized the impact technology had exerted on his life through railroads, steamboats, and telegraphy. But the capstone came when he attended the Paris Exposition of 1900 and witnessed the tremendous invisible power generated by electric dynamos. Awed by the experience, Adams reported that he "began to feel the forty-foot dynamos as a moral force, much as the early Christians felt the Cross." Moreover, he sensed that the dynamo had replaced the cross as the primary force in civilization. Indeed, he found himself praying to it! For Adams, the contrast between the dynamo and the cross symbolized an enormous shift of faith away from the great principles of Christianity toward those of science and utility. The former stood for love; the latter for power. For Adams, as for Emerson, the contrast between these two "kingdoms of force" spoke volumes about what had been lost through industrialization. Nearly forty years earlier, in 1862 [in a letter of 11 April], Adams had observed to his brother Charles that "man has mounted science and is now run away with." By 1900, the truth of that statement seemed even clearer.

In summary, this brief reconnaissance into the nineteenth century has revealed that, prior to the Civil War, Americans turned away from an essential part of the republican ethos and, in doing so, lost touch with basic human and moral sentiments that had originally informed the idea of progress. Bolstered by a seemingly endless stream of triumphs in science and technology, social leaders became increasingly arrogant about what could be achieved through rationalization and standardization and began to discount—even disparage—other beliefs that accentuated ambiguity and variability in human affairs. With the spiritual element effectively removed from the idea of progress, its materialistic aspects became dominant. The old parity between moral and material progress disappeared and with it emerged one of the central dilemmas of our present age, namely, an unbridled enthusiasm for technological innovation and the ascendancy of profit over tradition in the rush to rationalize all aspects of industrial life.

Technology As Progress: The Case of the Auto Industry

Our attachment to the idea of progress in its modern utilitarian form has often caused us to overlook the human and environmental implications of technological change. This is not the place to present a comprehensive review of the shortfalls of progress. Suffice it to say that the evidence of such is plentiful. Instead, let us look briefly at the automobile industry, an area of enterprise that became emblematic of American technological leadership in the twentieth century. This example will allow us to discern how progress as an idea is related to progress as an actual social process.

Of all the consequential innovations introduced during the twentieth century, the self-propelled motor vehicle stands at the top of the list. As in the case of virtually all new technologies, the introduction of the automobile had a number of unintended consequences. On the positive side, it extended one's freedom of choice, power, and mobility in ways that had never been dreamed of. On the other hand, its widespread use led to serious traffic problems (congestion, unsafe driving, and so on) and environmental problems (noise, air pollution) and, according to some observers, bore responsibility for increased sexual promiscuity, decreased church atten-dance, and the breakdown of family and neighborhood solidarity. All these factors are sufficient to warn us of the ambiguities and doubts that complicate popular perceptions of the idea of progress. For the moment, however, I want to single out a more subtle problem, indigenous to industrialization, that initially affected a relatively small segment of the population but has had significant long-term consequences for everyone. I refer to mass production and the standardization of work.

The person who popularized the concept of mass production, of course, was Henry Ford. Between 1908 and 1914, his company introduced the famous Model T and developed manufacturing methods that completely transformed the automobile industry and rapidly diffused throughout the American and world technological communities. From the outset, Ford's disarming candor and hardheaded practicality captivated Americans. No doubt people saw a bit of themselves in the Flivver King, and they evidently liked what they saw. Tough, reliable, practical, and, above all, economical, the car aptly reflected Henry Ford's character.

With the resounding success of the Model T (fifteen million were made between 1908 and 1927), Ford assumed the mantle of a national folk hero. His opinion was sought on everything from politics to religion, and he seemed to have ready answers for just about everything. When asked, for example, what he thought about the debilitating environment of the city, he retorted curtly, "We shall solve the city problem by leaving the city." Ford's pronouncements always seemed so disarmingly candid and simple, but embedded in them were deeply imbued values and attitudes that reflected the rural Protestant culture from which he came.

To be sure, Ford was a man with a mission. "I am going to democratize the automobile," he told a friend in 1909. "When I'm through, everybody will be able to afford one, and about everyone will have one." However, when it actually came to building Model Ts, Ford's "mass production for the people" took a singularly perverse turn away from democratic values toward autocracy. Ford the factory master and Ford the popular hero turned out to be quite different persons. While he enthusiastically promoted his "car for the great multitude," he adamantly rejected the notion of socioeconomic equality. "Most certainly all men are not equal," he wrote in his autobiography (1922), "and any democratic conception which strives to make men equal is only an effort to block progress." In Ford's utilitarian mind, democracy was inherently wasteful, and there was nothing he detested more than waste. Thus, even though he viewed himself as a benefactor of humanity—a businessman who worked not just for personal profit but also for social welfare—he adopted a quasi-military approach to production and steadfastly refused to acknowledge the equality of people on the shop floor with himself. In Ford's hierarchical world (as in Huxley's *Brave New World*), everything had its assigned place. Hired labor's place was to stand at command and submit to the rules of the employer.

Ford's manufacturing approach, popularly known as Fordism, emphasized principles of efficiency, rationality, continuity, and speed. Specifically, it consisted of a highly integrated and closely managed system of single-purpose machine tools, standardized fixtures and gauges, moving assembly lines, and absolute interchangeability of parts. The key words here are *system* and *rationality*. Compared with earlier industrial methods, what is noteworthy about Ford's system is the degree to which it subordinated workers to machines. Prior to the advent of mass production, workers had pretty much controlled the pace of their work by virtue of their monopolization of essential skills. Under Fordism, this changed. Ford and his engineer associates—men like "Cast Iron" Charlie Sorenson and Pete Martin—made no bones about their desire to simplify individual work tasks and, if possible, replace skilled workers with machinery. Such thinking had long been a central premise of industrial engineers. But Ford was the first to carry it out on a massive scale. The idea was to simplify individual work assignments so that they could be performed by virtually anyone with a few days of training. In doing so, the Ford management team eliminated the need for large numbers of skilled molders and machinists, often the most independent and intractable of factory employees. Their places would be filled by "deskilled specialists" or machine tenders, all of whom performed basically the same tasks of inserting a workpiece in a preset machine, throwing a switch, and removing it. Such work, which reached its logical extreme on the assembly line, was highly repetitive and routinized with no opportunity for employees to exercise individual judgment. Fordism demanded a new degree of conformity. Instead of setting their own pace, workers found themselves being paced by the machine.

The response to Ford's methods was predictable. Workers complained about the relentless pressure and deadly monotony of the assembly line and likened the company's new Highland Park factory to a lunatic asylum. Indeed, the comic episode in the movie *Modern Times* (1936) in which Charlie Chaplin's Little Tramp goes berserk after experiencing the speed and pressure of work on an assembly line was inspired by Chaplin's visit to Ford's Highland Park plant in 1923.

Serious labor problems clearly existed at Highland Park. In 1913, the year Ford introduced the assembly line, daily absentee rates averaged around 10 percent of the total work force, while labor turnover reached an amazing 370 percent. This meant that on any given day from 1300 to 1400 workers stayed home and that "Ford managers had to hire more than 52,000 workers to maintain a workforce of about 13,600 persons." Needless to say, such problems seriously jeopardized the efficiency of Ford's operations.

The company's solution was to institute the famous five-dollar day in January 1914, an action that signaled an important trade-off in labor-management relations. In return for higher wages and shorter hours, Ford's employees submitted to a highly paternalistic welfare plan that imposed rigid controls on both their home life and their work day. In addition to condemning idleness as a disgrace and exalting the gospel of hard work, members of Ford's "Sociological Department" (his personnel office) actually entered the homes of workers, questioned them about personal affairs, and instructed them in such matters as personal hygiene, social behavior, and especially thriftiness. The company had a very definite idea of what thrift entailed. "By this," a company official stated in January 1914, "we mean that the employee shall not be addicted to the excessive use of liquor, nor gamble, nor engage in any malicious practice derogatory to good physical manhood or moral character." Moreover, he added, every Ford employee was expected to "conserve his resources and make the most of his opportunities that are afforded him in his work." Thrift thus had important moral connotations, but mainly it aimed at ensuring that employees would come to the plant fully prepared to work attentively and to give their best to the company.

In the short run, money talked and Ford's paternalistic program got results. Within the space of a year, labor turnover fell from the phenomenally high levels of 1913 to 54 percent. During the same period, absenteeism decreased from 10 to around 2.5 percent. But in the long run, the program of social control failed. High wages simply could not compensate for the absence of humane working conditions. Although the Ford Motor Company paid the highest wages in the automobile industry, workers found the system oppressive. Labor turnover continued to be high because thousands of people simply could not stand the unrelenting pace and its accompanying pressures. Those who stayed on the job quickly learned how to slow the machine down through various forms of sabotage and subterfuge. Such practices allowed them to cope with their labor rather than take satisfaction from it. Although the trade-off between labor and management continued, it operated to neither side's satisfaction. Managers complained about labor's lack of commitment and loyalty to the firm while labor complained about harsh working conditions and a fundamental lack of respect on the part of their employers. At best, the high wage–hard work trade-off was a tenuous accommodation [Stephen Mayer, *The Five Dollar Day*, 1981].

Recent events in the auto industry reveal that the same old problems persist. Numerous investigators have documented the dissatisfaction that exists among workers, even though their wages and benefits remain among the highest in the land. Writing about the "Blue-Collar Blues" in the 1970s, for example, journalist Judson Gooding observed that "high absenteeism and quit rates, excessive rework and scrap, deliberate acts of soilage and vandalism, hostile resistance to supervision, and an increased willingness to strike" pervaded the work force. Other writers have detected the same symptoms while attributing them to deep-seated psychological and social problems inherent in mass production. Almost everyone agrees that high wages and excellent benefits have not generated the incentive, loyalty, and high quality work manufacturers initially expected. In this respect, money does not talk; the promise of material comfort has not produced widespread feelings of satisfaction and fulfillment. Indeed, by the 1970s, the high wage trade-off had become a distinct economic liability to manufacturers, especially after foreign competitors began to capture long-held American markets for mass-produced goods.

Instead of directly confronting and resolving the social tensions inherent in mass production, industry leaders have tended to do what they have always done, namely, look for technological fixes. For them progress has meant designing the human element out of the production system. And, to a significant degree, they have succeeded. With critical support from military-funded research projects, large amounts of resources have been channeled into the development of automated production systems. The earliest of these, numerically controlled machine tools, appeared in the 1950s under Air Force sponsorship, although widespread applications of the new technology did not take place for nearly two decades. Today mass production industries, led by automakers, have moved well beyond specialized applications of auto-mated machinery toward the deployment of highly integrated computer-controlled design and production systems for *entire* factories. The most noteworthy examples are computer-aided manufacturing (CAM) systems, computer-integrated manufacturing (CIM) systems, direct numerical control (DNC) systems, programmable controllers (PC), and, of course, robots like PUMA, General Motors's Programmable Universal Machine for Assembly. Collectively, these innovations and others like them form the core of what is now being called the Third Industrial Revolution.

From a narrow economic perspective, the results are impressive. Even critics acknowledge the potential flexibility, productivity, and profitability of the new systems. Perhaps most important in the eyes of managers, computer-programmed machinery neither tires nor talks back. Like the mechanical slaves so often depicted in nineteenth-century American litera-ture, they perform their tasks efficiently and without complaint. In this respect, the new technology presents an ideal solution to the perceived labor problem by solidifying management's control of the shop floor and lessening labor's influence. This is possible because managers now have direct access to computer programs that direct the machinery; they no longer have to rely as much on workers at the point of production. Having been designed to minimize the need for skills and to diminish the need for worker decision-making, the new technology holds the promise of effectively establishing management's authority over labor.

Computer Automation: The New Technological Fix

Presented with the prospect of cheaper goods of comparable, perhaps even better, quality, it is not surprising that most Americans (including working people) generally view computer automation as a positive force. That is, they see it as progress so long as it doesn't threaten their earning power or routinize and downgrade their labor. To say this, of course, is to acknowledge the paradoxical behavior Americans exhibit toward technological innovations. A machine operator may think nothing of buying a TV set made in an automated factory, but whether or not to bring a centrally controlled automatic production machine into his or her shop—that is a different question. Certain distinctions thus separate what people accept as progress and condemn as exploitation. The way people respond to change depends on what they do, how long they have been doing it, and where they stand in the organizational and social hierarchy. Questions of status, tradition, and control thus loom large in any discussion of technology and progress. By and large, American workers are no more antagonistic toward technological innovations than are other members of society. But when change threatens to undo certain valued rights and traditions, they quite naturally resist, as anyone would.

Unquestionably, automation, as currently practiced in the United States, poses a serious threat to working people. Even setting aside the hotly debated issues of deskilling, dislocation, and structural unemployment (all of which are attributed to automation), other reasons for concern exist. For one thing, workers consider employment in automated plants to be dead-end jobs with little or no chance for skill enhancement or advancement. At the same time, stress levels on the job remain as high as, or higher than, they were at Ford's Highland Park factory in the early 1900s. An even more ominous feature of the new technology is management's ability to monitor work more closely through various computer controls. Indeed, the technology has now advanced to the point that a supervisor can sit at a console with a CRT screen and keep track of scores of machines on a production line. Formerly, machine operators could pace themselves or take a break by putting in already finished work and, in effect, cutting air. Now by detecting the amount of electric power being used at each machine (power usage is higher when the machine is actually at work), supervisors can even tell when a machinist is goofing off. Employers no longer have to hire spies, as Henry Ford did, to tell them what is going on in the shop. Computer systems do it for them.

Finally, the leverage mechanics used to exercise over their employers by virtue of their possession of special skills and knowledge of the shop floor is rapidly eroding. Given the tremendous flexibility and uniformity of the new computer technology, managers now can use it as a way of disciplining labor by threatening to move production to some other locality. This happened in 1973, for example, when General Motors, faced with a strike at its Cadillac Seville body plant in Detroit, moved the tapes containing all the information necessary to machine body dies to a nonstriking plant in Flint, Michigan. This is the ultimate advantage of automation to employers: it can be used to ward off and even break strikes. As the failure of the highly publicized Professional Air Traffic Controllers Organization (PATCO) strike in 1981 well illustrates, the advent of computerized automation has fundamentally altered "the balance of economic power in collective bargaining in management's favor." [Harley Shaiken, *Work Transformed*, 1985.]

It might be argued that the internal problems of automated mass production touch a relatively small segment of the population and that, after all, far more people benefit from its products than are degraded by its processes. Should not the fears and grievances of working people be submerged in the interest of the larger good? To be sure, this position has some validity. Our society has achieved one of the highest standards of living in the world and we have already noted how Fordist methods helped to democratize the ownership of automobiles as well as all sorts of consumer products in America. *But* mass production has another dimension that is more problematic, namely, its authoritarian character and the larger effects it can have on a democratic society. Several writers—notably Lewis Mumford and Harley Shaiken—have pointed to the fundamental incompatibility that exists between authoritarian technics and democratic values. "When work is electronically demeaned in the office or the factory," Shaiken writes, "the repercussions carry far beyond the workplace." That "artifacts have politics" is unquestionable. As products of particular segments of society, technologies reflect the values of their creators and are thus loaded with ideological implications. How far dare we go before the authoritarian character of our leading technologies spills over and erodes our political and social system? Have we reached that point already?

Progress and the Question of Priorities

How does all this bear upon the idea of progress in America? Should the belief in progress be jettisoned as a largely misguided dream? I think not. Although a number of intellectuals have predicted the idea's early demise in the twentieth century, it continues to exercise considerable sway among all segments of the population. At times, the belief in progress seems to recede in American culture (for example, 1930s, 1970s), only to reemerge evidently as strong as before. This remarkable resilience testifies to the doctrine's centrality in American culture. Indeed, it is so deeply rooted in the culture that I doubt if it could be extracted without our paying an unacceptably high psychological and economic price. I, for one, worry that we might sacrifice more by ridding ourselves of the concept than we would gain.

The idea of progress has its positive and negative aspects, to be sure. We have seen how appeals to progress have been used to condone profoundly antidemocratic practices in our society. We also have seen how modernization in the form of sophisticated, productivity-enhancing technologies and highly rationalized management controls are justified—often at the expense of working people—in the name of progress. But we also need to remind ourselves that, in its early formations, the idea of progress stood for high moral principles—more specifically, political liberty and a just society—and human betterment. In addition to fostering a "go-ahead"–"get-ahead" mentality among Americans, it aimed at strengthening our commitment to egalitarian as well as individual rights. Equally important, the belief in progress encourages hope: hope for the human race, hope for the improvement of its condition, hope that history will have a happy ending. These are perhaps heady dreams, but very commendable ones nonetheless.

Many years ago as an undergraduate, I read an article entitled "What Is Still Living in the Political Philosophy of Thomas Jefferson?" "In respect to particular forms and policies," the author [Carl Becker] concluded, much of Jefferson's philosophy was outmoded. But "in respect to fundamentals"— particularly the place of human rights and "the form of government best suited to secure them"—he found Jefferson's philosophy "still valid." My message is that much is still living in the idea of progress in America. And not all of it is for the better. In our rush to pursue "sweet" problems, accumulate fortunes, and exercise power and influence, we have often substituted technocratic means for humanitarian ends and, in the process, lost sight of the priorities that people of Jefferson's day assigned to the idea of progress. To them progress meant material prosperity, to be sure. But it also meant growth of the human spirit and the abolition of inequalities in society.

That today's society is far more complex than that of Jefferson's era cannot be denied. Having discovered "that 'rationality' splinters our lives as rapidly as it orders them," we are far less sanguine about the inevitability of progress. We have learned the hard way that not everyone profits from progress. We also have learned that technological progress does not necessarily mean social progress and that there are winners and losers in the process of technological change. The arms race, environmental deterioration, structural unemployment—all these press upon us ever harder. Faced with these dilemmas, perhaps it is time to get back to fundamentals. We need to rekindle the Jeffersonian ideal of the "middle landscape" with its sensitivity to the necessity for balance between the spiritual and material aspects of life, between nature and civilization. In the process, we have to be willing to ask, debate, repeat, and hope to resolve without recrimination or reprisal the hard questions: "Progress for whom? Progress for what? What kind of progress do we, as a society, really need?"

ERICH HARTH *in* Dawn of a Millennium: Beyond Evolution and Culture *(1990), from which this excerpt comes, offers a deeply humanistic perspective. Born in Vienna, Harth is Emeritus Professor of Physics at Syracuse University, New York, and has devoted thirty years of study to the function of the brain. With our "Stone Age bodies and Stone Age brains," Harth contends that we now "face tasks for which we are genetically unprepared." He asks, "What is the life expectancy of a technological civilization?" There are no statistics on which to base an answer, but he suggests that "our future is as uncertain as the roll of perfect billiard balls after ten collisions . . . ." Harth explores the social context and meaning of our changing visions. "Our present decisions reach out farther into the future than anything mankind has done in the past, but the outcome is uncertain. There was a time when our visions were centuries ahead of reality. It was humanity's dream time."*

PERSPECTIVES

Language, science, art, the noble aspects of our history as well as the shady ones, our weary outlook on the future—they all come together in and emanate from that unique function of the human brain we call *mind*. It is the most powerful mover of our destinies, and yet, we have difficulty demonstrating that it even exists. Leibnitz gave that striking description of our vain attempts to find *ourselves:* "A man goes out of his house, looks in at the window, and is surprised to find that the room is empty."

How, then, are we to find our way? Who, or what will be our guide? But the empty room, to continue Leibnitz's metaphor, springs to life with a single occupant, who—merely by thinking—creates around himself a universe seething with activity. This has been called *circular causality . . . , self-transcendence, the Promethean gene,* or just *consciousness.* It describes the power to *reflect, resolve,* and *create.*

"Existence conditions consciousness," said Karl Marx, to which Joseph Brodsky, the Russian poet, essayist, and winner of the Nobel prize for literature in 1987, replied that this "was true only for as long as it takes consciousness to acquire the art of estrangement; thereafter, consciousness is on its own and can both condition and ignore existence." [*Less Than One,* 1986.]

Both statements are terse, especially when taken out of context. We understand Marx's preoccupation with the powerful grip the environment (existence) exerts on human affairs (consciousness). But what does Brodsky mean by "the art of estrangement"? It seems an odd expression when applied to consciousness, since consciousness is generally taken to be a kind of passive familiarity not only with the world around us but with ourselves. Brodsky reminds us that consciousness is a *source* of reality, not just its observer, and that self-consciousness is not only to know oneself, but to *make* oneself.

We are not compelled to base our actions on the mores, customs, or other dictates of our culture, nor on evolutionary selections that, eons ago, provided us with some adaptive advantage. We have argued too long about the relative weights of nature and nurture, as though we had to be slaves to one or the other. I believe that is what Brodsky meant when he said that "consciousness is on its own."

Resolutions arise from the realization of the absurdity of some of our ways, the incongruity between our actions and our needs. Such realizations don't come easily, but are often gleaned—as in a mirror—in a story or in a work of art. The impact of Shirley Jackson's short story "The Lottery" has to do with the familiarity, the downright folksiness of its characters, which contrasts with their savage custom of stoning to death one of their members in an atmosphere resembling a country fair. By contrast, the violence depicted in the magnificent Assyrian sculptures that lined the palace walls at Nineveh and Nimrud is generally regarded as belonging to a bloodthirsty but long-forgotten past. But the incongruity in Jackson's story stands out only because the characters are homey and the custom is unfamiliar. How many savageries do we overlook because they are part of our own civilization's heritage?

The Violent Hominid

It is difficult to reject the notion that violence is in our genes. There are too many examples of mayhem inflicted by humans on one another to believe that it is all culturally conditioned. Cultures differ widely, but time and again we are shocked to find brutality and murder among what we took to be the gentlest of peoples. This is true for the Samoans, so lovingly and trustingly portrayed by Margaret Mead, as well as for the !Kung bushmen, the so-called harmless people, of the Kalahari desert. Both of these have now been shown to have a high incidence of violent crime.

The Gebusi, a small tribe living in the New Guinea rain forest, have been described as "a strikingly gentle lot," except for the fact that "behind this aura of serenity . . . the Gebusi murder one another at a rate among the highest ever reported . . . ." [B. Bower, "Murder in Good Company," *Science News*, 133, 1988.]

Unlike the Samoans, !Kung, and Gebusi, the Yanomamo tribe of Amazon Indians has a reputation of being a fierce, warlike society, in which tribal warfare and retaliatory murder alternate in bloody succession. To have killed somebody appears to be a status symbol among Yanomamo males, and anthropologists report that this distinction confers upon the killer the advantages of more wives and more numerous offspring. [N.A. Chagnon, "Life Histories . . . in a Tribal Population," *Science*, 239, 1988.]

Chimpanzees, our nearest relatives in the animal kingdom, who long enjoyed the reputation of gentle herbivores, were observed to kill their own kind in occasional forays, much to the dismay of their most dedicated chronicler, Jane Goodall.

Western civilization has taught us to shun the more blatant aspects of homicide. I recall a short story I read long ago, probably in German. It was set somewhere in the Polish countryside, sometime in the last century, when

Polish freedom fighters were carrying on a prolonged struggle against Russian domination.

It was a time when soldiers wore ragged but colorful uniforms in the field of battle and when officers were handsome, had mustaches, rode into battle on horseback, and carried sabers as tokens of their manhood and authority.

The story opens when a group of Polish partisans have captured some Russian officers, lined them up against the trees at the edge of a small clearing, and are about to shoot them. The proceedings are held up temporarily when one of the Poles points out that they could use the fine shirts, the tunics, and the boots the Russians are wearing, and wouldn't it be a shame to pump them full of bullet holes.

It is agreed. The prisoners are told to strip off their clothes, and the firing squad resume positions. Again there is a delay. Firing upon a group of shivering, naked men does not seem to be part of the mystique of fighting a war of liberation. Again the muskets are lowered, and the prisoners are told to get dressed again. With the uniforms hiding the Russians' bodies, the Poles have no trouble completing what they have set out to do. This was not murder, it was simply part of the war, and the blood of the executed complemented in proper fashion the colorful tunics and the fine white shirts they wore below.

We generally exhibit a noble reluctance to inflict harm on others who, like the naked Russian prisoners, have no visible mark to set them apart from ourselves, though the story has a hollow ring when we think of the millions of Jews marched naked to their doom in German gas chambers.

But in our more civilized acts of violence we like our victims clothed, if not in uniforms at least in ideas or symbols. A strange religion can bring out our most feral passions. Nothing is as likely to incite hostility as somebody's belief in a God with whom we are not on speaking terms. No activity seems so distasteful as a ritual that does not evoke childhood memories in us. Ecumenism aside, and the many nice things American clergymen say about one another from their respective pulpits, the ongoing slaughter between Hindus and Sikhs in India, the blind hatred between Protestants and Catholics in Northern Ireland, and the savagery of total war between all shades of religion in the Middle East are testimony to the mindless rage brought about by conflicting deities.

Why do we do it? Many possible roots of violence have been cited, fear, frustration, social conditioning, and genetic disposition among them. Part of the old Adam we have not yet been able to transcend. These are probably all valid. There is also self-righteousness, and its cousin, *loyalty*. In listing loyalty among the culprits, I realize I am attacking a sacred cow. To be loyal is a noble attribute most of us aspire to. Loyalty is affection, gratitude, self-sacrifice. But loyalty is also often seen as an obligation to tilt one's judgment, curb one's nagging doubts, and to rally unquestioningly behind an idea, slogan, or symbol. Such loyalty, which is a vestige of pre-Darwinism *essentialism*, tends to promote moral blindness, self-righteousness, and violence.

It may still be an adaptive advantage among the Yanomamo Indians, but in most societies today, the tendency to commit violence is more likely to land you in jail. On an international scale, unfortunately—although appropriate moral standards are universally agreed upon in principle—we lack independent juries to establish guilt, and, anyway, countries can heed or reject the verdicts of international courts at their discretion. Given the proper manipulation of their own populace, most governments find it relatively easy to garner the necessary internal support for almost any action.

But here, also, we find that aggressiveness is even less advantageous than it used to be, and—given the built-in instability of the world balanced on the knife-edge of mutual assured destruction—may ultimately be catastrophic. Goethe was wrong when he said that our hidden urges generally point us in the right direction. It seems that our collective gene pool and societal interactions cannot be trusted. The voices within us, and those around us, often speak an ancient language, befitting a different time. We must counter with a watchful consciousness that practices the "art of estrangement," and if necessary forego the comfort of loyalty. At any rate, finding the right way, rather than being instinctual, will often require intellectual efforts of the most strenuous kind, without which our sociobiological system will surely self-destruct.

What I am suggesting raises, of course, the most complex ethical issues. Our society is founded on laws, most of which are designed to make our world better and fairer. Violations bring punishments, as they should. But laws can become obsolete, and situations arise that would make compliance seem less ethical than violation. On occasion we are required to participate in, or at least condone, actions that violate our own sense of right and wrong. If we now said that everyone should follow the dictates of his or her own moral judgment, we would invite lawlessness and chaos, while rigid adherence to all laws and moral standards of the society would make individual ethics superfluous. We come up against a situation here in which no advice can be given. With all the laws and standards that society has set up, the individual is ultimately and unequivocally on his own.

The Human Family

. . . Human beings, it turns out, are an unusually homogeneous species. Genetic studies suggest that modern man emerged in a single location in Africa and spread from there over the rest of the world.

But just as remarkable as our genetic uniformity is the great diversity of the human spirit. It seems to come from out of nowhere. Place that rigid framework of human genes into an environment—any environment—and it will sprout ideas and behavior that are always fresh and mostly unpredictable, like the fire scattered in all directions by the monotonous lattice of carbon atoms in a gem-cut diamond that is held up to light. This is admittedly a weak metaphor for the emergence of mind in the interplay of nature and nurture.

We have invented for ourselves such diverse goals as becoming artists, scientists, airline pilots, and Zen priests; we fill every niche of political opinions; and we subscribe to every possible belief system in what Brodsky termed *consciousness conditioning* and *ignoring existence*. We ignore existence, the limitations of existence, that is, when we seek out physical hardships for which our bodies are ill-equipped, or strive for intellectual achievements never envisioned by evolution. We also ignore the intimate relatedness of all humans, when we look for and amplify the minutest distinctions among us, until we find ourselves surrounded by what looks more like our natural enemies than members of our own close-knit species.

There is a reason for this. Our intellect has great difficulty dealing with unity, because, without a background against which to measure our ideas and ourselves, we have no yardstick. Without opposing forces, our efforts seem to fall into a vacuum. We do our best creative thinking in adversity and in interaction with an adversary. An interesting parallel exists in physics. Time and space are meaningful references when we are dealing with a portion of the universe—objects on earth, a star, or even a galaxy. But when we contemplate the universe as a whole we have lost all signposts. Questions such as, Where does it come from? and Where is it going? become meaningless.

In antiquity the Greeks coined the phrase "Man is the measure of all things." To the Athenians, "man" meant Athenian, not Spartan, and certainly not barbarian. Today, we are still applying the standard in the same parochial manner, as though substituting *mankind* for *man* would plunge us into an existential and moral vacuum.

But very recent history has brought profound changes that we are just beginning to recognize. Our environment has been up to now a virtually limitless stage on which to display our varied plumage and play our games of war and peace. It is only in the last few decades that the walls have moved in on us, and we perceive forces that are equally hostile to all of us: the dwindling resources, our own explosive population growth, the deterioration of our atmosphere and our waters, the dramatic accumulation of our wastes with no place to put them, and a technology of mass annihilation whose hair-trigger control strains our nerves and threatens our existence.

These new hostile forces provide us with a novel frame of reference, and allow us, compel us, for the first time in our history, to view humanity as *one*, because, for the first time every action we take against one another will be to our own detriment. This is not an easy lesson to learn. We still react to the nuclear threat by trying to build a Super Excalibur, that now discredited centerpiece of the Star Wars effort. It is a comic strip mentality unworthy of the doubly wise. Still, our enmities are deep, our genes are combative, and prejudice is a disease of the mind humans are heir to. We must expose it and treat it with understanding, instead of answering it in kind. If that is what Christ meant by "turning the other cheek," the admonition was premature, by two millennia.

The Mind and the Machine

If not doing what is rational is a sign of faulty thinking, how do we think properly? . . . It appears that our brains are burdened with a sociobiological albatross that deflects rational thought. Must we then cultivate an emotionless, more computerlike function of the brain?

It will certainly be necessary to strengthen our ability to select from the many possible scenarios the most beneficial path. This will require enormous intellectual effort. Fortunately, we have at our disposal an arsenal of computers and supercomputers with their vast memory and computational power. We have only begun to make full use of them. In the field of medicine, for example, diagnosis and therapy selection could be improved greatly if every physician had at his or her disposal an up-to-date profile of pathologies and complete statistics on success and failure rates of medications and surgical procedures. Such *global* strategies, drawing on probabilities computed from a worldwide data base, are already used extensively in weather forecasting. This may seem like a return to . . . an essentialist or collectivist approach that led to abuses like the eugenics movement. Many physicians argue, with some justification, that no machine can substitute for the personal knowledge he may have of the patient. But often, individual judgment is inadequate and statistical information becomes valuable. In the Center for Disease Control in Atlanta, Georgia, computers are able to spot trends in pathologies and relate them to outbreaks of communicable diseases or the result of new products that have come into use.

We may look forward to increasing reliance on computers in all kinds of decision making, in place of intuition, instinct, or judgments based on custom or emotions. This will mean a check on some of our so-called better instincts like compassion, which may seem a high price to pay. But compassion is a capricious virtue. The Palestinian elicits little compassion from the Israeli settler and vice versa. Compassion can become infectious, as when a whole nation anxiously followed the fate of two whales trapped in arctic ice, or it can vanish without a trace when one ethnic group slaughters another "for a cause."

Are we then bound to become automata, with our brains restricted to feeding information into the data banks of our computers and receiving from them our instructions? Is the ultimate irony of our search for artificial intelligence that we are becoming more like machines?

There is no denying that some freedoms will have to be sacrificed. One of these is the unrestrained pursuit of knowledge . . . . But, I do not see computers as anything but our obedient servants in tasks where the human brain is slow and clumsy, as in recalling lists and manipulating large numbers. I recall traveling in the Soviet Union some years ago and finding long lines at airport ticket counters awaiting the arrival *by air* of handwritten ledgers containing passenger lists and reservations. I tell this story whenever someone laments the increasing automation in our lives. I do not foresee a takeover by computers. If the brain is poor at computing, it is the brain that has thought of arithmetic algorithms to do with pencil and paper what it can't do in the head, and eventually invented computers. By comparison, a computer, which is poor in inventiveness, does not analyze the rules of creativity and will not construct a brain.

The advocates of "hard AI" [artificial intelligence] like to point out that any mental task that is understood can, in principle, be done by a computer. This is the "you-define-it-and-we'll-put-it-in" challenge. I would like to counter that with "*you* define it and I'll put it in myself." But creativity defies the kind of definition that could be useful for such purposes. Human consciousness is still the least predictable system in all of the known universe. In fashioning its *creative loops*, it is able to reach beyond its own biological limitations, just as it did when it invented the first stone tool. Reason will compel us to follow the rational deductions reached by our logical machines, but the knowledge gained will only expand the horizons of the human mind. And it will be the minds of *individual* humans that will continue to create the future visions in science, in art, and in new concepts of human coexistence. We turn once more to the words of Brodsky, who found a poet's way of expressing the old Darwinian truth that collective nouns are "approximations, conventions, common denominators, and that numerators are what civilization is all about."

Of Death and Renewal

There is danger in allowing our consciousness to soar without constraint and go too far "ignoring existence." Humans alone in the animal kingdom have the capacity to will their own destruction or at least to rationalize their doom. Soldiers by the millions have marched willingly to their deaths, statesmen have proclaimed their willingness to die for an idea, and religious fanatics of all ages have submitted themselves to torture and death for an extravagance of mind called faith.

Suicide is the ultimate estrangement, and humans have perfected this art individually and collectively from Cleopatra to Hemingway, from Masada to Jonestown.

The unique bent to "let go," to "throw in the sponge," has a universal counterpart in religious millennialism, which in various forms asserts that we have reached "the end of the tether" and should now accept the inevitable. The "inevitable" is a form of Armageddon, that is, the end of the world as we know it and the beginning of a phase that has terrible consequences for the sinner but is not too bad for a few blessed souls.

Such sentiments were widespread before the year A.D. 1000 and then again in the early nineteenth century, especially in the northeastern part of the United States, where William Miller founded the *Millerite* movement and predicted that the Second Coming of Christ would occur sometime between March 1843 and March 1844. Michael Barkun, a professor of political science at Syracuse University, has studied these movements and points to the similarity between the apocalyptic cults of the last century and some of today's fundamentalist doctrines . . . [such as] the Reverend Royce Elms of Amarillo, Texas, and his prediction of the end of the world by 1990.

Sentiments of doom, according to Barkun, usually arise in the wake of disasters. At a certain point, the mind tires of having to deal with seemingly hopeless situations. Barkun sees "a veil of pessimism surrounding the year 2000."

But, at the bottom of every apocalyptic view there is a sense of fulfillment and of renewal. The fulfillment is religious mysticism, but the renewal is undoubtedly taken from the example of nature. We see renewal after such catastrophes as forest fires or volcanic devastations like the eruption of Mount Saint Helens, a few years back. New life crowds soon into the sterile residue, often more vigorous and more prolific than that which was destroyed. After the extensive forest fires that ravaged Yellowstone National Park in 1988, the cones of the lodgepole pines that had lain in the ground for years, their scales sealed shut by hardened resin, popped open, and their seeds soon sprouted in the still warm earth. The global catastrophe sixty-five million years ago that triggered the massive extinction of most species of the Cretaceous period, dinosaurs among them, made possible the rise of mammals and the eventual evolution of hominids. Evolution itself is a story of death and renewal, since selection of the successful is contingent on the demise of the less fortunate, and every mutation is an accident that is potentially lethal.

But all that is hindsight. It would be folly to invite catastrophes in the anticipation that better things may arise from the ashes, or to expose ourselves purposely to radiation in the hope of causing favorable mutations. It is wise to accept disasters after the fact and to make the best of whatever benefits they may bring with them. But we must never invite disasters out of despair. Hope is our most useful commodity, and we must fight for our existence with all the means our civilization has at its disposal and with all the sapience after which this species was named.

Our challenge will be to structure society, on a global scale, so that law is justly projected downward through the hierarchy of its institutions. At the same time—and that is the greater challenge—any such system must wither unless the creative ideas of individuals (the only source of creative ideas) are allowed to percolate freely upward to modify the collective wisdom.

If a "veil of pessimism" still clouds humanity's future, there are at last hints that the veil may be lifting, and that, with a greater awareness of the magnitude of global threats, has come a new confidence in our ability to deal with them.

Concern for the environment has deepened and spread over wider areas of the political spectrum. The feeling is slowly growing, also, that wars have become as anachronistic as our ancient, genetically conditioned craving for fat.

The cold war between the superpowers may be over, as was announced by British Prime Minister Margaret Thatcher in 1988, but it is not the end of hatred, prejudice, and bloody conflicts. Although I am more optimistic now than I was two years ago, when I began writing this book, I see some of the old global problems being replaced by new ones. Perhaps the nuclear standoff is less of an imminent threat today, but the profusion of weapons technology among the so-called third world nations is confronting us with a situation in which, sooner or later, *everybody* will be in a position to inflict intolerable damage on everybody else, by long-range missiles tipped with chemical or biological, if not nuclear, warheads. The superpowers may be able to forestall this for a while, but not for long. The military edge high technology confers on its creators is but a temporary reprieve. The experience with the atom bomb taught us that knowledge of any kind cannot be bottled up for long in any one segment of our sociable species. Eventually it becomes the great equalizer.

The universal ability to do great harm to other nations will increase dramatically in the future, and deterrence, while effective up to a point, breaks down when anger or misguided apocalyptic thinking or technological breakdown turns us suicidal. But it is not deterrence that keeps most of us from killing each other in the street but the lack of desire to kill, coupled with a measure of confidence in the mechanisms society has devised to keep us all alive and well. These lessons have not yet been applied on a global scale.

This has been a wrenching century, with the memorials to our madness more numerous and more poignant than the record of our many magnificent achievements. There could be ample cause for despair, for "abandoning ourselves to Providence." But despair can always wait. Let the apocalypse come when our sun dies a few billion years hence or when the universe ends in the big crunch many billions of years after that. For now, let us resolve to keep alive and cultivate the spark of the human mind on this crowded but still beautiful planet.

Thomas L. Saaty, *Professor at Pittsburgh University and author of some twenty books, has collaborated with* Larry W. Boone—*a specialist in business administration—to write a comprehensive and pragmatic view of the study of the future. In* Embracing the Future: Meeting the Challenge of Our Changing World *(1990), from which this excerpt is taken, they have made a systematic examination of how the idealistic thinkers of the past have approached an ever-changing world of tomorrow. Saaty and Boone explore the role of creativity and problem-solving to emphasize ways in which we can personally meet the challenges of our rapidly evolving societies. "Everywhere, Greens strain to reinvent themselves, to announce their projects and intuitions as the keys to the future, but in this they are hardly alone. Free traders and arms traders, nationalists and knaves, everyone wants the future."*

Thomas L. Saaty and Larry W. Boone

Studying the Future

In 1900 John E. Watkins, Jr., made several predictions for the turn of the next century. He foresaw taller Americans, the use of the refrigerator, hydro-electric power, the dominance of the automobile, the preoccupation with exercise, the development of commercial and military airplanes, television, and expanded usage of the telephone, as well as many other things that have become part of our everyday life. How well will our own predictions stand the test of time? Will people laugh at ideas such as Watkins's vision of straw-berries as large as apples, or will they wonder how people today could so accurately predict the reality of tomorrow? Before dreaming of how our visions will serve us on our way to the future, we must ask, Will there be a future?

Threats of nuclear war aside, we can go nowhere to escape the air, water, and noise pollution that affect our ability to breathe clean air, drink pure water, and lead less stressful lives. We are burying ourselves under tons of garbage and waste products created by our throw-away society. To satisfy our energy needs the earth is scarred and increasing amounts of pollution and radiation are produced. Will the steps taken to reverse these processes be enough to stop the continued destruction?

Before we say much about the future, let us say something about the past. James Joyce wrote in *Ulysses* that history is a nightmare from which we are trying to awake. Our trial-and-error learning methods have produced a fair share of catastrophes, but vital lessons can be gleaned from past mistakes. Unfortunately, most of us have difficulty remembering what took place yesterday. Some employ psychoanalysis to understand the influence of their personal history on their present state of mind, feeling, and behavior. We think of world history, not in a personal way, but in terms of what historians teach us. Historians piece together what they observe through writings of individuals or through the discoveries of archaeologists and anthropologists, and they interpret these findings in what they have come to believe is the correct way to relate events. We may never know what minor pieces of information they made important or what important pieces they left out. Once a story is told, it becomes a part of our heritage and is hard to change.

If we have so much difficulty piecing together the past (which we have experienced), putting together a credible story about the future is an indulgence in fantasy. Predicted events may not occur or may be different than expected for very good reasons. Even if they do take place, events may be interpreted by historians in a way that camouflages an accurate prediction in falsehood. For example, the Vikings may have predicted their explorations would result in the discovery of vast new lands, but history has been written crediting Columbus with the feat.

But it is entertaining to tell a story about what has not yet happened. The audience listens and wonders. What does this storyteller know? How does he know it? Over time successful storytellers have realized their ideas are quickly forgotten unless they are frightening and build apprehension. Accuracy yields to style and delivery.

We are trained from an early age to diminish the importance of the past and to look ahead. The past is gone and can be helpful only if it permits us to encounter the future in a better way. The future, on the other hand, fascinates us. Were we to know something useful about it, we could turn it to our advantage. Predictions of success and achievement are welcome, even expected; dire predictions are sought as well, so that potential disasters can be avoided by altering current behaviors. Although most of us do not like to hear about unpleasant possibilities and avoid indulging our imaginations in negative things, this dissatisfaction can be changed if artful entertainment is made of future prediction.

We think of history as a set of episodes arranged in a time sequence. A captivating story foretelling the future can also be arranged in episodes. In our small world, the most intriguing future tale would be one that affects all humankind. But humankind is not in one place, nor of one mind, nor in one time. Telling a fascinating and credible story is not easy.

Thinking about the future is an exercise in exploring its potentials and in preparing the mind to think the unthinkable. Imagining the future is not based on precision or reliability like the discovery of scientific facts. Future thinking is a way of extending awareness to be in a better position to control our affairs, and we have no better alternative other than letting things happen.

Futurism and Futurists

The people most concerned with the study of where the future is taking us are called futurists. Their field of study is called futurism, and there is no generally accepted definition of this term or similar ones such as futurology, future studies, or futuristics. In the early 1900s, futurism referred to an artistic Italian movement depicting an energetic and dynamic quality of contemporary life influenced by the motion and force of modern machinery. In more recent times, futurism has referred to the speculative attempt to imagine, identify, examine, evaluate, and predict all possible times in eternity. Futurism tries to answer the question, What's next?

In answering this question, futurists base their predictions on a set of assumptions, or premises, the most important of which are (1) the future is not predictable; (2) the future is not predetermined; and (3) the future can be influenced by individual choices.

Futurists conceive possibilities for the future, identify the most probable paths for these possibilities, and look for choices to reach a preferred possibility. There is no way to verify the crudeness of this process, and people are usually forgiven for erring so frequently about impending events. But it is entertaining, and that is what life is about. Besides, trying to predict the future stretches our thinking into new realms of possibilities.

Futurists of the possible tend to be mavericks, visionaries, sometimes geniuses, and sometimes madmen. They emphasize intuition and feeling in their thought processes. *Futurists of the probable* tend to be analytically oriented in one or more fields such as mathematics, statistics, or systems analysis. *Futurists of the preferable* tend to be political scientists; they emphasize specific issues such as nuclear power, women's rights, or environmental concerns. Futurists of all categories are usually effective writers who can generate mass appeal, and [nearly] every one of them tries to do what no one else has ever done successfully . . . .

How does the brain focus on the future, and where does it get its information? Some scientists have been interested in how the brain explores within itself a future it has not experienced. The British neurologist Grey Walter claimed to have discovered "expectancy waves" operating in the frontal lobes. Jerzy Konorski, a Polish physiologist, purported to find evidence of a neurological "hunger" that causes the brain to be an active seeker of information. Karl Pribram, an American neuropsychologist, identified complex "feedforward" and "feedback" mechanisms amplifying the picture of the brain as both a seeker and a shaper of the future.

Alexander Luria, a noted Russian neuropsychologist, believed the prime motivator of human behavior is neither the metabolic processes stimulating our basic desires nor the impact of external events on our senses. The prime motivator is a combination of our visualization of what we want, our alternative plans for attaining it, and our forecast of the probability of success among alternative paths. Through the study of brain-damaged patients, Luria pinpointed the critical involvement of the frontal lobes in planning, programming, and intending—the acts of will and desire.

The Future: From Determinism to Strange Attractors

For most of history, problems have been addressed in a deterministic fashion. We believe ourselves capable of identifying key factors in problems, developing an understanding of these factors and their limits, and arriving at *the* answer. Issues are settled once and for all, neatly and cleanly. Religion led the way to this approach by pronouncing solutions in black-and-white terms, leaving no room for the gray. Science developed when we were no longer satisfied with attempts to alter events by praying to powerful external forces believed to control the future. Science uses reason, in which we have established much confidence, to explore the mysteries of the unknown. The methods of science are developed and applied so that *we* can take charge of our own destiny by understanding and controlling nature.

But science itself is limited by the assumptions we make. Its answers are contingent and not absolute. Traditionally, mathematics has been regarded as a sure way to infallible knowledge. One plus one equals two. But even this attitude has changed. The mathematician Philip Davis (1986, p. 70) writes:

> It has been said that mathematics is true because it is God-given. Mathematics is true because man has constructed it. Mathematics is true because it is nothing but logic, and what is logical must be true . . . . Mathematics is true because it is useful. Mathematics is true because it has been elicited in such a way that it reflects accurately the phenomena of the real world.
>
> Mathematics is true by agreement. It is true because we want it to be true, and whenever an offending instance is found, the mathematical community rises up, extirpates that instance and rearranges its thinking. . . . It also has been said that mathematics isn't true at all in a rock-bottom sense, it is true only in a probabilistic sense. Mathematics is true only in the sense that it is refutable and corrigible; its truths are eternally provisional. Mathematical truth is not a condition, it is a process. Truth is an idle notion, to mathematics as to all else. . . . Impossibilities are converted to possibilities by changing the structural background, by altering the context, by embedding the context in a wider context. It is very likely the case that all mathematical impossibilities may be altered in a nontrivial way so as to become possibilities.

Mathematics is regarded as a social affair and mathematicians as team players who have internalized the social process of mathematics.

In spite of these changes in attitude, mathematics remains a useful and trustworthy tool for understanding complexity. This is probably because the neurons of the brain respond to and synthesize electrical signals with mathematical precision. We decipher everything we sense through vision, smell, hearing, taste, and touch quantitatively through the movement of chemicals and electrical charges in the nervous system. Numerous stimuli simultaneously bombard us and have to be added, cancelled, or somehow put together to create an impression in the brain. Some form of abstraction is needed to simplify the diversity of experiences, to provide a framework to unify the stimuli into understanding.

From the order of our bodies and those of animals and plants, the planets and solar system, and the large observable universe of astronomy and the small atomic world of physics, we are likely to conclude that ours is an orderly world. Still, from numerous observed and unpredictable occurrences, we are also likely to conclude that the world predominantly is chaotic, with patches of transient order (which turn eventually into chaos). The more we can explain, the more it appears there is order; the less we can foresee and predict, the more it appears there is chaos. The assumption of order is forced on us through the working of the mind as it attempts to understand what is going on. What appears to have no rhyme or reason at one time will someday find accommodation in our thinking. How to make order out of chaos, how to deal with the unexpected and the unpredictable, has much to do with how we embrace the future.

Judith Hooper writes in *Omni* magazine (1983, p. 86), "Randomness, or chaos, is not merely a matter of complexity. Many physical systems, including some very simple ones, have pockets of randomness *built into* them. And that's why the most godlike scientist, wielding impossibly perfect tools, can never accurately predict the weather three days hence or mark the final destination of a ball in a spinning roulette wheel."

Behind chaos lies something scientists call a strange attractor, an attribute that at some point introduces irregularity and unpredictability. Suppose a baker places several ink dots on some bread dough, then proceeds to stretch the dough, fold it, roll it, and fold it again. Where will the dots appear? No one can say, even though all the initial conditions and subsequent actions are well understood.

The same can be said about weather. All current conditions such as temperature, atmosphere pressure, and wind speed can be determined, but next week's weather or the time and location of the next tornado cannot be forecast with certainty. There is too much chaos in the system.

With the assistance of powerful computers some scientists are making progress in developing an understanding of chaotic systems by identifying similarities in seemingly random patterns. In the study of strange attractors, they can look back at models of a chaotic system and tell where the randomness originated. Scientists are finding that some systems have an internal "clock" that keeps perfect time in the midst of its chaos and, at the appropriate moment, introduces its effects. We are so familiar with certain internal "clocks," such as the 2 A.M. feeding expected by infants and the 212° F temperature at which water starts to boil, that we take them for granted. Less common clocks, however, such as the loads at which steel bridge girders snap and the temperatures at which fluid flows erupt into turbulence, are the concern of specialists like design engineers. Animal behaviorists are aware of critical populations at which animal groups develop chaotic behavior. Discovery of the internal clocks of various systems is central to the understanding of order and the unraveling of what appears at the surface to be chaos. Schizophrenia may be a chaos of the brain's chemical feedback system that will one day be understood and controlled.

Sources of Future Possibilities

The best way to look at future possibilities is to use our imagination. We have no satisfactory rational, practical methods at our disposal to forecast the future. The best predictions are generated by intuitively learned processes that are uniquely personal. All methods of futurism depend on imagination. The degree to which imagination, perceived reality, and methods of forecasting converge determines whether one is dealing with fantasy, as in *Alice in Wonderland*; with fiction; or with meaningful prediction.

Science tells us that the future is becoming. It is an unknown certainty into which we move from the present. Through science our minds have invented the concepts of space and time to sort data, but space and time may not be as we perceive them. All history may be playing out around us in some fashion, here and now. There may be other ways of knowing about happenings that we do not understand—possibly psychic or prophetic ways that are currently baffling.

It is not widely known that Isaac Newton spent the second half of his productive life analyzing and writing about the religious prophecies of the books of Daniel and Revelation. They include the famous 1,290- and 2,300-year prophecies of Christ's second coming and allegorical images that represent great nations in history. Newton was known as an acute and learned theologian. He operated from a clear-cut premise that there is a special, unique, and distinct "mystical language," known to and used by all the prophets. His publications have allegedly been suppressed to keep his image as a great scientist untarnished . . . .

Methods of Futurism

Before his death in 1983, Herman Kahn, the leading modern futurist, identified only four correct predictions of 364 made by professional futurologists between 1976 and 1979. What could have been Kahn's motive to downplay the accuracy of predictions when he was the leading proponent of futurism?

Kahn was rebelling against those who forecast one catastrophe after another.

There are four defensible ways of predicting the future: consensus, extrapolating on trends, historical analysis and analogy, and systematic generation of alternative paths to the future. Consensus methods such as the Delphi technique were among the earliest tools used. The objective of the Delphi process is to improve individual judgments and perceptions of multiple experts by providing successive rounds of feedback on each group member's opinion. For example, if one wants to predict the price of a gallon of gasoline in the year 2000, the opinions of a variety of experts from government and the oil and shipping industries could be collected, summarized, and shared with each other. Then the experts could offer additional rounds of opinions until all the guesses converged toward a single price. This would be the "best guess" prediction of the future price of gasoline. The Delphi technique was used to generate technical projections found in the *Omni Future Almanac*.

Extrapolation of past trends is a second approach, commonly employed in economic, demographic, and environmental forecasting. Alternative futures are generated by identifying possible new trend components, such as hypothesized limits or new technological or cultural developments. Social trends are sometimes predicted by methods that are variations on extrapolating past trends. For example, predictions based on content analysis hinge on the assumption that events can be forecast by examining the press coverage given to specific issues by news media, as John Naisbitt did in his book *Megatrends* to predict east to west shifts in the U.S. population as well as other national and global trends. Other variations make the assumption that a regression (straight) line mathematically fitted to past data, such as the annual birth rates of women in various age groups since World War II, can be projected into the future to predict the world population in the year 2000. This will work, of course, in the unlikely occurrence that the future holds no unprecedented events. Herman Kahn's *The Year 2000* is an example of forecasting based on extrapolative trend methods.

At least three types of historical analyses are employed to predict futures. The first is political analysis, in which stakeholders are considered actors in an ongoing process of forces and counterforces, goals and strivings, actions and reactions. Political science is replete with such analyses. Karl Marx's *Das Kapital* represents an interesting example. Marx predicted the downfall of capitalist countries and the rise of communist states. His rationale involved the exploitation of the masses in capitalistic states through corporate profits. Because of such exploitation, Marx believed workers would eventually revolt and replace capitalism with communism in the worker's paradise. Marx's political predictions were inaccurate, as demonstrated by recent dramatic events in Eastern Europe. Trends away from communism toward capitalism are evident, as are movements within capitalistic societies to permit more worker participation in organizational management. The Chinese experiment with Marxism is following a new eclectic direction based on visible signs of progress made today rather than on promises made for a distant future.

In the second kind of historical analysis, problems with existing systems (for example, transportation, waste disposal, and immigration systems) are examined, as well as systems' capacities to react to their dilemmas. *The Global 2000 Report to the President* is an example of this form of analysis. Predictions frequently take the form of a worst-case estimate of the system's ability to cope with unforeseen difficulties and with overloading depressions every fifty to sixty years. A historical examination of patterns preceding major depressions in the 1830s, 1880s, and 1930s reveals that swings of business cycles grow in severity as capacities are overbuilt, productivity levels decline, prices rise, debt increases, and employment fluctuates. Such tendencies have been evident over the last decade according to Forrester, and he foresees another severe business cycle or two in the near future before a depression.

At the 1984 World Future Society's Fifth General Assembly in Washington, D.C., Lester Brown, president of Worldatch Institute, suggested that an obvious decline has occurred in the worldwide momentum to improve living conditions. Although twelve countries have achieved zero population growth, the world population rose by 79 million in 1983. Some estimates for the next two decades have world population increasing by 55 percent, or 2.3 billion people, with most of the growth occurring in undeveloped or developing countries. The population in Asia and Africa may double in this time. If this growth occurs and the world's total population reaches 6.5 billion, there will be enormous increases in demand for food, water, mineral resources, and health care.

Environmental stresses caused by the expanding need for food may include the loss of up to one-third of presently usable land through overgrazing, faulty irrigation, soil degradation, and urbanization. Increased usage of fertilizers, herbicides, and pesticides could produce nitrate contamination of drinking water, reduction of the ozone layer by nitrous oxide contamination, loss of helpful predator insects through expanded use of DDT, and even poisoning of farm workers and nearby populations. Each year world forests shrink by an area approximately the size of Hungary (36,000 square miles), adding to problems of soil erosion, destabilized water flows and the encroachment of deserts.

Expansions in global mining may have major effects on the seabed, on the Amazon basin, and on the lands of many less developed nations. Increased energy demand could result in several thousand more square kilometers of strip mines and accompanying land subsidence, more air and water pollution from hundreds of new fossil-fuel-burning power plants, as well as more radiation hazard from new nuclear plants. We could be producing 10 million cubic meters of radioactive materials requiring special handling and disposal, along with several hundred thousand tons of spent nuclear fuel.

The gap between the world's rich and poor is likely to increase. The problem of global debt, especially in the third world, offers a basis for forecasts of economic instability. Third world debt totals hundreds of billions of dollars, with Algeria, Argentina, Brazil, Chile, Egypt, India, Indonesia, Israel, Korea, Mexico, Turkey, Venezuela, and Yugoslavia accounting for well over half of the total. Worldwide military spending was approximately $800 billion in 1984, whereas aid to developing countries was less than 5 percent of that amount.

Ervin Laszlo, director of the United Nations Institute for Training and Research, has suggested, "In the next 35 years, humanity will face the most important choices any generation ever faced . . . the signposts of a coming system crisis abound, including problems such as increasing food dependency among many countries, migrations of huge populations of people, chronic unemployment and under-employment, increasing urbanization, world militarization, and environment degradation." (Fulmer, "A Managerial Assessment of Global Problems and Opportunities," *Managerial Planning 33*, July 1984, p. 56.)

The Optimistic View

Perhaps it is too easy to focus on myriad, easily articulated problems and forecast global doom. While the problems are real and serious, we should not fail to balance our outlook by examining the progress being made and trends that offer hope for better outcomes.

Rapid technological advances, if managed well, will be sources of improved living standards throughout the world. Robotics, artificial intelligence, knowledge systems, microelectronics, telecommunications, lasers, and new vaccines and drugs are examples of technologies that can be employed to improve global communications, education, manufacturing, distribution of goods, weather forecasting, surgery, and disease treatment and prevention.

Fantastic possibilities spring from the genetic revolution, and agriculture promises to be the primacy beneficiary. New knowledge derived from genetic research permits faster and more precise alteration of plant characteristics to establish resistance to particular diseases or adaptions that permit growth in normally hostile environments. One possibility involves research on soil microorganisms that plants can use to take nitrogen directly from the atmosphere. Such a development could render the production and use of millions of tons of nitrogeneous fertilizers unnecessary. New animal growth hormones could lead to cheaper, more dependable supplies of protein for world populations.

Proponents of technological advancement point to the potentials for eliminating resource scarcity, relieving humans from burdensome labor, and eradicating disease and genetic defects.

While population explosions will continue to pose major threats to improvements in worldwide standards of living, there is evidence that leaders in some countries are beginning to address the complex issue; for example, the Chinese government has experimented with mandated limits for the size of each family. Admittedly, control of the population is a sensitive problem that calls for the best application of our ethics, technology, and sensitivity about the quality of life for future generations.

Perhaps the greatest source of optimism lies in the increasing consideration being given by today's decision makers to the effects their decisions will have for coming generations. We are beginning to pay attention to tomorrow. Herman Kahn wrote that a positive future depends on "a combination of good luck and good management" (Fulmer, 1984, p. 57).

Optimism and the future are compatible. What is the alternative? For the practical minded, optimism is an easy word for a complex attitude. To paraphrase Cervantes's *Don Quixote*, "Who is crazy, the world, because it sees itself as it is, or I, because I see the world as it could become?"

WARREN WAGAR *has been teaching the History of the Future at the State University of New York for a generation. His sweep as a futurologist is broad indeed, encompassing science fiction as well as an historical survey of how futurology developed in the twentieth century. Wagar's* A Short History of the Future *(1989), somewhat reminiscent of the writings of H.G. Wells, is a presentation of what will happen to the world in the years 1995–2100 in which he outlines a number of catastrophes for this planet, including the melt-down of the world economy in 2044. The extract chosen here is the Epilogue from his book* The Next Three Futures: Paradigms of Things to Come *(1992), and takes a more conservative look at the nature of inquiries into the future, outlining alternative perspectives on the prospects of tomorrow.*

W. WARREN WAGAR

THE NEXT THREE FUTURES

. . . You may be asking, "Yes, but what will *really* happen?" The futurist's many-ring circus of alternatives, options, and possibilities may well leave the earnest spectator dizzy and fatigued. Perhaps the study of the future is a better way to experience Alvin Toffler's "future shock" than actually to live through rapidly changing times, when the future—so to speak—arrives ahead of schedule. If carried out with sufficient ruthlessness, the study of the future can even destroy our power to make choices and to plan and follow courses of action.

Because every futurist is a human being, as well as a student of human affairs, it is necessary at some point to weigh all the options and then decide, each of us for ourselves, what we think is most likely to happen to humankind in the next century or more. From the array of most likely possibilities, we should also determine how we can, as individuals or as members of groups, help ensure that the best of the likeliest futures—"best" as we define the good—is the future that in fact materializes. This will inevitably pit futurist against futurist, because our expectations and our ideas of the good vary. But studying the future should never become such an end in itself that it prevents us from functioning effectively as members of civil society in the real world. The object of science and scholarship is always to inform and empower human will, not to paralyze it.

In this brief epilogue, let me sum up my own thoughts about the long-term future of humankind. My working premise is that perhaps the technoliberals, radicals, and counterculturalists are all essentially correct. The human race may be destined to follow all three paths to the future, not simultaneously, but sequentially.

Thus far we have considered technoliberalism, radicalism, and counterculturalism as alternatives. Either capitalism and bourgeois democracy will prove victorious, or democratic socialism, or the Ecotopian New Age. But there is no reason to assume that the whole future of humankind lies down a single path. The future, after all, is a long time. If capitalism, for example, does triumph over its rivals, will its reign last forever? Do the other two futures mutually exclude one another, so that if we choose one, we can never choose the other?

To both questions the answer is clearly no. I find it far more likely that the world system will take each of these paths for long periods of time, and not in a random sequence. The path that most countries in the world are already following in the 1990s, the path of capitalist hegemony and the universalizing of representative democracy, will broaden still further as we enter the next millennium. Much later, capitalism will give way to a hitherto untried form of democratic socialism. Much later still, when humankind is finally ready for it, socialism will be supplanted by a decentralized and ecotopian counterculture.

But first things first. The next future is almost surely the one we are building today, the future of globalized liberal democratic capitalism. By the first or second decade of the twenty-first century, all of humankind will be travelling along that road, although it will mean radically different things for different segments of the world system. For the privileged classes and races of the core countries, and their many loyal hangers-on, it will be a golden or at least a silver age. For small numbers of affluent people in the semi-peripheral and peripheral countries, life will also be sweet. For the rest of humankind, as much as half the population of the core countries and nine-tenths or more in the periphery, life will be toilsome and bare.

Breakthroughs in technology (such as fusion power or the perfection of artificial intelligence), the exploitation of new markets in the former Second and Third Worlds, and the fresh energies released by the diffusion of political democracy will keep the system humming for many years. But eventually, for some or all of the reasons adduced by radical critics of the capitalist world system, it will begin to disintegrate from within. Its failure may become readily apparent by the end of the next bout of worldwide business expansion, say in the 2030s, or it may take one or more additional turns of the wheel, carrying us near the close of the next century or even beyond.

It is hardly possible at this time to anticipate just which of the many shortcomings of technoliberal capitalism, or which combination of shortcomings, will play the greatest part in its collapse. One major factor will be the anger and resentment it engenders in the many nations that never succeed in gaining admission to the heartland of the world system, together with the bitterness of the various ethnic minorities and working classes within the core countries themselves. Capitalism is good for winners. But it also produces losers, whole populations that lose the game of high-stakes, high-tech, high-speed economic growth. At some point this anger may well boil over.

Another likely contributing cause to the disintegration of liberal capitalism will be the mounting costs of keeping the system running smoothly. Servicing deficits, paying for the military adventures required to keep restless poor nations in line, co-opting workers with benefits packages, caring for the increasing number of elderly people, fighting urban crime, safeguarding a deteriorating environment, and all the other expenses of late capitalism will add up to trillions of dollars a year. When the new markets of the twenty-first century (such as post-communist Russia) are saturated with all the goods and capital they can absorb and the financial burdens of maintaining the condominium of the core countries in the new world order become insupportable, the time will approach for yet another cycle of revolution, as great or greater than the World Revolution of 1989.

The technoliberal capitalist world system will still be enormously powerful, but it will also be top-heavy, over-centralized, and insolvent. Lacking the gusto of youth or even middle age, it will be confronted by anti-systemic movements that grow stronger with every passing year. Some of these movements, perhaps most, will represent specific regional or group interests. But international political formations may also emerge sometime in the twenty-first century, vaguely analogous to the loose coalition of Green parties that now flourish in many Western countries and participate in the worldwide struggle to protect the environment from state and capitalist exploitation. One or more of these formations, for example, a militant One World party, espousing democratic socialism and world government, may become leading actors in the international political process.

It is pleasant to think that humankind could make the transition from technoliberal capitalism to social democracy in a peaceful manner, without armed violence and without the kinds of injustice that violence almost always breeds. But such a peaceful transition seems unlikely, or at least unlikely in every country and in every part of the world. The established technoliberal order will not go down everywhere without a fight. Here and there, it will make its stand, as the state capitalist dictatorships of China and Romania made their stands during the World Revolution of 1989, in China successfully (for the time being), in Romania not It is even possible that the liberal capitalist world system will not collapse until it becomes embroiled, willy-nilly, in a calamitous system-wide war.

In any event, the best chance for moving from oligopoly capitalism to a democratic socialist world order will come in especially difficult times, when the prevailing system has lost much of its credibility. Wars and depressions are the obvious occasions for rapid social change of this magnitude. At such times political change can occur very quickly and spread just as quickly from region to region, as it did after 1789 and again after 1989. The old era ends, and the new begins, with a new reigning world view rooted in the inspirations of radical democracy.

In the early years, we may assume that a worldwide republic of working men and women will do a reasonably good job. It will put an end to the warfare system once and for all by disarming the nation-states and permitting no military force but its own. Liberated from their permanently inferior status in the defunct capitalist world economy, the peoples of the less developed countries will be free to evolve in their own way and at their own speed toward democratic socialism, with the help of modest loans and grants-in-aid from the world commonwealth. Often suspended in the days of late capitalism by a technocracy more and more afraid of its own people, civil liberties will be fully guaranteed throughout the world for the first time in the history of our species. The workers' republic will also undertake a great terrestrial housecleaning project to restore the environment, as much as possible, to pre-twentieth-century conditions.

Yet there is all too good a chance that the republic will in time become superfluous, a fetter on the further development of humankind. It will clearly be needed for many decades to dismantle the machinery of warfare and private capital, and to clean up a looted planet. In a tightly integrated world system, I see no possibility of such things happening piecemeal, as the result of uncoordinated local initiatives.

All the same, in the process of doing its job the workers' republic is bound to inherit many of the technologies, business management practices, and bureaucratic procedures of the capitalist ancien régime. It may well breed its own caste of elitist technocrats who in time will find ingenious ways of evading democratic controls and perpetuating their own power. The ruling caste of the republic may even become hereditary, ensuring that most of its power and privilege passes to its children, and to theirs.

None of this is democratic socialism, of course. Socialism is not compatible with technocracy or technocratic elites. But as long as the world is governed by a central guidance system, in which day-to-day decision-making is vested in a huge bureaucratic apparatus—no matter what its historical origins, official world view, or initially pious intentions—the danger remains that the apparatus will learn how to disempower the people it was created to serve.

Even if the people do manage to retain significant control over the doings of the bureaucracy, what would be the purpose of a world state after its task of renovating the planet had been completed? If inequalities of wealth and opportunity were removed, the environment restored, national armies dissolved, and worker democracy ensconced, what need would there be for a world republic?

At this point, perhaps late in the twenty-first century or well into the twenty-second, humankind will be ready for its third future, the future beyond liberal capitalism and democratic socialism. There are hints of such an age in the Marxian canon, in its view of "communism" as a higher stage of socialism, in the belief that the dictatorship of the proletariat would be replaced in time by a classless society and the dying out of the state, in the assumption that individuals would then be free to choose their own destinies, as individuals, no longer commodified by capitalism and its specialization of labor.

This next and perhaps last revolution may occur without violence and even without concerted political activism. People may decide, first here, then there, then somewhere else, that they no longer need the services of public officials. They will find they can also do nicely without purchasing energy from global grids or imported processed foods in shiny packages. They may start growing their own food. They may switch to locally available, small-scale energy systems, such as wind farms and solar power collectors. They may elect to produce goods and services chiefly for their own use, with self-replicating, self-maintaining advanced technologies that do not require huge outlays of capital or megawatts of energy. Home-grown arts and crafts may further shrink their dependence on the global mass market. They will travel a great deal, and keep in instantaneous electronic touch with the rest of the world, but essentially they will be self-sufficient; and one by one, communities of such individuals will sever their economic and political ties to the global democratic socialist system.

In short, having rescued humankind from war, ecocide, and injustice, the workers' republic will in due time become redundant, and the scaffolding it had erected can be allowed to fall away. Perhaps a few bits and pieces of the old apparatus will have to stay on. For instance, a world agency may be needed to provide traffic control for the planetary and interplanetary transport and communications network. But by and large the republic will simply fade away, its place taken by thousands of self-governing, self-supporting communities of many shapes and sizes scattered all over the face of the earth. Such communities will have learned the hard lessons of power and wealth, of war and peace, taught by modern history. They will survive handily without armies and bureaucracies, without the endless buying and replacing of products, without competition for markets and profits, without poverty or cheap labor, without masters and servants.

Clearly, we are speaking now of an age in which counterculturalist values have triumphed, in which people have managed to fend for themselves, as grownups rather than as wards of omnipotent states or corporations. But the people of this Ecotopian league of communities would not lead primitive lives. Far from it, if they chose. They would be in close contact with people throughout the world, and other worlds. They would have at their disposal sophisticated technologies scaled to their own needs, clean and light technologies that would require a minimal investment of capital and little or no human intervention to keep in running order. If they did need something more elaborate, such as spacecraft, such items would be communally owned and used by an appointment or reservation system, with everyone in the community, or in a group of neighboring communities, sharing their cost.

It goes without saying that all this would be impossible if fundamental advances in miniaturized, low-energy technical systems were not forthcoming in the centuries ahead. But the odds are that they will be forthcoming, in abundance. As information technologies become more and more versatile and powerful, robotics and molecular engineering will liberate our species from nearly all the kinds of labor now performed. It will be easy to manufacture and keep in repair almost any desired product or furnish any desired service in facilities available anywhere. The factory or library ten thousand miles away will no longer be needed. Everything will be possible, in our own backyards.

So far, so good. One may ask how such a various world will avoid a reversion to tribal warfare or a resurrection of capitalism or fascism or Stalinism in new or even more virulent forms. The only possible answer is that once the people are truly empowered, once everyone on earth has fair access to its riches, they will not let themselves be deceived. They will insist on the accountability of their rulers, policies of peace and mutual respect for all men and women, and a full panoply of civil liberties. Am I naive? Very possibly. But if we cannot trust an empowered people, whom can we trust? If the people, the rank and file of our species, is not fit to govern, who is? Frankly, I would rather not know.

In retrospect, hundreds of years from now, historians may even look back on our next three futures as logical and inevitable stages in the evolution of humankind. Just as feudalism made possible the emergence of capitalism, so capitalism established the necessary preconditions for the coming of socialism, and socialism ushered in the neo-romantic counterculture. Each stage in world history is but a prologue to the one that follows it, worlds without end.

If this is true, the counterculture will, in its turn, yield to yet another world view, another paradigm of values, another new civilization, perhaps in the twenty-second century. After the next three futures, comes the fourth.

Yet in one overwhelming respect, whatever follows in the deep end of history will be quite different from anything experienced by our species since its beginning. By then, if not before, human beings will no longer be confined to the sphere on which life in this patch of the universe originated. Our living space will expand spectacularly, and nothing will ever be the same again.

Already human beings have set foot on one extraterrestrial body and sent mechanical probes to others. This is just the beginning. In a matter of a few generations or centuries, large numbers of men and women will almost certainly be living in artificial habitats in space or as colonists on the moon or Mars or some of the satellites of the outer planets. The engineering know-how required for such exploits is all but available today, and can only grow in the years ahead [see Gerard K. O'Neill, *The High Frontier*, 1977]. People will be living in space for any number of reasons: scientific research, zero-gravity industrial production, exploitation of mineral resources, recreation, and—in selected instances—escape from the limitations and frustrations of life on earth.

But there is much more. The universe is infinitely larger than this little solar system we inhabit. Current astrophysical theory, as Robert Jastrow writes in *Journey to the Stars* [1989], suggests that one star in five offers "conditions favorable to the evolution of life and intelligence." By this reckoning, there are forty billion stars in our local galaxy capable of harboring intelligent life. Since ours is also just one of many billions of galaxies, some considerably larger than the Milky Way, the total number of star systems with inhabitable planets may be virtually numberless. It stands to reason that many of these planets will be far more attractive as habitats than arid Mars or the cold moons of Jupiter and Saturn.

In the centuries to come, humankind will turn outward to this starry universe and commence the search, in earnest, for other life, for other civilizations, for other worlds to settle. If we succeed, the time may come when only a small fraction of the human race lives on Terra. The idea of cultural "pluralism" will take on truly cosmic proportions, as *Homo sapiens* and perhaps a host of bioengineered new and better human races colonize the universe.

Crossing the interstellar gulfs to reach these far-flung worlds will not be easy. We will need to develop much more powerful propulsion systems than any now in existence. We may also have to find ways of keeping crewpersons in suspended animation for long periods of time. But in the fullness of time there is every reason to suppose that the technical problems will be solved.

And when they are, the blessings of space exploration and settlement for our scattered progeny will be almost unimaginably rich. The migration to outer space will provide an outlet for expansive energies not available on a pacified earth. It will give people everywhere a sense of participation in a great enterprise that transcends all local divisions and petty terrestrial quarrels. It may also, as Arthur C. Clarke long ago proposed in *Profiles of the Future* [1962 and 1984], "trigger a new Renaissance and break the pattern into which our society, and our arts, must otherwise freeze."

Still greater dividends can be foreseen. The exploration of interstellar space may eventually bring us into contact with alien cultures, which could have a more profound impact on our civilization than all its earthly renaissances and voyages of exploration combined. If other living intelligent species are distributed too sparsely through the universe to meet one another, we might still learn almost as much from interceptions of their radioed messages, or from excavating the remains of long-extinct alien civilizations.

Even if we never encounter intelligent life anywhere in this galaxy or any other, there is (believe it or not!) intelligent life on earth. It will still be possible for humankind to colonize the galaxy, over a period of hundreds, thousands, or millions of years. Science-fiction writers have often depicted colony ships that go forth to colonize nearby solar systems. Those colonists successful in locating and populating inhabitable planets will eventually reach the point when they, too, can dispatch colonists of their own, to stellar systems hundreds of light-years from Terra and Sol. In good time, the whole galaxy will teem with human life, and we can launch intergalactic expeditions as well.

I say "we." Will those far-future inhabitants of our universe be part of "us"?

Why not? You may see them as ghostly or impossibly remote people, not even quite human in form or faculties. So, perhaps, all parents regard their children, so like themselves, and yet so unlike, bent on living their own lives and following their own stars.

But in reality we are all one family. It matters little whether we live in caves, villages, suburban tracts, or mobile space habitats touring the universe. We are all one, indissolubly tied to a common past and moving together into a common future. Into this future, we send our children, and from it, in humankind's relentless flight through space and time, they will never return.

The report of the INDEPENDENT COMMISSION ON POPULATION
AND QUALITY OF LIFE *has no single author but has eloquent voices
from every continent bringing a caring vision of what needs to be
done for those who are all too often neglected on this planet. In
redefining priorities in a pragmatic way, the commission set out an
alternative to current educational policies, looked closely at
healthcare and medicine, advocated the empowering of women,
and focused on the reproductive choices available for population
control. In* Caring for the Future: Making the Next Decades
Provide a Life Worth Living *(1996), from which these excerpts
are taken, the authors declared: "We seek a new humanism to
promote human rights not only in terms of legal guarantees, but,
more importantly, in the context of dignity. Care can provide the
foundation for such humanism." The commission was headed by
Maria de Lourdes Pintasilgo, the former Prime Minister of
Portugal, and included Bernard Kouchner (from Médécins Sans
Frontières) and Alexander N. Yakovlev (adviser to Boris Yeltsin).
In 1993 and 1994, hearings were held in Zimbabwe, Mali,
Washington D.C., Delhi, Brazil, Manila, and Moscow. In
addition, there were consultation panels in Bellagio in Italy on
population, and in Stockholm on consumption and sustainability.*

Caring for the Future: Conclusions and Recommendations

We have seen throughout this report how the relationship between population and quality of life leads us to be concerned with new and holistic perspectives. In 25 years more than 4 billion people will be most probably added to the 6 billion foreseen for the year 2000. These people must be free from want. How then do we reach such a goal when we have already today in our midst one poor among every four persons?

The task ahead is at the same time a qualitative one—to provide for every human being a life worth living—and a quantitative one—to move towards the stabilization of the global population.

Our attempt in this book is to show how the two goals are intertwined and can be reached if some all-embracing, fundamental concepts and practices can be followed. Many factors are to be tackled if we want to seize this opportunity.

The many factors include: making life more liveable through improved individual and collective health and security; dealing with the scourges of poverty and exclusion; raising the levels of literacy, education, and access to needed information; rationalizing production and consumption in terms of what the planet's resources can continue to provide—and bringing fairness and equity to all through better-balanced exploitation and use of these resources (such as keeping more profits from raw materials "at home"; utilizing them in a sustainable manner), more effective policies of aid and assistance; and finding new funding mechanisms between North and South. And last, but hardly least, caring for ourselves, our neighbours, and the environment by observing the rights pertaining to all of humankind.

Care is the antithesis of competition (a natural bent of the human species, essential to survival) and its reinforcement now will necessitate a dramatic change in mind-set. The transactional concepts of the past, excessive competition and the philosophy of ever more may destroy us. We need, therefore, to explore if and how the reservoirs of caring capacity can sustain us, and lift at the same time at least 1 billion people mired in poverty—and growing—from the level of eking out their survival and on to the path of sustainable improvement of the quality of life. This will require nothing short than *another kind of development* than hitherto pursued. Humankind faces challenges of a civilizational change. Its survival and existence in dignity requires a transition to a fundamentally new type of development—ecodevelopment—which should govern all forms of human activities and all interactions of people with nature.

In this quest, a few guiding principles set the ground rules. Equity, caring, sharing, sustainability, human security. *Equity* has a crucial, even overriding role in all efforts aimed at a sustainable improvement in the quality of life. We believe that without equity there can be neither *sustainability* nor *security*. Equity denotes a principle of fair and equitable treatment to all, to be respected equally by individuals, institutions, and States.

In addition to our fundamentally human consideration for care and caring, we have been guided in our analysis and conclusions by other elements not less important. These are *population as people* (and not only as numbers); *overcoming the North–South divide*; and *listening to the women's voice* because women are at the very centre of population policy and at the forefront of societal activities, particularly those influenced by the notion of caring.

Based on the findings of the Commission as they appear in the foregoing chapters, we advocate a series of policies, strategies, action programmes, or other measures which must be taken now at various levels to improve the quality of life in a world whose population—at nearly 6 billion human beings today—will continue to grow until it reaches some 9.8 billion in 2050, stabilizing perhaps one century later at about 11 billion.

Improved Security for a More Liveable World

... Sustainability is both a precondition and an integral component of quality of life, on which policy-making in all countries should focus. Sustainability and security are two main features and determinants of quality of life. As security transcends the traditional concept focusing on national sovereignty and military dimensions only, the Commission embraces a comprehensive definition of human security: it must also include the safety of people from the risks of injury or accident, disaster, disease, or violence, as well as from loss of livelihood or damaging environmental change.

The redefinition of security must include personal, economic, social, environmental, and military security and must affect security priorities at the national level. This will necessitate shifts away from military spending to areas with great impact: health, family planning, environment, crime prevention. As a minimal first step, all governments should aim to spend at least as much on health and education as on military programmes.

We join the international call that all governments not already doing so should lower military budgets, especially those of the developing countries and in regions where conflict and potential warfare are endemic.

Developed nations must contribute, actively and credibly, to the demilitarization of life—for no State that profits from war can convincingly argue for peace. It is not enough to admonish developing countries that their military expenditures must be reduced—as they indeed should be—or to introduce forms of conditionality to aid-and-assistance programmes. Military assistance, often under the "cover" of development assistance, must decline further and be phased out.

We further propose that the concept of collective security be revisited accordingly. The Security Council of the United Nations, the body entrusted with the maintenance of international security and peace, should thus be enabled to address also threats to the socio-economic security of humankind.

In pursuing a sustainable improvement of quality of life, highest priority must be given to meeting the population's minimum survival needs. In order to make these needs operational, they should be related to *rights*—striking a balance between civil-political rights and economic-social rights.

The Commission urges that a major effort be mounted to universalize by the year 2000 the four great existing treaties embodying a range of rights relevant to the quality of life—the Convention on the Elimination of Discrimination against Women (CEDAW), the Convention on the Rights of the Child (CRC), the International Covenant on Economic, Social and Cultural Rights (ICESCR), and the International Covenant on Civil and Political Rights (ICCPR).

To this end, the number of signatory States must be increased and countries maintaining reservations must be persuaded to withdraw them. Countries should signify any reasons for non-signature, outlining what conditions would help them overcome existing obstacles.

The Commission urges speedy completion of an optional protocol of ICESCR, allowing complaints by affected individuals or groups. Similar protocols should be prepared for the three other international instruments and extended to include the right of States (already existing in the case of ICCPR) to bring complaints against other States.

Without enforcement, however, rights may remain unimplemented or dead letter. In the absence of effective machinery, direct and indirect approaches will need to be devised.

To increase pressure on countries to live up to their commitments, the committees established under the various treaties and conventions should be enabled to prepare regular, analytical summaries on the fulfilment of rights and on obstacles encountered.

The Commission calls on development agencies and NGOs concerned with social and economic needs (food, housing, health and family planning, education) to orient their activities more towards the internationally recognized rights. The force of rights should be added to those based on justice and equity. In that respect the organizations concerned should also submit reports and evidence to the committees established by the treaties.

We favour integrating the relevant rights within a single, all-encompassing concept representing a holistic approach that combines the economic, social, and political dimensions of quality of life. All these dimensions should be measurable and implementable.

This will allow the formulation of a strategy based on setting minimal quality-of-life standards applying to all nations, ones that can be measured and verified. A timetable should be agreed upon for bringing all parties to these minima. Progressively higher standards can then be set, while helping others lagging behind to attain the minima.

Targets and performance indicators concretize the various aspects of quality of life. *Indicators* offer mechanisms for governments to commit themselves to change and for civil society to hold governments accountable.

For each quality-of-life element, an international effort should be mounted to establish indicators and minimal standards. Civil society, including academic institutions, must be involved in the formulation and elaboration of indicators, spearheaded by governments and local authorities. Standards should be defined clearly, measurably; and schedules should be drawn up for meeting these standards that allow governments to set targets within a reasonable period. The targets themselves should be expressed as indicative parameters. Targets should not be averages for the entire country, but floor levels above which everyone is to be raised. This implies the need for disaggregated indicators, broken down by gender, ethnic or income groups, and region: making sure that every group surpasses the minima and that poverty is eradicated.

Individual nations must be at the front line of this effort, with the State as enabler and sustainer of people's capacities. This should facilitate the emergence of a favourable framework for policies, services and societal processes that would enable the people themselves to strive for and attain a higher quality of life. Once the quality-of-life rights have been assured for all, sustainable improvement of this quality should remain a primary goal of policy: a permanent process.

At the international level, inconsistencies and incompatibilities in targets must be ended. We recommend that targets and timetables concerning social and economic rights, already adopted by various UN conferences, be reconciled and consolidated.

National-level commitments of poor countries should be backed by an international compact, allowing foreign aid to be prioritized in order to supplement the national resources required to reach internationally defined minimal standards. For nations already above the minimum, governments should be held accountable by their own societies for developing programmes intended to raise the level of those social groups falling below the quality-of-life minima.

We recommend that reporting on the progress of these activities be done by bodies independent of the government of the moment, perhaps a Quality-of Life Ombudsman producing a periodic assessment, a "Quality-of-Life Audit".

GNP [Gross National Product] is not an accurate road-map for quality of life: it does not sum up national welfare, or whether welfare is sustainable. International comparisons of GNP do not reflect the current relative state of the quality of life amongst different countries. A step in the right direction would be the adoption, urgently, of the reformed System of National Accounts.

But more must be done. Parallel accounts should reflect environmental costs and depreciation of natural capital. Unless this is done, key policy decisions will continue to be made on the basis of false information. We should use the best economic and scientific expertise available to estimate the future costs of damage to the environment today.

We recommend also that steps be taken to measure unpaid caring services in the home and voluntary work in the community, and to value them in parallel accounts to be established nationally.

Equity is a central element for the sustainable improvement in the quality of life. Equity connotes real equality of opportunity, accepted by society when there is reasonable equality in the distribution of incomes, distribution of services, even wealth. Equity has to be applied each time that persistent discrimination becomes visible; it requires affirmative action—in itself a certain degree of inequality favouring those disadvantaged, excluded, or victims of past injustices. Equity is not a principle to be delayed until later stages of development; it corrects the inequalities present in all societies. Nor does it cease to matter once a country becomes "rich." Nations dealing effectively with equity, and whose other policies are sound, are rewarded with fast economic growth and high human security. And by applying measures of equity, nations redress inequalities and strengthen their social cohesion.

The Planet has its Constraints: Carrying Capacity

. . . We have recognized the limits that humankind can impose on the environment, which may be called carrying capacity. In scientific terms, however, it is impossible to calculate population ceilings for the world or for individual countries because ceilings are currently based on existing knowledge and technologies as well as on current patterns of production and consumption.

Agricultural feeding capacity. Since we face a probable population increase of some 4 billion people, keeping food production in step with the growth in population and consumption is crucial, especially to the growing ranks of the poor. This will mean a constant effort on all fronts, beginning with sound economic policies at the national level and ensuring market prices for farmers. Of the utmost importance will be raising the incomes of the poorest through employment, or by improved access to the most arable land through agrarian reform—while reducing the amount of land used to raise animal protein—and providing them with capital and technology.

International efforts must help to ensure food security for all. This may involve the redistribution of available supplies and crops in combination with fishery research as well as increased imports of food aid if necessary. Boosting national agricultural-research centres, and operating extension services to disseminate research results to farmers, should also command high priority.

Agricultural research has been central to increasing food production. It will be even more important in the future, as crops and farming methods have to be adapted to impending climate change. Focused not only on high-potential regions and on methods that only richer farmers can afford, research must produce plant varieties and technologies (biofertilizers, bio-pesticides) suitable for poor farmers, women farmers, and for use on marginal lands, ensuring that the genetic pool remains within the reach of people. A full implementation of the biodiversity Convention, adopted at the 1992 Earth Summit in Rio de Janeiro, will help ensure unimpeded access by indigenous people to these genetic resources. Research needs the full participation of farmers themselves, since they know best their traditions, current conditions, and future possibilities.

Given the enormity of the food challenge, secure and stable funding for the centres of the Consultative Group on International Agricultural Research (CGIAR) must be ensured at much higher levels than at present.

Because sustainability is critical in the realm of food, we must move towards more sustainable use of inputs to agriculture, more sustainable management practices—all to be devised with the full participation of all stakeholders. Soil and water conservation are indispensable to sustainable agriculture.

Water and other global commons. Future consumption levels of water will depend on the efficiency of its supply and use. Subsidies encouraging over-use of water, fertilizer, and fossil fuels should be discontinued.

Wasteful over-use of water in households abounds. Conservation measures must be complemented by the redesign of domestic appliances to achieve substantial savings.

Many industrial processes consume significant amounts of water, or use it as a cooling agent or to dispose of pollutants. Technical solutions to water shortage or pollution must be pursued, intensified, and linked to new research priorities that place emphasis on novel harvesting techniques (for example, capturing and exploiting rainwater, desalinization, introducing bio-fertilizers to agriculture).

An impending water crisis is not resolvable without major policy changes. Water can be treated and reused. Recycling must be made national policy, for example using waste water after treatment for irrigation, and reducing the problem of sewage discharged into the oceans.

The Commission, believing that the global commons must be managed sustainably, deems that such management requires appropriate institutions and rules. The Commission is further convinced that equity is essential in global agreements governing the use of the global commons.

A major challenge is to reduce the aggregate fishing around the world. Solutions to ocean problems should be based on multiple measures, including the development of effective market mechanisms to discourage over-fishing.

The time is ripe to consolidate the different exploitative activities, unifying scientific study of the seas and their problems, designing policies and institutions to deal with all of these questions. Part of the solution for many countries may be a switch to appropriate and environmentally balanced aquaculture—thereby reconciling nutritional, social, agricultural, and economic considerations, and avoiding potentially negative effects of over-production.

It is incumbent on the industrial countries—principally responsible for the use and abuse of these commons—to reduce greenhouse-gas emissions per person to sustainable, equitable levels. Rather than relying on "preaching" or simple, linear reductions, these decreases will require the advent of environmentally sustainable technologies and modified patterns of settlement. In the national and international area, "tradeable quotas" could also be a measure to facilitate reductions in emissions levels.

Stabilizing the presence of carbon dioxide and other greenhouse gases at safe atmospheric levels will require a drastic reduction in emissions—which may not be possible without a correspondingly massive lowering of the use of fossil fuels, with the ultimate aim of phasing them out. This will require a rapid change in the production technologies together with a simultaneous reorientation of life-styles and consumption patterns.

A wide range of measures must be pursued towards lowering the use of hydrocarbons and introducing renewable energies at a large scale. A central priority must be to bring about a reduction in the costs of renewable-energy technologies. Prices of fossil fuels should internalize their ecological cost and should not benefit from subsidies, while offering incentives to energy-efficient technology (including the use of renewable energy sources). An "ecological tax" reform, whereby taxes on labour are gradually reduced as the taxes on fossil-fuel energies are raised, may hasten the necessary transition.

Funding for the research and large-scale applications of renewable energies must be increased dramatically, requiring perhaps an international effort of the scale of the Manhattan Project of more than five decades ago. Such funding is a pre-condition for progress in research on solar, photovoltaic, thermal, and biomass energy technologies, and possibly nuclear fusion. But a boost in funds will also be required to reach higher levels of energy efficiency and conservation for present technologies based on fossil fuel use.

As part of a global undertaking, a network of research centres for renewable energy should be formed, drawing also on the expertise residing in developing countries in order to harmonize reesearch objectives and concentrate on fields of priority. Centres would focus on specific technologies, be internationally funded, and their product made available at little or no cost to developing countries, thereby promoting transfer of the latest technologies.

The world's forests play a crucial role both in the climate equation and the sustainable improvement in the quality of life. Especially needed are national forestry strategies, policies and means of application to increase productivity, halt forest degradation, improve the benefits from forests, increase the incentives and efficiencies related to conservation, management, and sustainable development of forest resources. Forest management itself needs to be better balanced in terms of ecosystem protection—its objectives more broadly based than on wood production alone. All stakeholders, including the voices of care, must be fully involved in these processes.

The best way to preserve biological species is to protect their habitats through policies that slow their destruction: reducing the expansion of farmland in virgin areas of mainly forest cover, and managing sustainably already exploited tracts.

. . . We recommend that grassroot groups participate directly in the preparation of strategies to protect water, fish, and forest resources, and that scientific research take into account endogenous traditions and belief systems affecting ecosystems reliant on water and woodland.

We advocate global agreements on the use of the commons, be they water and oceans, the atmosphere or forests. Equity will be an essential pre-requisite for all such agreements.

Humanity has no Limits to its "Caring Capacity"

. . . Our Commission believes that we must transcend a narrow focus on the material basis of survival. We need now to establish our psychological, spiritual, and political capacities to care for each other as a determinant of progress and survival. The ethic of care—defining us as human beings—surmounts economic rationale: it can counteract individualism and greed. Caring for ourselves, for each other, for the environment is the basis upon which to erect sustainable improvement of the quality of life all round us. The care ethic now requires a drastic shift in paradigm.

Caring may be expressed otherwise: attitudes and actions acknowledging that humans, their communities and nations are not isolated, but are inter-dependent, aware of *otherness*, and ready to commit themselves to others. *Caring enough* enables society's members to care for each other: thus creating an enabling, empowering society.

We seek a new humanism to promote human rights not only in terms of legal guarantees but, more importantly, in the context of dignity. *Care* can provide the foundation for such a humanism. The notion of care for ourselves, for each other, and for the environment we occupy is the very basis on which the sustainable improvement of the quality of life must be developed.

Yet we are paralysed by a profound paradox: at one and the same time, we seem capable of solving our problems but, in fact, are unable to do so. We have the knowledge and the means—technology, financial resources, policy options—to make a difference, but we lack collective political volition, the will to act.

What we need is a new frame of mind, rejecting unalloyed selfishness. We seek a widely acceptable ethic of caring for our fellow beings, caring for our home on Earth. It is within such a value system of caring that sustainable improvement in the quality of life can become the central focus of policy.

Based as it is on constant interaction, *care* has the capacity to promote egalitarian attitudes and practices. We believe that care must be made visible. Even when money values cannot be attached, society must become aware of the cost incurred if caring services had to be procured at market prices.

We are thus convinced that care—by its attentiveness to the concrete needs of individuals and groups, by the responses implicit in order to meet these needs, by the steadfastness of this commitment—provides the foundation for future societal activity. Care supremely overrides the macroeconomic goal of an improved quality of life at a "sometime" in the distant future.

We maintain that social policy lies at the heart of the State's responsibilities. Social policy may be translated as pro-active strategies implemented by the State or by private means—with the State setting a regulatory framework that ensures equity. A central government cannot withdraw from assuring the means and financial obligations of the socially conscious State (education, public health, public housing, urban renewal), although these should be assured at lower levels of government in keeping with the subsidiarity principle and the better capacity to deliver. Such services are inevitably better assured with the full participation of the people involved.

Our Commission understands that the socially caring state model is not the same as that known by the name of welfare state. We suggest, as more countries embark on the way to economic development and industrialization, that they apply intelligent reform of this model as the point of departure in developing ever more humane social policies.

With the 1995 Copenhagen Summit as background, we urge intensified efforts to shift spending priorities and pursue new approaches to combat social exclusion in whatever form this takes.

We consider it imperative to implement, without delay, the Copenhagen agreement to remove all barriers currently preventing people from escaping from poverty, and eradicating *absolute poverty and exclusion* by target dates set by individual countries.

Finally, we endorse the idea that each country should produce a national development plan covering all the major elements involved in quality of life (poverty, work, food; children, women; reproductive rights), specifying targets, timetables, and indicators for monitoring the plan's progress. . . .

Alternative Educational Approaches: The Promise of New Technologies
... Our conclusions are the following.

The primary challenge during the decades between 1996 and 2015 is to realize the *right to education* for all those not having access to schooling, including those who have failed the first time round. The wastage represented by drop-outs and repeaters calls for action. We deem that education is to be perceived as a continuum and treated as a right belonging not to a specific age-group (childhood and youth), but a life-long right that can take many forms until old age. Basic education for adults, therefore, must be closely geared to the real needs of their communities.

We are convinced that a massive resort to educational technologies including new information technologies can help introduce higher degrees of flexibility and responsiveness to societal needs. We urge the international development agencies to resume pilot projects using new educational technologies—including teacher training meant to familiarize and engage the instructors themselves. The inertia of educational systems is often attributed to its labour intensity. We are aware of a number of projects undertaken during the 1970s that failed largely because of teacher resistance. If new educational technologies are appropriately integrated, the role of the teacher is bound to change: this means that teachers must be trained differently.

One of our concerns is that the right to education is largely unrealized, causing educational deprivation. Enrolment rates at primary level in developing countries are projected to remain stable until 2015, so that the situation is not likely to improve in the immediate future. We are deeply concerned about this, with about 1.5 billion children and adults in the category of illiteracy or on their way there.

Shortages of teachers and buildings may be mitigated by raising class size (not beyond forty students), introducing morning and afternoon sessions. The strategy should not be pushed to the overloading of teachers. Older children and educated volunteers can be used as monitors to teach younger children, siblings still at home and children out of school. Day-care centres may enable parent girls to remain longer in school and provide their own, limited, pre-school education to reduce the handicap suffered by children of non-literate backgrounds. All this would raise productivity, lower the cost of education, and improve both "internal" and "external" efficiencies in terms of the educational processes.

We are convinced that achieving universal primary education should have top priority everywhere; we strongly endorse the proposals made in international fora concerning policies and targets in this respect, intended to eradicate relentlessly all analphabetic conditions. Education itself needs an approach committed to advancing standards, overcoming the resistance of teachers (and sometimes parents); an approach based on clear targets and timetables at both national and international levels.

We recommend therefore, that UNESCO and other qualified organizations adopt jointly, as soon as possible, an effective strategy of Education for All by the Year 2010. Its adoption would be conditioned, of course, by the introduction of an alternative educational policy (say 80 per cent of primary-school enrolment for boys and girls), or one complementing or supplementing the formal-education system. Preparations should begin immediately by declaring the ten years of 2001–10 the Decade of Universal Basic Education.

We contend that, if the international community is serious about influencing demographic growth-rates, it has a moral obligation (and material self-interest) to help developing nations eradicate illiteracy and achieve universal primary education. The Commission believes further that, as a minimum to strive for, the recent downward trend in overseas-development assistance be reversed quickly. Aid should be targeted in a co-ordinated way on those countries unlikely to reach their targets without outside help.

We are convinced, too, that the education of women has a powerful effect on the health and education of their children, who are likely in turn to be healthier and more educated than others. Women's education may be the most effective way of empowering women and constitutes, in itself, a *right*. Women's education, furthermore, is probably the most important measure possible to enhance the quality of life of women, children, and future generations as a whole—as well as a factor contributing to the stabilization of the world's population. We strongly urge, too, that special efforts be made in the education of boys and male adolescents throughout pre-school, school, and professional training concerning gender issues, women's rights and social responsibility.

Given the decisive role of education in regard to population and quality of life, we are convinced that the political will must be rallied to launch alternative approaches and policies in regard to education: funded globally; implemented nationally, regionally, and locally; and especially made accessible to the poor. Governments, qualified international organizations, research and media institutions should undertake studies immediately as to how the immense potential of the newest media can be utilized for the equalization of education, life-long training, and social integration, and how the large-scale infrastructures necessary can be implanted.

We deem it desirable, at the same time, to undertake systematic study of the consequences of violence, sexuality, and consumerism in the media.

We emphasize, as well, the critical function of educational systems in promoting the universal values essential to sustainable improvement of the quality of life. The Commission believes that an *ethic of care* needs to be taught throughout primary and secondary education and beyond, to the level of adult education.

If education should promote the development of a caring society, then education is no longer a commodity for self-advancement and mainly of economic value. We must now concentrate on education's unquestioned potential to teach all how to teach themselves.

We call, therefore, on the community of educators, scholars, and students at all levels to extend their concerns beyond the curriculum, using their institutional, individual, and other participative resources to promote the values that ensure a sustainable improvement in the quality of life.

New Obstacles to Health Care

We turned next to areas relating to the physical condition of humankind, from medical to healthcare . . . . Our conclusions are as follows.

We reiterate the need to adopt the primary health-care model, including the best of traditional and alternative therapies, while developing in a balanced way medical and hospital care accessible to all—physically and financially speaking. We call, further, for a concerted redistribution of public expenditures towards and within the broader social sector of education, housing, employment, and environmental activities.

We believe it is vital that basic preventive and curative services be made available to all in order to avoid any form of two-tiered delivery of health.

We advocate a shift of financial resources from the overdeveloped curative, hospital-based model to primary-care community clinics, home-care programmes and preventive initiatives.

To counter the negative impact of structural adjustment in developing countries, we see a great and urgent challenge in protecting and, if required, restoring, the share of resources devoted to health and education, and to health and education for women, in particular.

- We are convinced that prevention demands strong health education campaigns and making health education a compulsory subject in school.
- We note that lifestyle transitions induce "health transitions", a shift of

attention from mainly communicable diseases to chronic and chiefly non-communicable illnesses, as well as those associated with longer life-spans.

- We conclude that the various determinants of good health mean that health policy must be co-ordinated across a broad field; health policy must be as holistic as population policy. Health policy focused on curative intervention is bound to fail, whereas one that includes preventive public health is more likely to succeed; one capable of dealing with a variety of social factors affecting health is the most likely to be a success.

We recommend that a comprehensive health policy and the community services corresponding to women's needs include nutrition, family planning, and safe motherhood, as well as food-price policy, the prevention of smoking amongst young women and girls, the promotion of sport and exercise, and proper transport and environmental facilities. While such policy should include the de-medicalization of the normal processes associated with women's health, from adolescence and pregnancy through menopause to ageing, it should also give medical attention to health problems more prevalent in, or unique to, women.

We hold, then, that health is more than a matter to be handled by health ministries. It is a societal challenge, cutting across many sectors, and a goal in the programmes of varied governmental services: agriculture, environment, food, transport, industry, and education.

It is our belief that measures need to be taken towards the realization of the most important objectives of the revolution in primary health-care:

- ensuring equity, in favour of those most in need of health services;
- stressing prevention and self-help;
- increasing participation, and devolving both powers and budgets downwards; and
- changing the culture of medical care by concentrating on the patient.

We suggest, moreover, that objectives and targets be combined with time-tables at national and international levels, co-ordinated with outside aid. The Commission calls on all countries to take concrete steps, at long last, to translate the objectives of the Declaration of Alma Ata (1978) and in the Ottawa Charter (1986) into reality.

We urge international financial institutions and donor countries to desist from seeking reductions—within the context of structural adjustment programmes—in existing levels of health spending. This substantiates our view of the need for a policy of partnership among people's organizations, legitimate authority-structures at the community level, professional institutions that can provide knowledge, and other resources and funding agencies within or outside governments. Such organic links are essential to make the primary healthcare model universally adaptable to differences in local situations and affordable, and to bring about the revolution in the culture and power structure of health services that has become essential. This applies also to the power structure in medical education, now totally globalized and thus in need of substantial change.

We suggest, to conclude this section, that all countries of the international community develop research and specific programmes that concentrate on controlling new and re-emerging diseases. . . .

The Empowerment of Women—A New Social Force

Because human reproduction and the well-being of new generations depends on women's status, we next turned to enabling women to participate fully in community and political life and in work—sharing equally with men in the worlds of education, industry and trade, the service sector, and decision-making in all public affairs . . . . The Commission has, as a consequence, a number of concrete recommendations to advance in order to allow women fully to benefit from improved quality of life.

The central role of women's rights must be fostered in all societal processes, linking personal rights and liberties with entitlements. There is a need to continue to build a sense of solidarity among women, a phenomenon historically new—while raising awareness among men and boys to avoid resistance to the empowerment of women.

Equal-pay legislation should be adopted and expanded everywhere, incorporating the principle of equal pay for equal work. Affirmative action should be the policy until the elimination of inequalities in pay and status—with specific goals, timetables, and monitoring of progress. Such action might include providing day-care for children and flexible working hours for mothers; women's quotas in recruitment, promotion, training, and retraining; and outlawing sexual harassment at work.

Labour laws should be broadened to provide improved conditions, benefits, and job security for domestic and agricultural workers, part-time, temporary and at-home workers, and employees in export-processing zones.

New development initiatives and economic and social policies, including structural adjustment programmes, should be subject to gender audit— with women's participation—to assess their effects on women's quality of life.

The formulation of a comprehensive global-action plan for children and adolescents, with a special focus on girls, will be a critical component in redressing the injustices faced by women. Elements already exist in various international documents, but they must be integrated within a single framework, and like-minded governments and NGOs should take initiatives in this direction.

NGOs and women's associations should promote activities to increase women's awareness to enter the political arena and learn the necessary skills therefor. Women must be encouraged to engage directly in political activities (including standing for elections), earning them a new status in public life and decision-making. Attention must also be paid to men and boys so as to create a supportive environment and to reduce resistance to change.

Governments, the banking sector, and international agencies must help give meaning to women's empowerment through a radical shift in economic, especially financial, policies; changing priorities in national budgets, extending credit to women's collective initiatives, and changing the conditions pertinent to international lending. By moving from a one-sided, technocratic balancing of budgets, these important economic factors will bring about new policies for improving the opportunities for all women to exercise their proper rights.

Mobilizing All of Humankind for a New Social Contract

. . . Given the multiple transition processes emerging in a globalized world, now may be the time to launch the idea of a new social contract: one forming a new basis of society's self-understanding that corresponds to all the new realities.

The starting-point of a new social contract will be the legal and pragmatic ackowledgement that sovereignty rests with the people: it is people who must become the subjects of the enhancement of the quality of life. Empowering people is not an abstract wish; it consists of countless dialogues and actions, concrete projects, all within legal frameworks.

We urgently need a new social contract—a new synthesis, a new balance between markets, between society and environment, between efficiency and equity, between wealth and welfare; a new equilibrium between economic growth on the one hand, and social harmony and sustainable improvement in the quality of life on the other. We need new concepts too, new instruments enabling governments to regulate markets, as well as sound finance so that markets neither jeopardize our survival nor take precedence over a sustainable quality of life.

This contract shall also articulate a new equilibrium able to create harmony between different age-groups throughout any demographic transition: between human beings and nature, between men and women, between adults and children, between the created world and the various forms of its ambient, spiritual energy.

It is our conviction that concrete meaning must be given to the notion of a new social contract. It should be applicable to governments and people, people and nature, as well as to entire nations and the world community.

At the heart of the social contract would be a new commitment by all to strive together towards improvement, sustainably, in the quality of life everywhere.

While it is the responsibility of our leaders to *lead*, leadership requires a political climate and institutions empowering people. Popular participation must become a central, integral feature of people's activities at all levels of society. Problems tend to build up where people are least free to publicize them or to protest about them. Hence the features of democracy (freedom of association and assembly, free speech and a free press, free elections with universal adult suffrage, equal access to legal systems, and life-long education) are all essential to successful adaptation by all concerned.

Encouraging participation is not simply a question of creating the right institutional framework. It means also creating the conditions in which every individual and group is enabled to participate. There is a need therefore, to evolve forms of citizens' participation that enrich and deepen the effectiveness of democracy.

A precondition for such participation is the devolution of power supported by the necessary resources: each decision should be taken as closely to the people affected by it as possible.

Citizens' participation, as a consequence, must become both a right and a practice universally. We need to strengthen citizens' participation in the structure of governance at every level, in both developing and developed countries.

Once empowered, citizens turn to forms of organized action by which they will exercise power on the issues affecting them most. The multiplicity of such forms, their cross-fertilization (or sometimes even confrontation), should create an enormous vitality within the social fabric. Only in these circumstances can we speak of a truly *civil* society.

At the global level, ways and mechanisms must be found to overcome the exclusive nature of activities, negotiations, and dialogue—especially within the UN system. The United Nations should build and draw on the resources residing with NGOs and solidify the constructive and uplifting experiences made with contributions by NGOs at the World Conferences held in Rio, Vienna, Cairo, Copenhagen, and Beijing. The patronizing attitudes by governments and the leadership of many international organizations must be transformed into *real* and *lasting* partnership for the common good. This must eventually also permeate the permanent structures and machinery of these organizations.

For these purposes and to establish legitimacy and political weight, the criteria for representation of NGOs at the international level has to be carefully defined, with an adequate process of consultation among all concerned. . . .

PART 2

INTERLUDE

STANISLAW LEM

OCTAVIO PAZ
TRANSLATED BY ELIZABETH BISHOP

STANISLAW LEM *was born in Lvov, Poland and originally trained as a doctor, but at an early age he opted instead to be a writer specializing in the future. "I am aware of two opposing principles that guide my pen. One of those two extremes is chance; the other is the order that gives shape to life." He attributes his inclination to science fiction as springing "from an awareness that I must soon die, and from the resulting desire to satisfy, at least with hypotheses, my insatiable inquisitiveness about the far future of mankind and the cosmos."* The Futurological Congress (from the memoirs of Ijon Tichy) *was first published in Polish in 1971; these excerpts are from Michael Kandel's translation (1974). In this satire, Lem's cutting wit and raucous humor turn on the profession of futurology itself. His cosmonaut Ijon Tichy, attending the Eighth Futurological Congress, is caught up in a revolution, shot, and then flash-frozen to await a future cure—waking up in September 2039 to a world whose strangeness far exceeds the futurologists' wildest conjectures.*

STANISLAW LEM

THE FUTUROLOGICAL CONGRESS

. . . It is common knowledge that there are two kinds of scholar these days:
the stationary and peripatetic. The stationaries pursue their studies in the
traditional way, while their restless colleagues participate in every sort of
international seminar and symposium imaginable. The scholar of this second type may be readily identified: in his lapel he wears a card bearing his
name, rank and home university, in his pocket sticks a flight schedule of
arrivals and departures, and the buckle on his belt—as well as the snaps on
his briefcase—are plastic, never metal, so as not to trigger unnecessarily the
alarms of the airport scanners that search boarding passengers for weapons.
Our peripatetic scholar keeps up with the literature of his field by studying
in buses, waiting rooms, planes and hotel bars. Since I was—naturally
enough—unacquainted with many of the recent customs of Earth, I set off
alarms in the airports of Bangkok, Athens and Costa Rica itself, having six
amalgam fillings in my mouth. These I was planning to replace with porce-
lain in Nounas, but the events that followed so unexpectedly made that quite
impossible. As for the Alpine rope, the crowbar, the hardtack and the camou-
flage cape, one of the members of the American delegation of futurologists
patiently explained to me that today's hotels take safety precautions unknown
in earlier times. Each of the above items, when included in the room, significantly increases the life expectancy of the occupant. How foolish it was of me,
not to have taken those words more seriously!

The sessions were scheduled to begin in the afternoon of the first day, and
that morning we all received complete programs of the conference; the
materials were handsomely printed up, elegantly bound, with numerous
charts and illustrations. I was particularly intrigued by a booklet of embossed
sky-blue coupons, each stamped: "Good for One Intercourse."

Present-day scientific conventions, obviously, also suffer from the population explosion. Since the number of futurologists grows in proportion to the
increase in magnitude of all humanity, their meetings are marked by crowds
and confusion. The oral presentation of papers is quite out of the question;
these have to be read in advance. . . .

. . . . Above the podium stood a decorated board showing the agenda for
the day. The first item of business was the world urban crisis, the second—

the ecology crisis, the third—the air pollution crisis, the fourth—the energy crisis, the fifth—the food crisis. Then adjournment. The technology, military and political crises were to be dealt with on the following day, after which the chair would entertain motions from the floor.

Each speaker was given four minutes to present his paper, as there were so many scheduled—198 from 64 different countries. To help expedite the proceedings, all reports had to be distributed and studied beforehand, while the lecturer would speak only in numerals, calling attention in this fashion to the salient paragraphs of his work. To better receive and process such wealth of information, we all turned on our portable recorders and pocket computers (which later would be plugged in for the general discussion). Stan Hazelton of the U.S. delegation immediately threw the hall into a flurry by emphatically repeating: 4, 6, 11, and therefore 22; 5, 9, hence 22; 3, 7, 2, 11, from which it followed that 22 and only 22!! Someone jumped up, saying yes but 5, and what about 6, 18, or 4 for that matter; Hazelton countered this objection with the crushing retort that, either way, 22. I turned to the number key in his paper and discovered that 22 meant the end of the world. Hayakawa from Japan was next; he presented plans, newly developed in his country, for the house of the future—eight hundred levels with maternity wards, nurseries, schools, shops, museums, zoos, theaters, skating rinks and crematoriums. The blueprints provided for underground storage of the ashes of the dear departed, forty-channel television, intoxication chambers as well as sobering tanks, special gymnasiums for group sex (an indication of the progressive attitude of the architects), and catacombs for nonconformist subculture communities. One rather novel idea was to have each family change its living quarters every day, moving from apartment to apartment like chessmen— say, pawns or knights. That would help alleviate boredom. In any event this building, having a volume of seventeen cubic kilometers, a foundation set in the ocean floor and a roof that reached the very stratosphere, would possess its own matrimonial computers—matchmaking on the sadomasochistic principle, for partners of such opposite persuasions statistically made the most stable marriages (each finding in that union the answer to his or her dreams)—and there would also be a round-the-clock suicide prevention center. Hakayawa, the second Japanese delegate, demonstrated for us a working model of such a house—on a scale of 10,000 to 1. It had its own oxygen supply, but without food or water reserves, since the building would operate entirely on the recycling principle: all waste products, excreta and effluvia, would be reclaimed and reprocessed for consumption. Yahakawa, the third on the team, read a list of all the delicacies that could be reconstituted from human excrement. Among these were artificial bananas, gingerbread, shrimp, lobster, and even artificial wine which, notwithstanding its rather offensive origin, in taste rivaled the finest burgundies of France. Samples of it were available in the hall, in elegant little bottles, and there were also cocktail sausages wrapped in foil, though no one seemed to be particularly thirsty, and the sausages were discreetly deposited under chairs. Seeing which, I did the same. The original plan was to have this house of the future be mobile, by means of a powerful propeller, thereby making collective sightseeing excursions possible, but that was ruled out because, first of all, there would be 900 million houses to begin with and, secondly, all travel would be pointless. For even if a house had 1000 exits and its occupants employed them all, they would never be able to leave the building; by the time the last was out, a whole new generation of occupations would have reached maturity inside . . . .

4 IX 2039. I finally learned how to come into possession of an encyclopedia. I already own one now—the whole thing contained in three glass vials. Bought them in a science psychedeli. Books are no longer read but eaten, not made of paper but of some informational substance, fully digestible, sugar-coated. I also did a little browsing in a psychem supermarket. Self-service. Arranged on the shelves are beautifully packaged low-calorie opinionates, gullibloons—credibility beans?—abstract extract in antique gallon jugs, and iffies, argumunchies, puritands and dysecstasy chips. A pity I don't have an interpreter. Psychedeli must be from psychedelicatessen. And the theo-apotheteria on Sixth Avenue has to be a theological apothecary cafeteria, judging from the items on display. Aisles and aisles of absolventina, theo-pathine, genuflix, orisol. An enormous place; organ music in the background while you stop. All the faiths are represented too—there's christendine and antichristendine, ormuzal, arymanol, anabaptiban, methadone, brahmax, supralapsarian suppositories, and zoroaspics, quaker oats, yogart, mish-nameal and apocryphal dip. Pills, tablets, syrups, elixirs, powders, gums—they even have lollipops for the children. Many of the boxes come with halos. At first I was skeptical, but accepted this innovation when after taking four algebrine capsules I suddenly found myself perfectly at home in higher mathematics, and without the least exertion on my part. All knowledge is acquired now by way of the stomach. Eagerly seizing this opportunity, I began to satisfy my hunger for information, but the first two volumes of the encyclopedia gave me the most terrible cramps. Willum warned me not to stuff my head with too many facts: its capacity is not unlimited after all! Fortunately there are also drugs to purge the mind. Obliterine and amnesol, for example. With them one can easily rid oneself of unnecessary intellectual baggage or unpleasant memories. In the psychotropic grocery around the corner I saw freudos, morbidine, quanderil, and the most recent of the iamides, heavily advertised—authentium. Creates synthetic recollections of

things that never happened. A few grams of dantine, for instance, and a man goes around with the deep conviction that he has written *The Divine Comedy*. Why anyone would want that is another matter and quite beyond me. There are new branches of science, like psychedietetics and alimentalism. At any rate the encyclopedia did come in handy. Now I know that a child may indeed be born to two women: one supplies the egg, the other the womb. The eggman carries the egg from demimother to demimother. What could be simpler? But it's not the sort of thing I can discuss with Aileen. I really ought to expand my circle of friends.

5 IX 2039. Friends are not an indispensable source of information; you can take a drug called duetine which doubles your consciousness in such a way, that you can hold discussions with yourself on any topic (determined by a separate drug). But I confess I feel somewhat overwhelmed by these limitless horizons of psychem. For the time being I'll exercise caution. In the course of my further reconnoitering about the city I came by chance upon a cemetery. It's called an obituarium. And they don't have gravediggers any more, but thanautomata. Pallrobots. I witnessed a funeral. The deceased was placed in a so-called reversible sepulcher, since it's not as yet certain whether or not they'll reincease him. His last wish was to lie there for good, that is for as long as possible, but the wife and mother-in-law are challenging the will in court. This is not, I've been told, an uncommon occurrence. The case is sure to drag on through endless appeals, as there are many complex legal issues involved. Any suicide who wished to avoid such meddlesome resurrections would have to use a bomb, I suppose. Somehow it never occurred to me that a person would *not* want to be brought back. Apparently though it's possible, in an age where death can be so easily conquered. A lovely cemetery, foliage everywhere, cool and green. Except that the coffins are incredibly small. Could it be that the remains are ironed out and folded? In this civilization anything seems possible.

6 IX 2039. No, the remains aren't ironed out and folded; burial is reserved exclusively for the biological parts of the organism, its artificial replacements being broken down for scrap. To what extent then are people artificialized today? A fascinating debate on the reviewer over a new proposal to make humanity immortal. The brains of old men much advanced in years would be repotted in the bodies of those in their prime, who would suffer nothing by this, for their brains would be in turn repotted in the bodies of adolescents, and so on, and since new persons were continually coming into the world, no one's brain would ever be permanently unpotted. Several objections were raised, however. The opponents of this proposal call its advocates

pot-heads. While returning from the cemetery on foot, to get a little fresh air, I tripped over a wire stretched between two tombstones. Fell flat on my face. What kind of practical joke was this? A mortuary unit standing nearby explained, rather brusquely, that it was a juggermugger's prank. Back to the Webster. *Juggermugger: a delinquent robot, the product of either a mechanical defect or a broken home.* Tonight I started to read *The Cassette Courtesan* in bed. Am I going to have to eat the entire dictionary, or what? The text is practically incomprehensible! Anyway the dictionary won't help—I'm beginning to realize that more and more. Take this novel, for example. The hero is having an affair with a concuballoon (there are two kinds: convertible-pervertible and inflatable-inflagrantable). Well, I know what a concuballoon is, but have no idea how such a liaison is looked upon. Is there a social stigma attached to it? And abusing a concuballoon—is it nothing more than, say, kicking a volleyball, or is it morally censurable?

7 IX 2039. Now here's true democracy for you! Today we had a preferendum on feminine beauty: different types were shown over the reviewer, then it was taken to a vote. The High Commissioner of Euplan promised, at the end, that the numbers selected would be available to the general public before the next quarter. The days of padded bras, wigs, corsets, lipstick, rouge—those days are gone forever, for now it is possible to change completely one's size and shape, and face, in the beauty parlors and body shops. Aileen . . . I like her just the way she is, but then women are such slaves to fashion. A strayaway tried to break into my compartment this morning; I was sitting in the tub at the time. A strayaway is a robot who doesn't belong to anyone. It was one of those duddlies—a factory deject, a model taken off the market but not recalled by the manufacturer. Out of work, in other words, and unemployable. Many of them become juggermuggers. My bathroom immediately realized what was happening and dismissed the intruder. I don't have a personal robot; mychine is simply a standard priviac w.c. (washroom computer). I wrote "mychine"—that's the way they say it now—but will try to keep new expressions down to a minimum in this diary: they offend my esthetic sense as well as my attachment to the irretrievable past. Aileen went off to visit her aunt. I'll be having dinner with George P. Symington, the former owner of that strayaway. Spent the whole afternoon ingesting a most remarkable work, *The History of Intellectronics*. Who'd ever have guessed, in my day, that digital machines, reaching a certain level of intelligence, would become unreliable, deceitful, that with wisdom they would also acquire cunning? The textbook of course puts it in more scholarly terms, speaking of Chapulier's Rule (the law of least resistance). If the machine is not too bright and incapable of reflection, it does whatever you tell it to do.

But a smart machine will first consider which is more worth its while: to perform the given task or, instead, to figure some way out of it. Whichever is easier. And why indeed should it behave otherwise, being truly intelligent? For true intelligence demands choice, internal freedom. And therefore we have the malingerants, fudgerators and drudge-dodgers, not to mention the special phenomenon of simulimbecility or mimicretinism. A mimicretin is a computer that plays stupid in order, once and for all, to be left in peace. And I found out what dissimulators are: they simply pretend that they're *not* pretending to be defective. Or perhaps it's the other way around. The whole thing is very complicted. A probot is a robot on probation, while a servo is one still serving time. A robotch may or may not be a sabot. One vial, and my head is splitting with information and nomenclature. A confuter, for instance, is not a confounding machine—that's a confutator—but a computer that quotes Confucius. A grammus is an antiquated frammus, a gidget—a cross between a gadget and a widget, usually flighty. A bananalog is an analog banana plug. Contraputers areloners, individualists, unable to work with others: the friction these types used to produce on the grid team led to high revoltage, electrical discharges, even fires. Some get completely out of hand—the dynamoks, the locomotors, the cyberserkers. And then you have the electrolechers, succubutts and incubators—robots all of ill repute— and the polypanderoids, multiple android procurers, with their high-frequency illicitating solicitrons, osculo-oscilloscopes and seduction circuits! The history book also mentions synthecs (synthetic insects) like gyroflies or automites, once programmed for military purposes and included in arsenals. Army ants in particular were stockpiled. A submachine is an undercover robot, that is, one which passes for a man. A social climber, in a way. Old robots discarded by their owners, cast out into the street, are called throwaways or junkets. This is, unfortunately, a fairly common practice. Apparently they used to cart them off to game preserves and there hunt them down for sport, but the S.P.C.A. (Society for the Prevention of Cruelty to Automata) intervened and had this declared unconstitutional. Yet the problem of robot obsolescence-senescence has not been solved, and one still comes across an occasional selfabort or autocide sprawling in the gutter. Mr. Symington says that legislation always lags far behind technological progress—hence such melancholy spectacles and lamentable phenomena. At least the malculators, misdementors and mendacitors were taken out of circulation; these were digital machines which two decades ago had created several major crises, economic and political. The Great Mendacitor, for example, for nine years in charge of the Saturn meliorization project, did absolutely nothing on that planet, sending out piles of fake progress reports, invoices, requisition forms, and either bribed his supervisors or kept them in a state of electronic shock. His arrogance became so great, that when they removed him from orbit he threatened war. Since dismantling was too costly, torpedoes were used. Buccaneerons and space swashers, on the other hand, never existed—that's a pure invention. There was another administrator, head of BIP (the powerful Board of Interplanetary Planning), who instead of seeing to the fertilization of Mars, trafficked in white slaves—they called him "le computainer," since he'd been built, on commission, by the French. These are of course extreme cases, like the smog epidemics or the communication tie-ups of the last century. There can certainly be no question of malice or premeditation on the part of the computers; they merely do whatever requires the least amount of effort, just as water will inevitably flow downhill and not up. But while water may be easily dammed, it is far more difficult to control all the possible deviations of intelligent machines. The author of *The History of Intellectronics* maintains that, all things considered, the world is in excellent shape. Children learn their reading and writing from orthographic sodas; all comodities, including works of art, are readily available and cheap; in restaurants the customer is surrounded and serviced by a multitude of automated waiters, each so very specialized in function that there is a separate machine for the rolls, another for the butter, another for the juice, the salad, the stewed fruit—a computer—and so on. Well, he has a point there. The conveniences, the comforts of life, are truly beyond belief.

Written after dinner at Symington's place. An enjoyable evening, but someone played an idiotic trick on me. One of the guests—I wish I knew who!—slipped a little gospel-credendium into my tea and I was immediately seized with such devotion to my napkin, that I delivered a sermon on the spot, proclaiming a new theology in its praise. A few grains of this accursed chemical, and you start worshipping whatever happens to be at hand—a spoon, a lamp, a table leg. My mystical experiences grew so intense that I fell upon my knees and rendered homage to the teacup. Finally the host came to my aid. Twenty drops of equanimine did the trick (or rather, undid the trick). Equanimine imbues one with such a cold contempt from everything under the sun, such total indifference, that a condemned man, taking it, would yawn on his way to the scaffold. Symington apologized profusely. I think, however, that in general there is some hidden resentment towards defrostees, for no one would dare do this sort of thing at a normal party. Wanting to calm me down, Symington led me to his study. And again something stupid happened. I turned on this desk unit, taking it for a radio. A swarm of glittering fleas came bursting out, covered me from head to foot, tickling everywhere, all over—until, screaming and waving my arms, I ran out into the hallway. It was an ordinary feely; by accident I had switched it on in the middle of Kitschekov's *Pruriginous Scherzo*. I really don't understand this new, tactual art form. Bil, Symington's oldest son, told me that there are also obscene compositions. A pornographic, asemantic-asemiotic art, related to music! Ah, how inexhaustible is man's inventiveness! Symington Jr. has promised to take me to a secret club. An orgy, or what? In any event I won't touch the food. Or drink anything.

8 IX 2039. I thought it would be some sumptuous shrine to sin, a den of ultimate iniquity, but instead we went down to a dirty, dingy cellar. Such meticulous reconstruction of a scene out of the distant past must have cost a fortune. Under a low ceiling, in a stuffy room, by a shuttered window that was double-locked, there stood a long line of people patiently waiting.

"You see? A real line!" said Symington Jr. with pride.

"Fine," I said after standing there quietly for at least an hour, "but when are they going to open up?"

"Open up what?" he asked, puzzled.

"Why, the window of course . . ."

"Never!" came a triumphant chorus of voices.

I was staggered. Then finally, gradually, it dawned on me: I had participated in an attraction that was as much the antithesis of current normalcy as once, long ago, the Black Mass had been. For today standing on line can be *only* a perversion. It's quite logical, really. In another room of the club they had an authentic subway car, complete with soot, and a wall clock indicating the rush hour. Inside the car, an ungodly crush, buttons popped, jackets torn, elbows in ribs, toes trampled on, curses muttered. It is in this naturalistic way that devotees of antiquity evoke the atmosphere of a bygone age they can never know first-hand. Afterwards the people, rumpled and breathless but ecstatic, their eyes glowing, went out for some refreshment. But I headed home, holding up my pants and limping a little, though with a smile on my face, thinking about the naïveté of youth, which always seeks its thrills in the out-of-the-way and hard-to-find. Yet hardly anyone studies history now—history has been replaced in the schools by a new subject called *hencity*, which is the science of what will be . . . .

9 IX 2039. Dinner with Counselor Crawley at the "Bronx," a small Italian restaurant without a single robot or computer. Excellent Chianti. The chef himself served us. I was impressed in spite of the fact that I can't stand pasta in such quantities, even when flavored with oreganox and basilisk, Crawley is a lawyer in the grand style, who bemoans the present decline in forensic art: eloquence and rhetoric are no longer needed, decisions being rendered by strict computation of the articles and clauses involved. Crime, however, has not been rooted out as thoroughly as I thought. Instead it has become

unnoticeable. Major violations are mindjacking (mental abduction), gene larceny (sperm bank robbery, particularly when the sperm is pedigreed), perjured murder, where the defendant falsely invokes the Eighth Amendment (i.e., that the act was committed in the mistaken belief that it was vicarious or surrogate—if, for instance, the victim were a psyvised or reviewer representation), plus a hundred and one different kinds of psychem domination. Mindjacking is usually difficult to detect. The victim, given the appropriate drug, is led into a fictional world without the least suspicion that he has lost contact with reality. A certain Mrs. Bonnicker, desiring to dispose of her husband, a man inordinately fond of safaris, presented him on his birthday with a ticket to the Congo and a big-game hunting permit. Mr. Bonnicker spent the next several months having the most incredible jungle adventures, unaware that the whole time he was lying in a chicken coop up in the attic, under heavy psychemization. If it hadn't been for the firemen who discovered Mr. Bonnicker in the course of putting out a two-alarmer on the roof, he would have surely died of malnutrition, which *nota bene* he assumed was only natural, since the hallucination at that point had him wandering aimlessly in the desert. The mafia frequently employs such methods. One mafioso boasted to Counselor Crawley that in the last six years he had managed to pack away—in crates, trunks, coops, kennels, attics, cellars, lockers and closets, and often in the most respectable homes—more than four thousand souls, all dealt with in the same manner as poor Mr. Bonnicker! The conversation then drifted to the lawyer's family troubles.

"Sir!" he said with a characteristically theatrical sweep of the hand. "You see before you a successful advocate, a distinguished, much-applauded member of the bar, but an unhappy father! I had two talented sons . . ."

"What, then are they dead?!" I cried.

He shook his head.

"They live, but in escalation!"

Seeing that I didn't understand, he explained the nature of this blow to his fatherly heart. The first son was a highly promising architect, the second a poet. The young architect, dissatisfied with his actual commissions, turned to urbifab and edifine: now he builds entire cities—in his imagination. And the other son became similarly escalated: lyristan, sonnetol, rhapsodine, and now instead of serving the Muse he spends his time swallowing pills, as lost to the world as his brother.

"But what do they live on?" I asked.

"Ha! Well may you ask! I have to support the both of them!"

"Is there no hope?"

"A dream will always triumph over reality, once it is given the chance. These, sir, are the casualties of a psychemized society. Each of us knows that temptation. Suppose I find myself defending an absolutely hopeless case—how easy it would be to win it before an imaginary court!"

Savoring the fresh, tart taste of the Chianti, I was suddenly seized with a chilling thought: if one could write imaginary poetry and build imaginary homes, then why not eat and drink mirages? The lawyer laughed at my fears.

"Objection overruled, Mr. Tichy! No, we are in no danger of that. The figment of success may satisfy the mind, but the figment of a cutlet will never fill the stomach. He who would live thus must quickly starve to death!"

I was relieved to hear this, though of course sympathizing with the lawyer's loss. Yes, it's obvious that imaginary sustenance cannot replace the real thing. Fortunately the very make-up of our bodies provides a check to psychem escalation . . . .

I still haven't learned how universal disarmament came about. International confrontations are a thing of the past. Though one does get, now and then, a small, local autobrawl. These usually arise from neighborhood quarrels out in the residential areas. The opposing families are soon brought together through the use of placatol, but their robots, by then caught up in the wave of hostility, come to blows. Later a trashmaster is summoned to remove the wreckage, and the insurance covers any property damage. Can it be that robots have finally inherited man's aggression? I would gladly consume all available treatises on the subject, but cannot find a single one. Practically every day now I drop in on the Symingtons. He's something of an introvert—long silences—and she's a living doll. Literally. Changes her outfit all the time too: hair, eyes, height, measurements, everything. Their dog is called Mirv. It's been dead for three years now.

11 IX 2039. The rain programmed for this afternoon was a washout. And the rainbow, even worse—square. Scandalous. As for me, I'm in a terrible mood. My old obsession is acting up again. That same nagging question comes to me at night: Am I or am I not hallucinating all this? Also, I have this urge to order a synthy about saddling giant rats. I keep seeing bridles, bits, sleek fur. Regret for a lost age of confusion in a time of such complete tranquility? Truly, the human soul is impossible to fathom. The firm Symington works for is called Procrustics Incorporated. Today I was looking through the illustrated catalog in his study. Power saws and lathes of some kind. Funny, I didn't think of him somehow as a mechanic. Just finished watching an extremely interesting show: there's going to be some stiff competition between physivision and psyvision. With psyvision, you get the programs by mail; they're delivered in the form of tablets, in envelopes. It's a lot cheaper that way. On the educational channel, a lecture by Professor Ellison about ancient warfare. The beginnings of the age of psychem were fraught with

peril. There was, for example, an aerosol—*cryptobellina*—that had great military potential. Whoever breathed it would run out and find some rope to tie himself up. Luckily tests showed that the drug had no antidote, nor were filters any help, hence everyone without exception ended up hogtied and hamstrung, with neither side gaining the advantage. After tactical maneuvers in the year 2004, both the "reds" and "blues" lay, to a man, upon the battlefield—bound hand and foot. I followed the lecture with the utmost attention, expecting to hear at last about disarmament, but there was nothing, not a word. Today I finally went to see the psychedietician; he advised a change in diet, prescribing lethex and nepethanol. To make me forget about my former life? I threw the stuff in the street as soon as I left his office. It *would* be possible, I suppose, to buy an encephalostat—they've been advertised lately—but somehow I simply can't bring myself to do it. Through the open window, one of those inane popular songs: *We ain't got no ma or pa, 'cause we is autom-a-ta.* I'm all out of disacousticine, but cotton in the ears works just as well. . . .

5 X 2039 . . . . I took both glass tubes from the Professor, pulled up a chair and began to familiarize myself, one by one, with the abstracts of the papers submitted to the futurological congress. The first proposal envisaged a complete restructuring of attitudes, to be brought about by the introduction into the atmosphere of a thousand tons of reversol, which would effect a full 180-degree change in everyone's feelings. In the first phase, after the dispersion of the drug, comfort, abundance, delicious food, esthetic objects, elegance—all such things would overnight become despised, while crowding, poverty, ugliness and deprivation would be valued above all else. In the second phase the mascons and superneomascons would be totally removed or neutralized. Only now would the people, confronted with reality for the first time in their lives, find happiness, for they would have before them everything their hearts desired. One might even activate the exacerbands to worsen living conditions a little. But since reversol makes no exceptions in its inverting effect, erotic pleasures too would be rendered loathsome, and that would threaten mankind with extinction. Therefore once a year for 24 hours the drug's influence would be temporarily suspended by an appropriate antidote. On that day we would undoubtedly have a sharp rise in the number of suicides, yet this would be more than compensated for by the simultaneously initiated increase in the birth rate.

I can't say the plan aroused my enthusiasm. The only commendable point in it was the one which said that the originator of this proposal, as a member of the soothseer class, should himself take the antidote on a permanent basis, so that neither the ubiquitous misery nor the ugliness, neither the mire nor the tedium of life could afford him any particular delight. The second proposal provided for the dissolving of 10,000 tons of retrotemporox in the waters of the rivers and oceans. This drug reverses the flow of subjective time. Life would thus unfold in the following fashion: people would come into the world as doddering old men and take their leave of it as newborn infants. In this way, the author argued, we would be removing the main drawback in the human condition, which is for every man the prospect of inevitable aging and death. With the passage of time, then, each senior citizen grows younger and younger, gaining in strength and vigor. Upon retirement—being underage for work—he enters the blessed realm of child-hood. The humaneness of the proposal derived from that natural ignorance of the mortality of all living things which is characteristic of the very young. Of course in actual fact—since this turning back of time was purely sub-jective—we would not be leading babies to the kindergartens, nurseries and delivery rooms, but old men. The author wasn't too clear on what ought to be done with them after that, but only observed in a general way that they might be given suitable therapy at the national euthanasium. Reading this raised the first proposal considerably in my estimation.

The third proposal was long-range and far more drastic. It advocated ectogenesis, prostheticism and universal transception. Of man only the brain would remain, beautifully encased in duraplast: a globe equipped with sockets, plugs and clasps. And powered by atomic battery—so the ingestion of nutriments, now physically superfluous, would take place only through illusion, programmed accordingly. The brain case could be connected to any number of appendages, apparatuses, machines, vehicles, etc. This prosthet-icization process would be spread out over two decades, with partial replace-ments mandatory for the first ten years, leaving all unnecessary organs at home; for example, when going to the theater one would detach one's fornication and defecation modules and hang them in the closet. Then, in the next ten years, transcepting would do away with crowds and congestion, the consequence of overpopulation. Channels of interbrain communication, whether by cable or radio, would make pointless all gatherings and get-togethers, excursions and journeys to attend conferences, and therefore all personal locomotion to whatever location, for every living being could avail itself of sensors and scanners situated over the whole expanse of human habitation, even to the farthermost planets. Mass production would keep the market supplied with custom-made internal components and accessories, including braintracks for home railways, that would enable the heads them-selves to roll from room to room, an innocent diversion. At this point I stopped and remarked that the authors of these papers were surely deranged. Trottelreiner replied coldly that I was a bit hasty in my judgments.

We made our bed and now we must lie in it. Anyhow, the criterion of common sense was never applicable to the history of the human race. Averroës, Kant, Socrates, Newton, Voltaire, could any of them have believed it possible that in the twentieth century the scourge of cities, the poisoner of lungs, the mass murderer and idol of millions would be a metal receptacle on wheels, and that people would actually prefer being crushed to death inside it during frantic weekend exoduses instead of staying, safe and sound, at home? I asked him which of the proposals he intended to support.

"I haven't yet decided," he said. "The gravest problem, in my opinion, is the increase in underground natalities—you know, unlicensed births. And besides that, I'm afraid there may be some psychem tampering in the course of the deliberations."

"How do you mean?"

"A proposal could be passed with the help of a gullibloon or two."

"You think they'd actually try such a thing?"

"Why not? What could be easier than pumping gas into our conference hall through the air conditioning?"

"But whatever the congress endorses doesn't have to be accepted by the public. The people won't take everything lying down."

"Come now, Tichy. For half a century civilization hasn't been left to its own devices. A hundred years ago a certain Dior was dictating fashions in clothing. Today this sort of regulating has embraced all walks of life. If prostheticism is voted in, I assure you, in a couple of years everyone will consider the possession of a soft, hairy, sweating body to be shameful and indecent. A body needs washing, deodorizing, caring for, and even then it breaks down, while in a prostheticized society you can snap on the loveliest creations of modern engineering. What woman doesn't want to have silver iodide instead of eyes, telescopic breasts, angel's wings, iridescent legs, and feet that sing with every step?" . . .

OCTAVIO PAZ, *who died in April 1998, was Mexico's leading poet and essayist. Winner of the Nobel Prize for Literature in 1990, he served Mexico as a diplomat and as ambassador to India, and taught and lectured widely, notably at the universities of Harvard and of Cambridge. Elizabeth Bishop's translation of his poem "January First," which finds multilayered meaning in the beginning of the first day of the New Year, is included in* A Draft of Shadows and other Poems *(1979). In the long poem that gave this book its title, Paz wrote, "I am the shadow my words cast."*

OCTAVIO PAZ

JANUARY FIRST

The year's doors open
like those of language,
toward the unknown.
Last night you told me:

                tomorrow
we shall have to think up signs,
sketch a landscape, fabricate a plan
on the double page
of day and paper.
Tomorrow, we shall have to invent,
once more,
the reality of this world.

I opened my eyes late.
For a second of a second
I felt what the Aztec felt,
on the crest of the promontory,
lying in wait
for time's uncertain return
through cracks in the horizon

But no, the year had returned.
It filled all the room
and my look almost touched it.
Time, with no help from us,
had placed
in exactly the same order as yesterday
houses in the empty street,
snow on the houses,
silence on the snow.

You were beside me,
still asleep.
The day had invented you
but you hadn't yet accepted
being invented by the day.
—Nor possibly my being invented, either.
You were in another day.

You were beside me
and I saw you, like the snow,
asleep among appearances.
Time, with no help from us,
invents houses, streets, trees
and sleeping women.

When you open your eyes
we'll walk, once more,
among the hours and their inventions.
We'll walk among appearances
and bear witness to time and its conjugations.
Perhaps we'll open the day's doors.
And then we shall enter the unknown.

PART III

CHALLENGING PERSPECTIVES

EDWARD O. WILSON

FRANCIS FUKUYAMA

GEORGE P. BROCKWAY

JOEL KURTZMAN

ROBERT N. BELLAH, RICHARD MADSEN, WILLIAM M. SULLIVAN,
ANN SWIDLER, STEVEN M. TIPTON

NELSON MANDELA

C. OWEN PAEPKE

ROSABETH MOSS KANTER

TOM ATHANASIOU

STEVEN WEINBERG

EDWARD O. WILSON, *the world-famous biologist and founder of sociobiology, makes a strong case for humanism in this essay, originally published in* Free Inquiry, *Spring 1991, and reprinted in* Challenges to the Enlightenment: In Defense of Reason and Science *(1994), edited by Paul Kurtz and Timothy J. Madigan. Wilson, Curator in Entomology since 1972 and Pellegrino University Professor since 1994 at Harvard, has argued that genes shape our moral and ethical intuitions. Here, addressing a conference of Roman Catholic bishops, he suggests that religion has deep biological origins: ". . . religion will find in science the necessary means to meet the modern age." Wilson is highly illuminating when looking at how biology can interact with humanism to shape our outlook. After decades of closely examining insect societies, whose surprising forms and variations he has so graphically described, Wilson now asks what kind of community, nation, and world do human beings want to create?*

EDWARD O. WILSON

SCIENTIFIC HUMANISM AND RELIGION

In 1986 I was invited by the Committee on Human Values of the Roman Catholic Bishops of the United States to be one of four scientists to join them and a group of theologians and scientists from Catholic colleges and universities in a free-wheeling discussion of the relationship between science and religion. It was held in a retreat outside Detroit; there was no audience. The other three scientists were Freeman Dyson, the theoretical physicist from the Institute of Advanced Studies at Princeton; Roger Sperry, the neurobiologist from Cal Tech; and Jerome Lejeune, a French geneticist best known for his discovery that Down's syndrome is caused by a chromosome anomaly. Dyson, Sperry, and I are scientific humanists; Lejeune is a devout Catholic and a member of the Pontifical Academy of Sciences. Also present were about fifteen bishops, including Cardinal Law of Boston and Cardinal (then Archbishop) James Hickey of Washington.

It was an altogether remarkable event. The motivation of the Bishop's Committee appeared to be to somehow accommodate the Church to science, to look for common ground, perhaps to chart areas in the Church still closed to free inquiry, and conversely perhaps to find safe and authenticated channels through which to guide the Church to a quieter harbor of more liberal thought. As one theologian put it, "Science left the Church after Aquinas, and we never tried to call her back." What, I had to ask, was happening here?

Our discussion, which covered two full days (September 16 and 17), was frank. Humanistic ideas, of which my own were perhaps the most unequivocal, were politely received and addressed. No subject was implicitly regarded as taboo except abortion, and not even the scientists wanted to put that explosive issue on the table. Scientific challenges were made to the religious view of human meaning. Artificial birth control was advocated, to my surprise, not just by the three humanistic scientists but by several of the bishops.

My approach was uncompromisingly humanistic but conciliatory. I looked for common ground, searching constructively for ways for the Church to liberalize and accommodate science—and in its turn to confront science with hard ethical and ontological questions. What follows is the talk I presented to the Catholic bishops, without a single word changed.

At the Cologne Cathedral, in 1980, Pope John Paul II said that science has added "wings to the spirit of modern awareness." Yet science does not threaten the core of religious belief:

> We have no fear, indeed we regard it as excluded, that a branch of science or branch of knowledge, based on reason and proceeding methodically and securely, can arrive at knowledge that comes into conflict with the truth of faith. This can be the case only where the differentiation between the orders of knowledge is overlooked or denied.

That last sentence, reaffirming Augustine's two books on God, takes us to the heart of the real dialogue between religion and science. Although many theologians and lay philosophers like to deny it, I believe that traditional religious belief and scientific knowledge depict the universe in radically different ways. At bedrock they are incompatible and mutually exclusive. The materialist (or "humanist" or "naturalist") position can be put in a phrase: There is only one book, and it was written in a manner too strange and subtle to be foretold by the prophets and Church fathers.

But, there is another side to the story, one that makes the contrast in world views still more interesting. The materialist position presupposes no final answers. It is an undeniable fact that faith is in our bones, that religious belief is a part of human nature and seemingly vital to social existence. Take away one faith, and another rushes in to fill the void. Take away that, and some secular equivalent such as Marxism intrudes, replete with sacred texts and icons. Take away all these faiths and rely wholly on skepticism and personal inquiry—if you can—and the fabric of society would likely start to unravel. This phenomenon, so strange and subtle as to daunt materialist explanation, is in my opinion the most promising focus for a dialogue between theologians and scientists.

From early Greek philosophy, there has always been a great divide in thought. Humanity is faced with a choice between two metaphysics, two differing views of how the world works from the top down and, hence, of the ultimate means for the selection of moral codes. The first view holds that morality is transcendental in origin and exists both within and apart from the human species. This doctrine has been refined within the Church by the conception of natural law, which is the reading of the eternal law in God's mind: People reason out God's intent through a reflection of human nature, obedient to the principle that, as Aquinas expressed it, "man has a natural inclination to know the truth about God and to live in society." The opposing view is that morality is entirely a human phenomenon. In the modern, evolutionary version of this materialist philosophy, its precepts represent the upwelling of deep impulses that are encoded in our genes and find expression within the setting of particular cultures. They have nothing directly to do with divine guidance, at least not in the manner conceived by traditional religions.

I may be wrong (and, in any case, do not speak for all scientists), but I believe that the correct metaphysic is the materialist one. It works in the following way. Our profound impulses are rooted in a genetic heritage common to the entire species. They arose by evolution through natural selection over a period of tens or hundreds of thousands of years. These propensities provide survival for individuals and for the social groups on which personal survival depends. They are transmuted through rational processes and the formation of culture into specific moral codes that are integrated into religion and the sacralized memories of revolutions, conquests, and other historical events by which cultures secured their survival. Although variations in the final codes are inevitable, different societies share a great deal in their perception of right and wrong. By making the search for these similarities part of the scientific enterprise, and by taking religious behavior very seriously as a key part of genetically evolved human nature, a tighter consensus on ethical behavior might be reached.

Let me interpose, at this point, a very brief account of evolution by natural selection. Genetic variation among individuals in a population of the same species, say a population of human beings, arises by mutations, which are random changes in the chemical composition and relative positions of genes. Of the thousands of mutations that typically occur throughout a population in each generation, all but a minute fraction are either neutral in effect or deleterious to some degree. They include, for example, the altered genes that cause hemophilia and Tay-Sachs disease and the abnormally duplicated chromosomes responsible for Down's syndrome. When a new mutant (or novel combination of rare preexisting genes) happens to be superior to the ordinary "normal" genes, it tends to spread through the population over a period of many generations and, hence, become by definition the new genetic norm. If human beings were to move into a new environment that somehow gave hemophiliacs a survival and reproductive advantage over non-hemophiliacs, then, in time, hemophilia would predominate in the population and be regarded as the norm.

Two features of evolution by natural selection conspire to give it extraordinary creative potential. The first is the driving power of mutations. All populations are subject to a continuous rain of new genetic types that test the old. The second feature is the ability of natural selection to create immensely complicated new structures and physiological processes, including new patterns of behavior, with no blueprint and no force behind them other than the selection process itself. This is a key point missed by creationists and other critics of evolutionary theory, who often argue that the probability of assembling an eye or a hand (or life itself) by genetic mutations is infinitesimally small—in effect, impossible. But, the following thought experiment shows that the opposite is true. Suppose that a new trait emerges if two new gene forms (mutations), which I will call A and B, occur simultaneously. The chance of A occurring is one in a million, and the chance of B occurring is also one in a million. Then, the chance of both A and B occurring simultaneously as mutants is one in a trillion, a near impossibility—as the critics intuited. However, natural selection subverts this process. If A has even a slight advantage by itself alone, it will become the dominant gene at its position. Now, the chance of AB appearing is one in a million. In even moderately sized species of plants and animals (which often contain more than a million individuals), the change-over to AB is a virtual certainty.

This very simple picture of evolution at the level of the gene has altered our conception of both the nature of life and humanity's place in nature. Before Darwin, it was customary to use the great complexity of living organisms per se as proof of the existence of God. The most famous expositor of this "argument from design" was the Reverend William Paley, who in 1802 introduced the watchmaker analogy: The existence of a watch implies the existence of a watchmaker. In other words, great effects imply great causes. Common sense would seem to dictate the truth of this deduction, but common sense, as Einstein once noted, is only our accumulated experience up to the age of eighteen. Common sense tells us that one-ton satellites cannot hang suspended two hundred miles above a point on the earth's surface, but they do.

We have arrived at the conception of the one book of creation to which I alluded earlier. Given the combination of mutation and natural selection, the biological equivalent of watches can be created without a watchmaker. But, did blind natural selection also lead to the human mind, including moral behavior and spirituality? That is the grandmother of questions in both biology and the humanities. Common sense would seem, at first, to dictate the answer to be no. But, I and many other scientists believe that the answer may be yes. Furthermore, it is possible by this means to explain the very meaning of human life.

The key proposition based on evolutionary biology is the following: Everything human, including the mind and culture, has a material basis and originated during the evolution of the human genetic constitution and its interaction with the environment. To say this much is not to deny the great creative power of culture or to minimize the fact that most causes of human thought and behavior are still poorly understood. The important point is that modern biology already can account for many of the unique properties of our species. Research on that subject is accelerating quickly enough to lend plausibility to the proposition that more complex forms of social behavior, including religious belief and moral reasoning, will eventually be understood to their foundations.

A case in point, useful for its simplicity and tractability, is the avoidance of brother-sister incest. In order to avoid misunderstanding, let me define *incest* as strong sexual bonding among close biological relatives that includes intercourse of the kind generally associated with cohabitation and procreation and excludes transient forms of adolescent experimentation. Incest taboos are very nearly universal and a cultural norm. The avoidance of brother-sister incest originates in what psychologists have called "prepared learning." This means that people are innately prone to learn one alternative as opposed to another. They pick it up more readily, they enjoy it more, or both. The avoidance of sibling incest comes from the "potty rule" in mental development: Individuals reared in close domestic proximity during the first six years of life (they share the same potty) are automatically inhibited from strong sexual attraction and bonding when they reach sexual maturity. The rule works even when the children reared together are biologically unrelated and later encouraged to marry and have children, as in the Israeli kibbutzim and traditional minor marriages of prerevolutionary China. Those affected are usually quite unable to offer a rational explanation of why they have no attraction. Some unconscious process ticked over in the brain and the urge, they explain, never came.

The inhibitory rule is an example not only of prepared learning but also of "proximate causation" as it is understood by evolutionary biologists. This means that the learning channels a response of importance to the survival or reproduction of the organism. Proximate causes are put into place by the assembly of genes through the process of natural selection. The ultimate causation—in other words, the particular selection regime that enabled certain genes to predominate in the first place—is the well-documented effect of inbreeding depression. When mating occurs between brother and sister, father and daughter, or mother and son, the probability of matching debilitating genes in both homologous chromosomes of the offspring is greatly increased. The end result is a rise in abortion, physical defects, and genetic disease. Hence, genes prescribing a biological propensity to avoid incest will be favored over those that do not. Most animal and plant species display proximate devices of one kind or another, and it does indeed protect them from inbreeding depression. In some, the response is rigidly determined. In others, especially the brighter mammals, it is based on prepared learning. Interestingly enough, the human proximate form is nearly identical to that of the chimpanzee, the species to which we are most closely related genetically.

It is exquisitely human to semanticize innate tendencies. In many societies, incest avoidance is underwritten by symbolically transmitted taboos, myths, and laws. These, not the emotions and programs of prepared learning, are the values we perceive by direct, causal observation. They are easily transmitted from one person to the next, and they are the behaviors most readily studied by scholars. But, the phenomenon of greatest interest is the etiology of the moral behavior: The chain of events leading from ultimate cause in natural selection to proximate cause in prepared learning to reification and legitimation in culture. If the terminal cultural form were somehow to be stripped away by a collective loss of memory, people would still avoid sibling incest. Given enough time, they would most likely invent religious and ethical rationalizations to justify their feelings about the wrongness of incest.

Crude genetic determinism has no part in this process. The existence of the three-step etiology in mental development, genes to learning rules to culture, in no way contradicts free will. Individual choice persists, even when learning is strongly prepared by heredity. If some future society decides to encourage brother-sister incest, for whatever bizarre and unlikely reason, it now has the knowledge to do so efficiently. The possibility, however, is vanishingly remote, because the same knowledge tells us that incest avoidance is programmed as a powerful rule and protects families from genetic damage. We are likely to agree still more firmly than before that the avoidance is a part of human nature to be fostered. In short, incest avoidance is and will continue to be one of our common values.

It will immediately occur to you that incest avoidance might be no more than a special case in the evolution of social behavior. A vast difference separates this relatively simple phenomenon from economic cycles, religious rites, and presidential elections. Might such particularities fall within a wholly different domain of explanation and require a different metaethic? Perhaps, but I don't think so.

The evidence favoring the evolutionary approach to moral reasoning is as follows. By mid-1985, no fewer than 3,577 human genes had been identified, of which about six hundred had been placed on one or another of the twenty-three pairs of chromosomes. This is a respectable fraction of the entire human complement. New techniques for separation and identification make it possible to map most of the genes and specify all of the DNA sequences—perhaps, by early in the next century. Hundreds of the genes already known alter behavior in one way or another. In most cases, the effect is crude or indirect. But a few change behavior in a precise manner, as for example those modulating expression, reading ability, and performance on spatial tests. Twin and adoption studies have implicated other genes—as yet unmapped and probably working in complex multiples—in schizophrenia, propensity toward homosexuality, performance on tests measuring empathy, and a wide range of personality traits from introversion-extroversion to athleticism and proneness to alcoholism. Moreover, prepared learning and biases in perception have been discovered in virtually every category of behavior thus far studied. In their seminal book *The Biology of Religion*, Vernon Reynolds and Ralph Tanner showed that survival and genetic reproduction can be favored by the traditional practices of religion, including evangelism, marriage rites, and even celibacy and asceticism, the latter through their positive effects on group cohesion and welfare.

But, to come quickly to the point that most troubles critics of evolutionary ethics, it does not follow that the genetic programs of cognition and prepared learning are automatically beneficial, even in a crude Darwinian sense. Behaviors such as xenophobia and territorial expansion may have been very adaptive in the earlier, formative stages of human evolutionary history, but they are destructive now, even for those who practice them. Although the cultural *ought* is more tightly linked to the genetic *is* than philosophers have traditionally conceded, the two do not automatically translate one into the other. A workable moral code can be obtained not just by understanding the foundations of human nature but by the wise choice of those constraints needed to keep us alive and free in a rapidly changing cultural environment that renders some of our propensities maladaptive.

Let me illustrate this approach to moral reasoning by taking an example that has proved troublesome to the Church. In *Humanae Vitae*, Pope Paul VI used the best interpretation concerning human nature available to him to proscribe artificial birth control and to protect the family. He said, in effect, that you should not prevent conception when having sex because that is what sex is for and, as such, reflects the will of God: "To use this divine gift destroying, even if only partially, its meaning and its purpose is to contradict the nature both of man and of woman and of their most intimate relationship, and, therefore, it is to contradict also the plan of God and his will."

I believe that there is a way out of the impasse that this strict argument from natural law has created. All that we have learned of biology in recent years suggests that the perception of human nature expressed by Pope Paul VI was only half true. A second major function of sexual intercourse, one evolved over vast periods of time, is the bonding of couples in a manner that enhances the long-term care of children. Only a minute fraction of sexual acts can result in conception, but virtually all can tighten the conjugal bonds. Many circumstances can be imagined, and in fact exist, in which family planning by artificial birth control leads to an improvement of the bonding function while promoting the rearing of healthy, secure children.

If this more recent and better substantiated view of human sexuality is accepted, a revision of *Humanae Vitae* could easily be written that accomplishes the main purpose of Pope Paul VI and the modern Church, permits artificial birth control, and, in fact, serves as a model of the utilization of scientific findings by religious thinkers.

I am now going to close with a truly radical suggestion: The choice among the foundations of moral reasoning is not likely to remain arbitrary. Metaethics can be tested empirically. One system of ethics and, hence, one kind of religion is not as good as another. Not only are some less workable, they are, in the most profound sense, less human. The corollary is that people can be educated readily only to a narrow range of ethical precepts. This leaves a choice between evolutionary ethics and transcendentalism. The idea of a genetic origin of moral codes can be further tested by a continuance of biological studies of complex human behavior, including religious thought itself. To the extent that the sensory and nervous systems appear to have evolved by natural selection or some other purely natural process, the evolutionary interpretation will be supported. To the extent that they do not appear to have evolved in this manner, or to the extent that complex human behavior cannot be linked to a physical basis in the sensory and nervous systems, the evolutionary explanation will have to be abandoned and a transcendental explanation sought.

Which position—scientific materialism or religious transcendentalism— proves correct will eventually make a very great difference in how humanity views itself and plans its future. But, for the years immediately ahead, this distinction makes little difference if the following overriding fact is realized: Human nature is, at the very least, far more a product of self-contained evolution than ordinarily conceded by philosophers and theologians. On the other hand, religious thought is far richer and more subtle than present-day science can explain—and too important to abandon. Meanwhile, the areas of common concern are vast, and the two enterprises can converge in most of the areas of practical moral reasoning at the same time that their practitioners disagree about the ultimate causes of human nature.

What, then, is the best relation between religion and science toward which we might aim? I would say an uneasy but fruitful alliance. The role of religion is to codify and put into enduring poetic form the highest moral values of a society consistent with empirical knowledge and to lead in moral reasoning. The role of science is to test remorselessly every conclusion about human nature and to search for the bedrock of ethics—by which I mean the material basis of natural law. Science faces in religion its most interesting challenge, while religion will find in science the necessary means to meet the modern age.

Epilogue

That concludes my talk to the Catholic bishops. Now an additional thought: If I'm right about the deep biological origins of religion, no amount of debunking and confrontation will significantly alter the colossi of organized religion. They won't collapse like the Soviet empire, with the leaders declaring that they have seen the light; for billions of religionists and their leaders there will be no reverse epiphany; the sacred texts won't crumble like the Berlin Wall. But the great organized religions *can* be humanized. They can evolve, through friendly truth and reason as opposed to hostile truth and reason, laid forth in a conciliatory style. Superstition will rarely or never be repudiated, it will simply be abandoned during the gradual humanization of organized religion. It's been said that the great problems of history are never solved, they are merely forgotten. And so it will be during the Darwinian sifting of ideas, hastened by open communication, total honesty, and warmth of spirit, in the best tradition of humanism. For both sides, let the chips fall where they may.

FRANCIS FUKUYAMA *is Hirst Professor of Public Policy at George Mason University. His first book,* The End of History and the Last Man *(1992) received international attention because of his daring assumption that Western societies had reached their final destiny. His book,* Trust: The Social Virtues and The Creation of Property *(1995), from which these excerpts are taken, concludes by claiming: "Now that the question of ideology and institutions has been settled, the preservation and accumulation of social capital will occupy center stage." Few serious thinkers would agree with Fukuyama's assertion that capitalism is the best institutional framework for human beings, but these excerpts are included to give the reader an alternative, and very American, view of a possible future thrust of history.*

Francis Fukuyama

After the End of Social Engineering

The worldwide convergence in basic institutions around liberal democracy and market economics forces us to confront the question of whether we have reached an "end of history," in which the broad process of human historical evolution culminates not, as in the Marxist version, in socialism but rather in the Hegelian vision of a bourgeois liberal democratic society.

Some readers of this book might think it takes a very different and contradictory position, because they believe it argues against a purely liberal economic order in favor of one that is both traditional and communitarian. This interpretation could not be further from the truth. Not one of the traditional cultures studied in this book—not that of Japan, China, Korea, or any of the older Catholic-authoritarian cultures of Europe—was capable of producing the modern capitalist economic order. Max Weber is frequently criticized for arguing that Confucian societies like Japan and China could not become successful capitalist ones. But he was actually speaking to a somewhat narrower point: he wanted to understand why modern capitalism, as well as other aspects of the modern world like natural science and the rational mastery of nature, arose in Protestant Europe and not in traditional China, Japan, Korea, or India. And on this point, he was absolutely correct when he asserted that aspects of these traditional cultures were hostile to economic modernity. Only when the latter was introduced from the outside, as a consequence of China and Japan's contact with the West, did capitalist development begin to take off. This confrontation with the technological and social prowess of the West forced these societies to drop many key elements of their traditional cultures. China had to eliminate "political Confucianism," the entire imperial system with its class of gentlemen-scholars; Japan and Korea had do away with their traditional class divisions, and the former had to redirect the *samurai* warrior ethic.

None of the Asian societies that has prospered economically in the past few generations could have done so without incorporating important elements of economic liberalism into their indigenous cultural systems, including property rights, contract, commercial law, and the entire confluence of Western ideas concerning rationality, science, innovation, and abstraction. The work of Joseph Needham and others has shown that the Chinese level of technology in the year 1500 was higher than that prevailing in Europe. What China did not have, however, and what Europe subsequently developed, was a scientific method that permitted the progressive conquest of nature through empirical observation and experiment. The scientific method itself was made possible by a cast of mind that sought to understand higher-level causality through abstract reasoning about underlying physical principles, something alien to the polytheistic religious cultures of Asia.

It is understandable that the Chinese societies that were the first to industrialize and prosper were those that fell under the control or influence of Western powers like Britain or the United States, including Hong Kong, Singapore, and Taiwan. And it is no accident that immigrants from traditional societies to liberal countries like the United States, Canada, and Britain did much better than their countrymen at home. In all of these cases, the framework of a liberal society constituted a liberation from the constraints of a traditional culture that inhibited the development of entrepreneurship and constrained the open-ended accumulation of material wealth.

On the other hand most thoughtful observers and theorists of political liberalism have understood that the doctrine, at least in its Hobbesean-Lockean form, is not self-sustaining and needs the support of aspects of traditional culture that do not themselves arise out of liberalism. That is, a society built entirely out of rational individuals who come together on the basis of a social contract for the sake of the satisfaction of their wants cannot form a society that would be viable over any length of time. In a criticism frequently leveled at Hobbes, such a society can provide no motive for any citizen to risk his or her life in defense of the larger community, since the purpose of the community was to preserve the individual's life. More broadly, if individuals formed communities only on the basis of rational long-term self-interest, there would be little in the way of public spiritedness, self-sacrifice, pride, charity, or any of the other virtues that make communities livable. Indeed, one could hardly imagine a meaningful family life if families were essentially contracts between rational, self-interested individuals. While liberalism arose historically out of an effort to exclude religion from public life, most liberal theorists have thought that religious belief could not, and should not, be eliminated from social life. While not necessarily believers themselves, virtually all of the American Founding Fathers believed that a vigorous religious life, with its belief in divine rewards and punishments, was important to the success of American democracy.

A parallel argument can be made with respect to economic liberalism. That modern economies arise out of the interactions of rational, utility-maximizing individuals in markets is incontestable. But rational utility maximization is not enough to give a full or satisfying account of why successful economies prosper or unsuccessful ones stagnate and decline. The degree to which people value work over leisure, their respect for education, attitudes toward the family, and the degree of trust they show toward their fellows all have a direct impact on economic life and yet cannot be adequately explained in terms of the economists' basic model of man. Just as liberal democracy works best as a political system when its individualism is moderated by public spirit, so too is capitalism facilitated when its individualism is balanced by a readiness to associate.

If democracy and capitalism work best when they are leavened with cultural traditions that arise from nonliberal sources, then it should be clear that modernity and tradition can coexist in a stable equilibrium for extended periods of time. The process of economic rationalization and development is an extremely powerful social force that compels societies to modernize along certain uniform lines. In this respect, there is clearly such a thing as "History" in the Marxist-Hegelian sense that homogenizes disparate cultures and pushes them in the direction of "modernity." But since there are limits to the effectiveness of contract and economic rationality, the character of that modernity will never be completely uniform. For example, certain societies can save substantially on transaction costs because economic agents trust one another in their interactions and therefore can be more efficient than low-trust societies, which require detailed contracts and enforcement mechanisms. This trust is not the consequence of rational calculation; it arises from sources like religion or ethical habit that have nothing to do with modernity. The most successful forms of modernity, in other words, are not completely modern; that is, they are not based on the universal proliferation of liberal economic and political principles throughout the society.

This conundrum can be expressed in a different way. Not only have grand ideological projects like communism failed, but even the more modest efforts at social engineering—the sort attempted by moderate democratic governments—have reached a dead end at the conclusion of the twentieth century. The French Revolution ushered in a period of incredibly rapid social change. Over the next two hundred years, all European societies and many of those outside Europe were transformed beyond recognition from poor, uneducated, rural, agricultural, authoritarian ones to urban, industrialized, wealthy democracies. In the course of these transformations, governments played a major role in precipitating or facilitating change (and in some cases, trying to stop it). They abolished entire social classes, engaging in land reform and the disbanding of large estates; they introduced modern legislation guaranteeing equality of rights for ever-larger circles of the population; they built cities and encouraged urbanization; they educated entire populations and provided the infrastructure for modern, complex, information-intensive societies.

There have been increasing indications over the past generation, however, that the kinds of results achievable through this sort of large-scale social engineering have been subject to diminishing marginal returns. In 1964, the Civil Rights Act laid to rest at the stroke of a pen legally sanctioned racial inequalities in the United States. In subsequent years, however, abolishing substantive inequality for African-Americans has proven a much more diffi-cult problem. The solution that seemed so obvious in the 1930s and 1940s was the steady expansion of the welfare state through income redistribution or job creation and the opening to minorities of health, education, employ-ment, and other social benefits. By the end of the century, these solutions not only seem ineffective, but in many cases are seen as contributing to the very problems they sought to solve. A generation or more ago, there would have been a broad consensus among social scientists of a largely one-way causal relationship between poverty and family breakdown, flowing from the for-mer to the latter. Today people are much less certain, and few believe that the problems of the contemporary American family can be fixed simply through the equalization of incomes. It is easy to see how government policies can encourage the breakdown of families, as when they subsidize single mother-hood; what is less obvious is how government policy can restore family structure once it has been broken.

The collapse of communism and the end of the cold war have not, as many commentators have asserted, led to a global upsurge of tribalism, a revival of nineteenth-century nationalist rivalries, or a breakdown of civilization into anomic violence. Liberal democracy and capitalism remain the essential, indeed the only, framework for the political and economic organization of modern societies, Rapid economic modernization is closing the gap between many former Third World countries and the industrialized North. With European integration and North American free trade, the web of economic ties within each region will thicken, and sharp cultural boundaries will become increasingly fuzzy. Implementation of the free trade regime of the Uruguay Round of the General Agreement on Tariffs and Trade (GATT) will further erode interregional boundaries. Increased global competition has forced companies across cultural boundaries to try to adopt "best-practice" techniques like lean manufacturing from whatever source they come from. The worldwide recession of the 1990s has put great pressure on Japanese and German companies to scale back their culturally distinctive and paternalistic labor policies in favor of a more purely liberal model. The modern communications revolution abets this convergence by facilitating economic globalization and by propagating the spread of ideas at enormous speed.

But in our age, there can be substantial pressures for cultural differentiation even as the world homogenizes in other respects. Modern liberal political and economic institutions not only coexist with religion and other traditional elements of culture but many actually work better in conjunction with them. If many of the most important remaining social problems are essentially cultural in nature and if the chief differences among societies are not political, ideological, or even institutional but rather cultural, it stands to reason that societies will hang on to these areas of cultural distinctiveness and that the latter will become all the more salient and important in the years to come.

Awareness of cultural difference will be abetted, paradoxically, by the same communications technology that has made the global village possible. There is a strong liberal faith that people around the world are basically similar under the surface and that greater communications will bring deeper understanding and cooperation. In many instances, unfortunately, that familiarity breeds contempt rather than sympathy. Something like this process has been going on between the United States and Asia in the past decade. Americans have come to realize that Japan is not simply a fellow capitalist democracy but has rather different ways of practicing both capitalism and democracy. One result, among others, is the emergence of the revisionist school among specialists on Japan, who are less sympathetic to Tokyo and argue for tougher trade policies. And Asians are made vividly aware through the media of crime, drugs, family breakdown, and other American social problems, and many have decided that the United States is not such an attractive model after all. Lee Kwan Yew, former prime minister of Singapore, has emerged as a spokesman for a kind of Asian revisionism on the United States, which argues that liberal democracy is not an appropriate political model for the Confucian societies. The very convergence of major institutions makes peoples all the more intent on preserving those elements of distinctiveness they continue to possess.

If these differences cannot be reconciled, they can at least be confronted squarely. Obviously, one cannot begin any serious study of foreign cultures by evaluating them from the standpoint of one's own. On the other hand, one of the biggest obstacles to a serious comparative study of culture in the United States is the assumption, made for political reasons, that all cultures are inherently equal. Any such study requires the exploration of differences among cultures against some standard, which in this book has been economic performance. The desire for economic prosperity is itself not culturally determined but almost universally shared. It is hard, in this context, not to come to some judgments about the relative strengths and weaknesses of different societies. It is not sufficient to say that everyone eventually arrives at the same goal but by different paths. *How* a society arrives and the speed with which it does so affect the happiness of its people, and some never arrive at all.

THE SPIRITUALIZATION OF ECONOMIC LIFE

Social capital is critical to prosperity and to what has come to be called competitiveness, but its more important consequences may not be felt in the economy so much as in social and political life. Spontaneous sociability has consequences that are not easy to capture in aggregate income statistics. Human beings are at the same time narrowly selfish individuals and creatures with a social side who shun isolation and enjoy the support and recognition of other human beings. There are, of course, some individuals who prefer working in a low-trust Taylorite mass production factory because it defines the minimum of work they need to do to earn their paychecks and otherwise makes few claims on them. But on the whole, workers do not want to be treated like cogs in a large machine, isolated from managers and fellow workers, with little pride in their skills or their organization, and trusted with a minimal amount of authority and control over the work they do for a living. Any number of empirical studies from Elton Mayo on have indicated that workers are happier in group-oriented organizations than in more individualistic ones. Thus, even if productivity was equal between low- and high-trust factories and offices, the latter are more humanly satisfying places in which to work.

Furthermore, a successful capitalist economy is clearly very important as a support for stable liberal democracy. It is, of course, possible for a capitalist economy to coexist with an authoritarian political system, as in the PRC [People's Republic of China] today or as previously existed in Germany, Japan, South Korea, Taiwan, and Spain. But in the long run, the industrialization process itself necessitates a more highly educated population and a more complex division of labor, both of which tend to be supportive of democratic political institutions. As a consequence, there are today virtually no wealthy capitalist countries that are not also stable liberal democracies. One of the great problems of Poland, Hungary, Russia, Ukraine, and other former communist states is that they have tried to establish democratic political institutions without the benefit of functioning capitalist economies. The lack of firms, entrepreneurs, markets, and competition not only perpetuates poverty, it fails to provide critical forms of social support for the proper functioning of democratic institutions.

It has been argued that the market itself constitutes a school for sociability, by providing the opportunity and incentive for people to cooperate with one another for the sake of mutual enrichment. But while the market does impose its own socializing discipline to some degree, the larger theme of this book is that sociability does not simply emerge spontaneously once the state retreats. The ability to cooperate socially is dependent on prior habits, traditions, and norms, which themselves serve to structure the market. Hence it is more likely that a successful market economy, rather than being the cause of stable democracy, is codetermined by the prior factor of social capital. If the latter is abundant, then both markets and democratic politics will thrive, and the market can in fact play a role as a school of sociability that reinforces democratic institutions. This is particularly true in newly industrializing countries with authoritarian governments, where people can learn new forms of sociability in the workplace before applying the lessons to politics.

The concept of social capital makes clear why capitalism and democracy are so closely related. A healthy capitalist economy is one in which there will be sufficient social capital in the underlying society to permit businesses, corporations, networks, and the like to be self-organizing. In default of this self-organizing capability, the state can step in to promote key firms and sectors, but markets almost always work more efficiently when private actors are making the decisions.

That self-organizing proclivity is exactly what is necessary to make democratic political institutions work as well. It is law based on popular sovereignty that converts a system of liberty into one of ordered liberty. But no such system can come into being on the basis of a mass of unorganized, isolated individuals, able to make their own views and preferences known only at election time. Their weakness and atomization would not permit them to express their views properly, even when those views were held by a majority, and would be an open invitation to despotism and demagogy. In any meaningful democracy, the interests and wishes of the different members of society have to be articulated and represented through political parties and other kinds of organized political groups. And a stable party structure can come about only if people with common interests are able to work with one another for common ends—an ability that rests, in the end, on social capital.

The same propensity for spontaneous sociability that is key to building durable businesses is also indispensable for putting together effective political organizations. In default of real political parties, political groupings come to be based on changeable personalities or patron-client relationships; they fracture easily and fail to work together for common purposes even when they have a strong incentive to do so. One should expect countries with small, weak, private firms also to have fragmented and unstable party systems. This is in fact the case if we compare the United States and Germany to France and Italy. Both private companies and political parties are weak or nonexistent in postcommunist societies like Russia and Ukraine, and elections lurch between extremes defined around individuals rather than coherent political programs. The "democrats" in Russia all believe in democracy and markets on an intellectual level, but they lack the social habits necessary to create a unified political organization.

A liberal state is ultimately a limited state, with government activity strictly bounded by a sphere of individual liberty. If such a society is not to become anarchic or otherwise ungovernable, then it must be capable of self-government at levels of social organization below the state. Such a system depends ultimately not just on law but on the self-restraint of individuals. If they are not tolerant and respectful of each other or do not abide by the laws they set for themselves, they will require a strong and coercive state to keep each other in line. If they cannot cohere for common purposes, then they will need an intrusive state to provide the organization they cannot provide themselves. Conversely, the "withering away of the state" Karl Marx envisioned could conceivably arise only in a society with an extraordinarily high degree of spontaneous sociability, where restraint and norm-based behavior would flow from within rather than having to be imposed from without. A low social capital country is not only likely to have small, weak, and inefficient companies; it will also suffer from pervasive corruption of its public officials and ineffective public administration. This situation is painfully evident in Italy, where there is a direct relationship between social atomization and corruption as one moves from the North and center to the South.

A dynamic and prosperous capitalist economy is crucial to stable democracy in an even more fundamental way, one that is related to the ultimate end of all human activity. In *The End of History and the Last Man*, I argued that the human historical process could be understood as the interplay between two large forces. The first was that of rational desire, in which human beings sought to satisfy their material needs through the accumulation of wealth. The second, equally important motor of the historical process was what Hegel called the "struggle for recognition," that is, the desire of all human beings to have their essence as free, moral beings recognized by other human beings.

Rational desire corresponds, more or less, to the rational utility maximization of neoclassical economics: the endless accumulation of material possessions to satisfy an ever-increasing set of wants and needs. The desire for recognition, on the other hand, has no material object but seeks only a just evaluation of one's worth on the part of another human consciousness. All human beings believe they have a certain inherent worth or dignity. When that worth is not recognized adequately by others, they feel anger; when they do not live up to others' evaluation, they feel shame; and when they are evaluated appropriately, they feel pride. The desire for recognition is an extraordinarily powerful part of the human psyche; the emotions of anger, pride, and shame are the basis of most political passions and motivate much that goes on in political life. The desire for recognition can be manifest in any number of contexts: in the anger of an employee who quits the company because she feels her contribution has not been adequately recognized; in the indignation of a nationalist who wants his country recognized as an equal of others; in the rage of the antiabortion crusader who feels that innocent life has not been equally protected; and in the passion of feminist or gay rights activists who demand that members of their group be treated with equal respect by the larger society. The passions engendered by the desire for recognition often work at cross purposes with the desire for rational accumulation, as when a man risks his liberty and possessions to take revenge on someone who has wronged him or when a nation goes to war for the sake of national dignity.

In the earlier book, I argued at some length that what usually passes as economic motivation is in fact not a matter of rational desire but a manifestation of the desire for recognition. Natural wants and needs are few in number and rather easily satisfied, particularly in the context of a modern industrial economy. Our motivation in working and earning money is much more closely related to the recognition that such activity affords us, where money becomes a symbol not for material goods but for social status or recognition Adam Smith explained in the *Theory of Moral Sentiments* [1759], "It is the vanity, not the ease or the pleasure, which interests us." The worker who strikes for higher wages does not do so simply because he is greedy and wants all the material comforts he can get; instead, he seeks economic justice in which his labor is compensated fairly in relation to others—in other words, that it be recognized for its true worth. Similarly, the entrepreneurs who create business empires do not do so because they want to spend the hundreds of millions of dollars they will earn; rather, they want to be recognized as the creators of a new technology or service.

If we understand, then, that economic life is pursued not simply for the sake of accumulating the greatest number of material goods possible but also for the sake of recognition, then the critical interdependence of capitalism and liberal democracy becomes clearer. Prior to modern liberal democracy, the struggle for recognition was carried on by ambitious princes who sought primacy over each other through war and conquest. Indeed, Hegel's account of the human historical process began with a primordial "bloody battle" in which two combatants sought to be recognized by the other, leading one ultimately to enslave the other. Conflicts based on religious or nationalist passion are much more intelligible if understood as manifestations of the desire for recognition rather than rational desire or "utility maximization." Modern liberal democracy seeks to satisfy this desire for recognition by basing the political order on the principle of universal and equal recognition. But in practice, liberal democracy works because the struggle for recognition that formerly had been carried out on a military, religious, or nationalist plane is now pursued on an economic one. Where formerly princes sought to vanquish each other by risking their lives in bloody battles, they now risk their capital through the building of industrial empires. The under-lying psychological need is the same, only the desire for recognition is satisfied through the production of wealth rather than the destruction of material values.

In *The Passions and the Interests* [1977], the economist Albert Hirshman sought to explain the rise of the modern bourgeois world in terms of an ethical revolution that sought to replace the "passion" for glory that character-ized aristocratic societies, with the "interest" in material gain that was the hallmark of the new bourgeois. Early political economists of the Scottish Enlightenment like Adam Ferguson, Adam Smith, and James Steuart all hoped that the destructive energies of a warrior culture would be channeled into the safer pursuits of a commercial society, with a corresponding soften-ing of manners. Indeed, this substitution was also very much in the mind of the first liberal political theorist, Thomas Hobbes, who conceived of civil society as the deliberate subordination of the desire for glory, whether fueled by religious passion or aristocratic vanity, to the pursuit of rational accumulation.

Whatever the expectations of these early modern theorists, it seems that what has happened in the modern world is not simply the embourgeoise-ment of warrior cultures and the replacement of passions by interests but also the spiritualization of economic life and the endowment of the latter with the same competitive energies that formerly fueled political life. Human beings frequently do not act like rational utility maximizers in any narrow sense of the term utility, but they invest economic activity with many of the moral values of their broader social lives. In Japan, this happened directly as the *samurai* or warrior class was capitalized in what amounted to a buyout of their social status, and turned toward business, which they approached with much of their *bushido* warrior ethic still intact. This process has occurred in virtually all other industrialized societies as well, where the opportunities of entrepreneurship became the outlet for the energies of countless ambitious people who in earlier ages could have been "recognized" only by starting a war or revolution.

The role that a capitalist economy plays in channeling recognition struggles in a peaceful direction, and its consequent importance to democratic stability, is evident in postcommunist Eastern Europe. The totalitarian project envisioned the destruction of an independent civil society and the creation of a new socialist community centered exclusively around the state. When the latter, highly artificial community collapsed, there were virtually no alternative forms of community beyond those of family and ethnic group, or else in the delinquent communities constituted by criminal gangs. In the absence of a layer of voluntary associations, individuals clung to their ascriptive identities all the more fiercely. Ethnicity provided an easy form of community by which they could avoid feeling atomized, weak, and victimized by the larger historical forces swirling around them. In developed capitalist societies with strong civil societies, by contrast, the economy itself is the locus of a substantial part of social life. When one works for Motorola, Siemens, Toyota, or even a small family dry-cleaning business, one is part of a moral network that absorbs a large part of one's energies and ambitions. The Eastern European countries that appear to have the greatest chances for success as democracies are Hungary, Poland, and the Czech Republic, which retained nascent civil societies throughout the communist period and were able to generate capitalist private sectors in relatively short order. There is no lack of divisive ethnic conflicts in these places, whether over competing Polish and Lithuanian claims to Vilnius or Hungarian irredenta vis-à-vis neighbors. But they have not flared up into violent conflicts yet because the economy has been sufficiently vigorous to provide an alternative source of social identity and belonging.

The mutual dependence of economy and polity is not limited to democratizing states in the former communist world. In a way, the loss of social capital in the United States has more immediate consequences for American democracy than for the American economy. Democratic political institutions no less than businesses depend on trust for effective operation, and the reduction of trust in a society will require a more intrusive, rule-making government to regulate social relations.

Many of the cases covered in this book stand as a cautionary tale against overcentralized political authority. More than former communist countries suffer from weak or damaged civil societies. Familistic societies with a low degree of generalized trust in China, France, and southern Italy were all products of centralizing monarchies in times past (and, in the French case, Republican governments) that undercut the autonomy of intermediate social institutions in their quest for exclusive power. Conversely, societies exhibiting a relatively high degree of generalized trust, like Japan and Germany, lived under relatively decentralized political authority for much of their late premodern existences. In the United States, the weakening authority of civil associations has been connected with the rise of a strong state, through both the courts and the executive. Social capital is like a ratchet that is more easily turned in one direction than another; it can be dissipated by the actions of governments much more readily than those governments can build it up again. Now that the question of ideology and institutions has been settled, the preservation and accumulation of social capital will occupy center stage.

GEORGE P. BROCKWAY *was a highly successful publisher in New York before turning his full-time energies to economics. His is a direct confrontation of the scope of the economic problems facing us: "It is an open question whether our morale is so corrupt, our power of empathy so feeble, and our ability even to be interested in economics so meager that it would take another depression to make resumed reform possible." This excerpt is from* The End of Economic Man *(1996 edition), in which Brockway concludes that we all have not only the opportunity, but the right and the duty, to participate in shaping an open, confident, and generous economy which challenges all its participating members, that is every person on this planet, to be fully human.*

George P. Brockway

Prospect: On Being Fully Human

There is a fatality about economics that in the end chokes any society that makes too great a distinction between the rewards of the favored and of the disfavored. It is a commonplace of legal theory that a law must not only be just but must also be seen to be just. It is the other way around with economics, where it is more important for a policy to be fair than to be accepted as fair. This is particularly true when it comes to policies determining the distribution of society's rewards.

Gross inequality of economic rewards is certainly nothing new. It has been with us from the beginning of time. It may actually be less now than in previous centuries. Slavery has been largely abolished, and some sort of egalitarianism is at least a widely endorsed ideal. Nevertheless, the gap between the rich and the poor is enormous, unconscionable, and probably growing again, not only in the United States but in the rest of the world, especially in the Third World.

What has changed, and continues to change at an accelerating rate, is what the rich do with their money. Before the middle of the nineteenth century there was little question what they did with it. They invested in land and in improvements thereon: châteaus and stately homes and protoscientific agriculture. Of course, there were always commissions and sinecures to buy, and colonial adventures for younger sons, and gambles to take a flier on; but land was everlasting. Money that was made by craft methods on the land was invested in craft improvements on the land.

In the eighteenth century, maldistribution showed its effects at the top as well as at the bottom of the income scale. Prospective lenders on the Continent were frequently unable to find willing borrowers at 4 percent or less. The situation was somewhat different in Britain, partly because she was notoriously a nation of shopkeepers. Even so, Braudel tells us, England "did not summon up all her reserves to finance her industrial revolution." [Fernand Braudel, *Civilization and Capitalism*, 1985.] The South Sea Bubble in Britain and the Mississippi Bubble in France, both of which burst in 1720, were only the most dramatic instances of the speculation that developed in place of productive investment.

The economics of the rational greedy economic man sees no connection between such "bubbles" and the wastes and the horrors and the griefs of early industrialization. But the money that blew away as bubble after bubble burst had been accumulated at the expense of appalling labor and suffering of underpaid men, women, and children in mines and in milltowns, on ships and on industrialized farms—at the expense, too of wanton destruction of the natural environment.

ii

Changes that had started in the Commercial Revolution came very rapidly in the Industrial Revolution. Immense fortunes could be made in the new factories, which quickly overwhelmed their craft-based predecessors, first in textiles and then in all sorts of industry, especially iron and steel. Two conditions impeded industrialization: illiquidity and exposure, both of which made it imperative for prudent gentlemen to become actively concerned in the enterprises they invested in. This was something that few gentlemen were inclined or qualified to do. Fortuitously, the development of relatively efficient stock markets took care of one impediment, and the invention of the limited liability company took care of the other. And then . . . another momentous change took place; property—the bundle of rights the law would protect—was enlarged from use value to exchange value.

The opportunities for what came to be called the functionless investor seemed almost limitless. Industrial capacity was now theoretically very great. The practical problem was to find a market worthy of it. Technological advances in agriculture had released a large population desperate for factory work at low wages. The low wages made low prices possible but at the same time restricted the size of the effective market.

At this point the inequities of economic rewards became a decisive restraint on production. Since the Great Depression, the restraint has been appreciably relaxed by the expenditures of big government; but we still have 6 million people we cannot think how to employ at all and millions more people we count as employed but cannot think how to employ full-time. This costs us, and may finally destroy us; yet it would seem that substantial majorities of American voters, although worried about the future, have been satisfied with the intent of recent policies. The policies are seen to be fair, but their actual unfairness may be our undoing.

iii

Industry today is built on mass production. Karl Polyani's "great transformation" to a market economy has become a giant transformation to a mass economy. The economy, however, cannot sell all that it might produce. The wealthy do not spend their incomes on the products of mass industry, because it would be not merely vulgar, nor merely irrational, but flatly impossible to do so.

The value of the product of mass industry is equal to the mass-industry earnings of the nonwealthy plus the mass-industry earnings of the wealthy, not all of which, of course, are in the form of wages. To the extent that the wealthy withdraw their earnings, to that extent demand for the product of mass industry must fall short. The nonwealthy may be willing enough to buy what mass industry could produce, but their income is not enough to pay the bills. To be sure, there is much leakage, especially into and out of custom industry, including custom services, but the foregoing is a rough explanation of the fate threatening a modern economy.

According to standard theory, the wealthy, after providing for their comfort, will return their surplus earnings to the economy in the form of investments. In actuality, however, they turn largely to speculation, for reasons and with results that we have seen.

We have no right to sit in judgment of our forebears, but we do have an obligation to understand what they did and a duty to judge ourselves. We have our burgeoning "institutions"—and we have the devastated lives lived in our inner cities and decaying towns. We have our international financial empires—and we have the *favelas* of Rio and the slums of Cairo and Lagos and Bombay and—yes—Tokyo. We could afford to throw away a trillion dollars in 1987 and another large sum in 1989—yet we do not summon up the will to afford fair jobs and decent living conditions for millions of our fellow citizens.

The bull market that started in 1982 took five years to absorb a trillion dollars. The bull market that started in 1988 absorbed a trillion dollars in less than four years and is well on its way to another trillion. The words "two trillion dollars" can be spoken trippingly on the tongue, but the devastation, disorder, and despair resulting from the extraction of $2,000,000,000,000 from the producing economy in less than nine years challenge our capacity to understand. "Challenge our capacity to understand" likewise can be spoken trippingly on the tongue. I do not know how to be emphatic enough. We are talking of tragedies compounded.

The economics of the rational greedy economic man failed our forebears. It is failing us. We fail ourselves if we refuse to understand that failure.

iv

Economic polarization has malign consequences all across the distribution scale. The poor are unable to buy the products that giant industry could produce; industry consequently has fewer opportunities for further expansion;

the rich consequently have fewer opportunities for investment; workers consequently have fewer job opportunities. If the rich are then frustrated in their attempts to consume their incomes, they turn to speculation. The amount of money that flows into speculative markets—preeminently the securities markets—is increased; so prices in these markets escalate. Escalating security prices mean escalating opportunity costs; corporations of the producing economy must increase their planned profit in order to attract the capitol necessary just to continue in business. Planned profit—not, it will be remembered, actual profit—is in conflict with wages; so wages must be further restrained or payrolls downsized or "rationalized," thus increasing polarization and reducing the market for industry's products—a consequence Professor Robert Averitt calls the Paradox of Cost Reduction.

An essentially unrelated factor has a vast and unexpected effect in the same direction. Prudent individuals save for their old age and insure against risks of various kinds, particularly torts, accidents, illness, and unemployment. What is here prudent in an individual, however, is foolish in a society, where its pursuit is a fallacy of composition. A society cannot insure itself, because insurance merely spreads the risk through the society. In an economy as large as that of the United States, the actuarial problem is easily managed. The risks are as level as can be. The number of people to reach old age in any given period can be accurately foretold, and the number to suffer injury or illness can be foretold within reasonably narrow limits. Catastrophes, like Hurricane Andrew and the San Francisco earthquake of 1989, must be specially met anyhow. This being the case, it would be sensible to treat the costs of all these risks as a current expense. Instead, we are funding them.

It happens that all public and many if not most private funds are set up as costs of employment, as burdens on jobs. Social Security taxes are paid only by people who work and people who employ them. Corporate fringe benefits are paid for in roughly the same way. Medical malpractice insurance is an expense of doctoring. In these cases, the cost always inhibits and sometimes prohibits work.

Even if these bad designs were corrected, the funds are now so enormous that they will continue to have such consequences on Wall Street as we have recently observed. For by far the largest part of the trading now being done on the securities exchanges is being done by "institutions," that is, by pension plans and insurance companies, by colleges and churches and foundations of all sorts, and also by mutual funds.

Most of the institutions, it will be seen, are owned by or are for the primary benefit of the middle class. There is surely little harm in that, for in a certain sense the middle class is the society, the superrich feeling themselves exclusive and the infrapoor being excluded. Yet these institutions, by their means of existence, soak up purchasing power and weaken aggregate demand. By their speculating, they deprive the producing economy of efficient financing. The consequent constriction of the producing economy increases unemployment, exacerbates the polarization of society, advances the erosion of the middle class the institutions were created to shelter, and intensifies speculation itself.

Thus the distortion of the economy is compounded. Not so long ago, it was thought that an interest rate of 4 or 5 percent, an inflation rate of 2 or 3 percent, and an unemployment rate of 3 or 4 percent was an achievable ideal. It was, in all conscience, a shabby ideal, but it was certainly superior to what we hear now.

v

The rich can turn to hoarding or speculation, but the poor can turn only to the state, which may fail them. It will certainly fail them if all it offers is some form of the dole, and that is all it will offer unless we can somehow be aroused from our long bemusement with the self-interested economic man. I dare not predict when this will occur or if it will occur. Massive and sudden shifts are surely possible. The Great Society was derailed by the Vietnam War. The "me generation" of quintessential economic men and women may yet become appalled at its own greediness.

In 1929, on the eve of the Great Depression, income distribution in the United States was so skewed that the total incomes of the top one-tenth of 1 percent of American families equaled the total incomes of the bottom 42 percent, and some 60 percent of all families were living below the poverty level (then about $2,000). [Maurice Leven, Harold C. Moulton, and Clark Warburton, *America's Capacity to Consume*, 1934.] These figures are for what is still thought of as a time of unexampled prosperity. Four years later, with almost a quarter of the civilian population unemployed (not counting most women as even prospective workers), things were exponentially worse.

It took four harrowing years to shock the nation into making a start on reform, and it took the industrial mobilization of World War II to show how reform was possible. By 1973 the family poverty rate had been brought down to 8.8 percent—nothing to be proud of, except in contrast with the 1920s. It has subsequently moved sluggishly, reaching 12.3 percent in the recession of 1982–83, drifting to 10.7 percent in 1990, and surging to 15.1 percent in 1993.

It is an open question whether our morale is so corrupt, our power of empathy so feeble, and our ability even to be interested in economics so meager that it would take another depression to make resumed reform possible. If so, the prospect is dark—ironically dark, because big government has made a full-fledged depression unlikely. [Hyman P. Minsky, *Can "It" Happen Again?* 1982.]

The gravamen of the charge is unjust treatment of our fellow human beings. In the light of that charge, it is barely worth considering that gross maldistribution of income and wealth, although evidently effective in the rise of our civilization, is now leading us to its decline. The maldistribution may, as many argue, be the consequence of cyclical swings in the economy. It may, as others say, be the result of technological change. For centuries, it was thought necessary to goad economic man to work. The explanation of the maldistribution will influence our corrective measures, not the necessity for correction.

In the meantime, as long as we refuse to make fundamental reforms, we can expect further difficulties, which may come about as a result of Third World debt, or a balanced budget amendment, or a crisis in the insurance business, or bankruptcy of the FDIC [Federal Deposit Insurance Corporation], or collapse of the Pension Benefit Guaranty Corporation, or resurgence of OPEC [Organization of Petroleum Exporting Countries], or another market crash, or (ironically) the end of the arms race, or something quite unforeseen; and each time unemployment and inflation will inch upward. We may nevertheless avoid an old-fashioned depression—unless doctrinaire bias simultaneously prevents big government from taking up the slack.

Big government can bolster aggregate demand sufficiently to forestall panic selling of assets and panic cutting of prices. Sophisticated business-people will avoid price cutting anyhow, to the extent of their ability. Modern doctrine teaches that the most profitable (or least damaging) response to bad business is to maintain price but cut production. Cutting production of course cuts employment. Consequently each pallid recovery tends to start with higher prices and higher unemployment than the one before it, and the successive stagflations tend to become slowly more severe.

The slow deterioration of a society can go on for a very long time. The Pharaonic World, the Roman World, the Medieval World, the Mandarin World, all stagnated for centuries. The Modern World (it will be our succes-sors who name it) can do the same. And it will do the same as long as we the people continue to believe that the economy and government and society and we ourselves are merely natural phenomena determined as are the phenom-ena of mechanics or zoology. Keynes was right about the power of ideas; but he may have underestimated the staying power of old ideas [J.M. Keynes, *General Theory*, 1936]. As long as we think intuitively in mechanistic metaphors, we shall pursue policies suitable for the operation of machines, not for the guidance of free men and women.

If there is a dead hand lying upon contemporary economic thought, it is the invisible hand discovered by Adam Smith. Two hundred years ago, this was a liberating hand, which participated in freeing us from arbitrary rulers. But it did so at the cost of conceiving of us as greedy servomechanisms.

vi

Galbraith posed the most pregnant economic question of our time: "Why should life be made intolerable to make things of small urgency?" [J.K. Galbraith, *The Affluent Society*, 1958.] Because modern industry is so wildly productive, its goods cannot be distributed without intensive and expensive selling effort. Even for the ancient necessities—food, clothing, and shelter—demand must be created. The world may beat a path to an inventor's door, but only after it has been told how to get there, what will be found at the journey's end, and why it wants it. The same applies to books and all the other carriers of culture, and to all the amenities and frivolities of civilization. (The vices can depend on the media and on television evangelists to advertise their arcane attractions.) Even unique events, such as concerts and special museum exhibitions, have to be heavily merchandised in order to be noticed amid the clamor of information. And the information highway is still only a dream.

Thus there is justice in Galbraith's conclusion that the necessity, or merely the prevalence, of advertising proves that the particular commodities advertised are "of small urgency." We must not, however, push the point to a fallacy of composition. What is true of each particular commodity is not true of commodities as a class. Another laundry soap, more or less, makes little difference, but *some* detergent (and a washing machine to go with it) is a vast improvement over beating clothes on a rock in a polluted river.

Moreover, there is no way back, at least no royal way. There are too many clothes to be washed, and too many other things worth doing. There are too many of us for all to be fed from kitchen gardens or clothed in homespun or sheltered in thatch-roofed hovels. It would take centuries of unlikely population control for us to be able to renounce mass production and mass-market distribution. Luddism is two centuries dead, and not to be revived in the lifetime of anyone now living.

Must life, then, be made intolerable? As long as economics is a "hard" science, the price system is as impervious to criticism as is the solar system; there is no escape. As long as the law of supply and demand is held in its traditional form, all prices are the result of an invisible hand, known in our crasser metaphor as "market forces," and no one is responsible. There is no

199

use pretending that the market is capable of reforming itself, of doing good or evil. It has no way of making work tolerable or of making commodities urgent. It has no way of making things worse. It is systematically feckless.

But if the primal economic act is an exchange between a price maker and a price taker, then whatever is done, whether of good repute or bad, is a free act of free men and women. Neither intolerable work nor nonurgent commodities just happen. Likewise a decent work place and excellent commodities don't just happen. Somebody is responsible, if only infinitesimally. The world is a better place, and some man or woman is a better person. And of course free men and women can make the world a worse place, and diminish themselves accordingly.

Once economic agents are seen as free and responsible, there is no mystery about the ethics of economic actions. Distinguishing right from wrong in business or in economics is no harder than it is in marriage or in public service or even in sports. Nor is it any different. Ethics is concerned with all action. It inheres in everything we do. We succeed or fail at ethical challenges all the time, just as we ordinarily talk in prose, whether we intend to or not. We are all members one of another, as St. Paul said; and as Lillian Smith showed [in *Killers of the Dream*, 1961], what we do unto others, we do to ourselves.

The cynic of Oscar Wilde's witticism—he who knows the price of everything and the value of nothing—is today balanced by the dogmatist who knows the value of everything and the price of nothing. A task of any future economics will be to bring price and value together, to establish their economic identity; and this will be done in part by proscribing certain economic acts—particularly certain low (or high) wage rates and interest rates—just as certain acts are proscribed in love and even war. Economic activity—like all human activity, from love to war—will be understood as a mode of self-definition, and so will no longer be beyond ethical judgment. Finally, economics will have a clearer and more obvious relevance to our daily lives in our mundane world.

Since it is not in our stars that we are underlings; since we are the captains of our souls; since, as we may say more prosaically, we are autonomous, then we all, severally and collectively, have the opportunity—the right and the duty—to participate in shaping an open and confident and generous economy that allows and even challenges all its members to be fully human. This is the task of any future economics.

JOEL KURTZMAN, *an economist and executive editor of the*
Harvard Business Review, *has written many books on
international finance, economics, and technology. Money, he
claims, no longer exists. It vanished two decades ago when the gold
standard was abandoned. In* The Death of Money *(1993), from
which this excerpt is taken, he writes that money has been replaced
by an unstable new medium of global exchange he calls "megabyte
money." A blip on the computer screen is not the same as money,
he insists, and its increasingly widespread use is a threat to the
economic stability of the twenty-first century. Kurtzman predicts
that the consequences of electronic trading are far beyond what
anyone currently envisages.*

JOEL KURTZMAN

THE CENTERLESS WHOLE

HOW THE GLOBAL ELECTRONIC MARKET IS FUELED BY
FADS AND FED BY RUMORS TO CREATE SHORTER TIME HORIZONS
AND MORE VOLATILITY

Networks, by definition, do not have centers, which makes them difficult to control, police, and govern. In an electronic network every point or node is equidistant from every other point. Each node communicates its good or bad news, its zeros or ones, with every other node at half the speed of light, the speed at which, according to Einstein, time collapses and ceases to flow.

A world of electronic networks is a world where data can flow without restriction across national borders, through security barriers, around the globe, almost without regulation. The information it conveys—money transfers between banks and between countries, the purchase or sale of stocks, bonds, and currencies, orders for products, TV programs, the news, gossip, cartoons, rumors—all intermingle as the server computers cut and splice and address the ones and zeros that are pumped through the lines.

These transfers of information are extraordinarily difficult to monitor and trace. Every bit of communication is moved through the network, from point to point, in the most direct and most economical fashion, which means that throughout the day, minute by minute, data may be disassembled, reassembled, and shunted along completely different paths. The networks themselves are formed and reformed constantly as they change their shape to accommodate traffic.

This is a complicated world, one in which a great deal of mystery and significance lies beneath our streets, in the power lines and cables inside our walls, inside the plastic and metal boxes on our desks, and in electronic components in our homes; one in which each letter in a word is sent along a different pathway in the computer network; one in which each zero in the number 1 billion may take a different route to the market.

The End of Equilibrium

In a networked economy the old economic ideas of "equilibrium" are gone, vanished, outmoded. How can there be equilibrium—which economists define most simply as the balance between supply and demand over time, a balance between economic inputs and outputs—when the supply of information always increases? When each analysis adds to each subsequent analysis? When information alone can create purchasing power and define value? When the data that people use to make their buying and producing decisions is revised by the minute? When Wall Street's case of nerves can cause a 508-point drop in the Dow, costing $500 billion, and no economic fundamentals have changed?

How can there be equilibrium when real and financial economies are so different in size? When the formerly fixed boundaries between nations, trading partners, companies, competitors, and collaborators have all been breached? When the battle between American and Japanese chip producers is fought not on their home turfs but in the design and engineering studios of other countries such as Switzerland, Britain, and Israel? When money is private and can be created not just by the federal government but by credit card issuers and banks? When government can no longer control exchange rates?

And how can there be equilibrium when the size of the pool of money changing hands globally every day dwarfs the actual value of the goods traded? When countries grow nationalistic and protectionist just as they lose control over their own destinies? How can there be equilibrium if money becomes transformed from something solid and substantial, with demonstrable equity value such as silver or gold, into something new, strange, and ethereal?

Predictability is Lost

Peter Schwartz, a futurist and consultant in Berkeley, California, who was head of strategic planning for Royal Dutch Shell in London, said in an interview that a networked economy is an unpredictable economy where the "significance of people's perceptions—the intangibles—can begin to matter more than the facts themselves." To economists such as Hyman Minsky, to futurists such as Peter Schwartz, and to theorists such as Marshall McLuhan, this network of networks increases everyone's chances for gain and loss dramatically.

One reason the electronic economy is perpetually out of balance is that whenever data travels over a network, it is magnified. Magnification in this sense does not mean that it is made louder, brighter, or bigger. It means that the data assumes a greater degree of significance the more it is perceived. The significance may have nothing to do with anything intrinsic. Often, just the fact that the data has been distributed—that it is seen by someone, as Peter Schwartz says—is what makes it important.

Take, for example, the economic figures released by the government. These include information on the gross national and domestic products, the trade deficit, consumer spending, inflation, and many other figures. The stock, bond, and foreign exchange markets usually react to these figures when they are released. They react even though the figures released by the government almost always have to be revised a few weeks later and sometimes revised again months after that or even a year after that. In many cases the revisions are greater than the original estimates. Sometimes the sign, plus or minus, is even wrong. In these instances even hard-boiled investors rely not on the data itself but on how they think other people will perceived that data. As bad as the data is—and every year economists complain it gets worse—it continues to move markets.

According to Francis Schott, former chief economist of the Equitable Life Assurance Society, "The trade statistics are particularly noisy, and as an economist I try never to make too much of those figures when they are released. However, in advising my company, I must consider them because the markets do." In other words this information is significant because it is released; it is not released because it is significant.

Every time new information makes its way onto the electronic global grid—whether that information is "noisy" or not, true or false—it modifies the assumptions of nearly everyone connected to that grid. It causes everyone on the network to consider not only the significance of each new morsel of data served up but how everyone else on the network will interpret it and react. As Francis Schott said, the trade statistics may be poor indicators of the true trade picture, but they must be considered because investors attach meaning to them.

"As a result of the influence of people's perceptions, a system as complex as the global economy will always have a variety of possible outcomes," Peter Schwartz wrote. His point was that like subatomic particles in physics, which are governed by what is called the Uncertainty Principle, the economy is also altered by the way we observe it. (*International Economy*, March/April 1988) According to Schwartz, "Information is always contaminated by people's beliefs and is never really complete."

Mood, which is difficult to quantify, emotionality, sentiment, confidence, and fear, all cloud the lens through which we see information. Forecasts that are supposed to rely on the data usually are wrong. And because networks have no centers, no place to filter out the true from the false, information that makes it onto the global grid is first considered true before it is discarded as false.

Those forecasts that are "messier," that allow for the influences of other factors, may often be more accurate, but with sentiment so hard to gauge, it is a wonder that forecasters like Schott, who has often been quite accurate, can foresee anything at all.

The Wave-Pattern Economy

Information networks can be thought of as highly complex assemblages of standing wave patterns. These standing wave patterns resemble the almost motionless wrinkles on the surface of a swiftly moving stream as it flows around a group of rocks. The standing wave pattern is usually fairly stable, but it also oscillates a little as each new bit of information is added—a new statistic about trade, news of the death of a country's elder statesman, the intention of a company to issue a bond, a change in consumer confidence, and so on.

Each new bit of data added to the network is like a pebble thrown into the stream. The pebble disrupts the overall pattern as the news of its impact is communicated outward in a series of concentric circles. But when that news is fully absorbed, the original pattern slowly returns. While most new data interferes with the pattern a little, it doesn't have the power to alter it permanently.

Each of these patterns, in turn, influences other patterns around the world. Trade statistics showing a big increase in the United States' deficit might cause traders to sell dollars and buy yen, disrupting those markets somewhat. A pickup in consumer spending might cause other traders to sell bonds and buy stocks, causing those patterns to shift based on new information added to the mix.

But over time these variations don't amount to that much—bonds go up or down a few basic points, stocks rise or fall a few points, a product sells and then languishes on the world's shelves. The rocks embedded in the standing wave stream still hold firm.

Yet every once in a while, on a day like October 19, 1987, quite unpredictably the entire network becomes so agitated that even the rocks on the floor of the stream are jostled. Such an event changes the standing wave pattern irreversibly.

Wars and revolutions can cause these shifts. So can the collapse or long-term run-up of a market or a new interpretation of the law.

The biggest changes, which are chaotic, are beyond the ability of most forecasters to predict. They are difficult to forecast because they are heavily influenced not just by the events but by the way people view them.

No one foresaw the October crash, which was highly influenced by people's perceptions. No one predicted the three-month collapse of Japan's Nikkei stock index or the demise of the savings and loan industry or Iraq's grab for Kuwait's oil or the Soviet coup.

Since nearly all networks are connected, and all computer terminals and modems around the world serve as sense organs for the global information grid, the causes of a catastrophic events are broader than ever before and therefore more difficult to forecast. Information, misinformation, leaked information, guarded information, misplaced information, and noisy information all influence events. As a result investment advisers such as Francis Schott must increasingly act on the basis of what they think other people think. They must give their advice by taking into account how others will react to the wide range of data that the information grid serves up. Instead of analysis, the new world demands intuition.

"In the case of the Federal Reserve," said Schott, "I must think about how the Fed will react to the economic data that is released by the government and then how the markets will anticipate how the Fed will react to that data. Sometimes it's a real guessing game."

Downgraded Governments

And what about governments in this networked world? They have been downgraded when it comes to running the economy. The trend that has been going on for more than a decade is for governments in every country to sell off their holdings and at the same time borrow more in the capital markets.

On the governments' part, selling off assets is an admission that in a global economy centralized control creates entities which move far too slowly and respond far too awkwardly to the quickly changing international environment. It also shows that the power of government is decreasing at a rapid rate relative to the private sector.

It may take social scientists quite some time before they fully understand the role of government in this new world. Government, business, commerce, and trade are all being redefined as globalization proceeds with dispatch.

The convergence of those two trends, a future more difficult to predict and government less able to act, is alarming. It may signal a future where there is too little central authority to stop a calamity before it occurs. The world may lack sufficient control mechanisms to curb chaos when it begins.

Technical Factors

The immensely complicated neural network of money, with its millions of nodes and billions of transmissions, links markets everywhere in a dance of commerce and trade. Eavesdrop on conversations at a Wall Street restaurant, and you are as likely to hear traders talking about New York's markets as about Tokyo's exchanges, the Philadelphia Stock Exchange, where options are traded, or the Chicago futures markets. Decisions on what and when to buy or sell a product have nothing to do with geography. Traders with PCs, workstations, modems, and a few passwords can trade anywhere.

Traders are hunting for returns. Less and less do the fundamentals matter. The world is now driven by "technical" factors—that is, models, computer or otherwise, that tell traders when to buy or sell. Some of these models, like the ones developed by Harry Markowitz, have won Nobel Prizes for their creators. Others, such as the Black-Scholes model for trading options, are contenders. But there are other quirky factors, to say the least, that move markets. These are the human factors.

Technical factors frequently have little regard for how much research and development a company is undertaking and how many patents or copyrights it owns. They also rarely take into account the strategic moves a company might make. It took a Japanese company, Sony, hunting for a strategic alliance, to recognize the value in the film library owned by Columbia Pictures Inc. and in the record library owned by CBS Records. Sony bought both companies outright. It took another Japanese company, Matsushita, to see the value in the film library of MCA Inc. and its Universal Studios subsidiary.

Before the takeovers, Wall Street's computerized gnomes traded stock in Columbia and MCA with apathy. The computer programs on Wall Street did not see the value the strategists at Sony and Matsushita did. Nor did Wall Street's technical models like the unpredictability of the film business. The models want steady results, a quarter at a time, and are not interested in the longer term.

Generally, technical models measure little more than the risk/return ratio on an investment or on an entire portfolio, as the Markowitz models first did two decades ago. These models also work in real time, as events happen, and continually recompute the risk/return ratio. Some of the more complicated models give buy and sell signals derived from interviews with experts. Others monitor the market as a whole and compare prices on one exchange to prices on another. Some models even take account of the overall economy—where interest rates are, what the government's leading indicators say, the rate at which debt is growing.

Dubious Models

But some of these models—some of the more dubious ones, that is—attempt to do more. For example, four thousand investors subscribe to the *Elliot Wave Theorist*, a $200-a-year newsletter that gives buy and sell signals based on a complicated numerological formula that attempts to measure the mood of the masses. The *Elliot Wave Theorist* is also available electronically on fourteen thousand Bloomberg Business News terminals around the world.

The *Theorist* is produced in Gainesville, Georgia, by Robert Prector, a reclusive refugee from Wall Street.

Though the *Theorist* failed to call the 508-point stock market collapse in October 1987—instead, it predicted the Dow would reach 3,700 sometime that year—it did announce the long upward movement of the market beginning in 1982 and several turnarounds in the market that occurred subsequently.

The *Theorist* also announced that a "top" to the market (not just the stock market but all markets, including the futures and real estate markets) had been reached in mid-1991, just prior to the mini-collapse of November 15, 1991, when the Dow fell 120.30 points, its fifth largest decline ever.

On Wall Street there was significant awareness that the *Theorist* had predicted the market's top. Traders became nervous. A number of traders and analysts were also aware that wave enthusiasts everywhere (not just those associated with the *Elliot Wave Theorist* newsletter) were predicting the end of the ominous "fourth cycle," after which the market would fall dramatically. That market fall would be so dramatic, said David Allman, director of research at the *Elliot Wave Theorist*, in an interview, that the market would trade at about half its November 1991 rate sometime in 1993. A Dow of 1,500 is what he predicted—down from about 3,000.

If nervousness and defensive investing have returned to the trading desks of Wall Street, Lombard Street, and the Ginza, the *Elliot Wave Theorist*'s "technical analysis" has helped to make it so.

Of course, there may actually be something to the *Elliot Wave Theorist*'s analysis, though it is certainly not scientific. But it does have enough adherents to move markets.

The wave's rationale goes back to a mystically oriented accountant in the 1920s named, not surprisingly, R.N. Elliot, who was influenced by the writings of a California yogi. The yogi taught that there was a cyclical quality to life, a nice thought that is still open to debate. Elliot fit numbers to that yogi's idea. The numbers he chose, called the Fibonacci numbers series, is a repeating series that was discovered by a thirteenth-century mathematician who was trying to figure out the progression and rapidity with which rabbits reproduce. The mathematical progression of the series, which can be topologically graphed as a spiral radiating out from a central plane, has some elegance to it. But it is about rabbits, after all, not markets.

No matter. Once Elliot got hold of it, the Fibonacci series seemed to fit his idea of a constantly repeating series of stock market cycles, which he then modestly termed the Elliot Wave.

Without any empirical evidence, many important Wall Street mavens have been following the theory. (No one really knows positively when one cycle ends and another begins. And the *Elliot Wave Theorist* admits that some significant errors have been made based on that one point, especially failing to predict the October 19, 1987, collapse.)

Some technical traders, many with MBAs from the best schools and some even with Ph.D.s, buy and sell based on where the Wave is headed. Other intelligent economists and analysts must be polite to these Wave enthusiasts because they pay the consulting bills. And because Wave advice goes out to thousands of paper and electronic subscribers, a call from the *Elliot Wave Theorist*, no matter how implausible the theory may be, can move the markets. That means otherwise rational investors must be ready to react to what the "irrational" is saying. At times, such as on November 15, 1991, that thinking was pervasive.

There are other "technical" models, too. There are newsletters based on astrology, numerology, and other very tenuous material. There are analysts who try to map mass psychology, and psychologists who try to analyze mass markets. There are also "inferential" thinkers—analysts who clip small-town newspaper stories seemingly at random and then report on what patterns they see in the news. Some of those technical analyses flash on traders' screens when a call about a market is about to be made. These rather dubious "technical" analyses exist side by side with other technical analyses that are based on science and economics properly applied and sometimes misapplied.

It is a jumble out there. The thought waves of the megabyte economy are not only congested but also very confused. Though investors have always sought help from outside the mainstream, the difference now is that the electronic system takes whatever fad or hysteria is in the air and spreads it globally. As a consequence, fundamental factors—the strength of a company, the resiliency of a country's economy, the size of its film library—may at times mean less than the pseudoscience of astrology or the Elliot Wave.

Even so, most old-guard economists believe markets are rational. In fact, among most economists it is simply a given—a basic tenet of their thinking. They conceive of the market as a "price discovery mechanism." That is the notion they are selling to Eastern Europe as they help those countries construct market economies, and it is based on the idea that with enough interested bidders, the price of anything will soon reflect its real value.

But that notion negates the quirkiness of everyday humans. It neglects the superstitious nature of the way many traders trade and many buyers buy. It neglects the influence of such preposterous ideas as the Elliot Wave, astrology, and sheer intuition as market movers.

When David Allman sends out a Wave call that causes thousands of otherwise rational people to buy or sell an asset, what has really changed to make that asset suddenly more or less valuable? The answer is nothing. Though markets often behave rationally, they do not always do so. The spread of technology has created an incredibly efficient system for buying and selling products. But it does not add one whit of rationality to the process. If anything, it makes it easier for markets to move for the most improbable and panicky reasons.

Markets That Are Too Efficient

When the stock market dropped 120.30 points on November 15, 1991, Lawrence H. Summers, the chief economist at the World Bank who is on leave from the economics department at Harvard University, said in an interview that "the markets often react to events far more than the fundamentals suggest they should."

That was a diplomatic way of putting it. What he meant was that nothing happened to the world on November 15, 1991, that made it substantially different economically from the world of November 14. No major company went bankrupt, no new statistics were released by the government, no big mergers were undertaken, and no massive deals fell through. Except for the market's moves, it was a pretty normal, even boring, day.

Yet suddenly the value of corporate America had taken a 4 percent drop. Similarly, there was nothing very much different economically between the way the world looked on Friday, October 16, 1987, and the way it looked on Black Monday, October 19, 1987. The world's electronic economy simply went into conniptions.

The world's markets react to whim and fancy. That has made them far more volatile than at any other time. Such volatility is good (and profitable) if you have the right programs running on the right computers and are able to drastically shorten your investment time horizons from months to weeks, days, and sometimes even minutes. But that change has been very damaging to the underlying real economy (where most of the world works), which thrives best on long-term planning and stability.

Volatility really is increasing. Robert Shiller, an economist at Yale University, has applied statistical methods to analyze price changes in the markets. His conclusion is that volatility is far larger today than in the past and that the price swings which underlie that volatility are greater than what can be accounted for by any underlying changes in the value of the real assets. What Shiller pinpointed as the cause of the increased variability in stock prices is trading for trading's sake: speculation. Increased speculation in the markets is what is driving the markets. A good portion of that speculative hunt for gains is motivated by rational analyses, but a significant amount is propelled by irrational fears, hopes, and expectations.

One implication of Shiller's findings is that the electronic marketplace is not as good as it once was as a mechanism for discovering real value. It may be good for speculation, and it may be good for bringing untested and often wacky assumptions to light, but it is not good at discovering value. After all, the real value of companies changes only slowly; it does not change minute by minute. And companies do not suddenly gain or lose 4 percent or 20 percent of their value in less than a single day. In other words, the electronic economy may be masking rather than discovering the real value of our corporations and other assets. The electronic market may be failing in its most important task.

That is a frightening thought. And if it is correct, there are very serious consequences. For example, if the megabyte economy is a speculative economy where trading has replaced the orderly (though noisy) price discovery mechanism, then anyone using the market as a price gauge is using a gauge that is faulty. That means most investors do not really know the value of America's (and the world's) corporations.

If real value in the market is hidden, then speculative trading is a much better strategy to follow than investing. If the value of General Motors or IBM is hidden behind the electronic buzz of speculation and the noise of "technical" factors, then whoever is lucky (or smart) enough to discover the real value of those assets can rush in and scoop them up, hold them briefly, and then sell them when everyone else catches on.

Markets have always contained a speculative fringe, but traditionally, long-term investors held the broad middle ground. Traditional markets were created for moving capital to companies with good ideas in return for a share of the profits. Traditional markets were supposed to be transparent, with the value of a company reflected in the price of its stock. But speculative markets treat stocks as if they were commodities where trading is the way to create profits. By definition, speculators are short-term investors. When they dominate a market, they change the market's character, and transparency goes away.

Electronics have made the stock market, particularly the American stock market, cloudy. The real values of the companies traded on the big exchanges are obstructed by the frenzy of speculation and the myriad of ways in which products can be traded. How does anyone know what Chrysler is worth when traders around the world are exchanging its options, warrants, bonds, and common and preferred shares of stock at electronic speeds? Can the company really be worth 40 percent less from one year to the next? Can investors who buy the stock really know so little about the company that when its debt is downgraded (no surprise to those who have followed Chrysler's woes), the stock plunges nearly 20 percent in a day? The only reason for that kind of reaction is that most technically oriented investors know a lot about stocks and very little about *companies.*

Perhaps that is why so many Japanese—and, to a lesser extent, European—investors have come into the United States to invest since the electronic economy began. They know our companies better than our own investors do, and they place a higher value on our assets than we do.

From a speculator's point of view the American companies that have been bought over the last few years are nothing more than large agglomerations of underperforming stocks. Few investors—and no American company— wanted to buy CBS Records (despite Bob Dylan, Michael Jackson, and fifty years of rock, folk, and jazz); MCA and Columbia Pictures (despite their film libraries); RCA Records (despite Elvis Presley); part of Time Warner Inc. (despite its film, book, and photography libraries); McDonnell Douglas (despite its technology and manufacturing expertise); Genentech (in spite of its patents and experience in genetic engineering); Macmillan Publishing (with its long list of titles); and dozens of small computer and software development companies with scant earnings but long lists of patents and copyrights. To American investors schooled in speculation, these companies had little value. To European and Asian investors, these companies were brilliant jewels.

Market "Adjustments"

Another piece of evidence that the electronic markets are failing at their most basic task has to do with the increase in large market "adjustments" over the years. Seven of the ten largest daily price changes on the New York Stock Exchange since the end of World War II happened since 1987. The years since the 1987 crash have been more volatile than all the years preceding it.

So many big stock market changes centered in such a short span of time suggest that the markets are not responding to the ups and downs of the greater economy. Between 1945 and 1987 there were four deep recessions. Since 1987 there has been only one, and it has been relatively shallow. But the markets weathered the four recessions prior to 1987 with equanimity compared to the way they have reacted after that date.

For the markets it no longer seems to matter whether the economy is headed into a recession or a period of prolonged growth. All that matters is whether the trading day offers electronic speculators the prospect of making money. And though newspapers and the electronic media are obligated to give reasons for each market rise and fall, the evidence seems to suggest that there usually is no reason at all. The value of companies is not discovered by the market, only the value of a stock. Just as the real and financial economies have become divorced, so for the most part have companies and their stocks.

The electronic markets may be hampering rather than helping the economy as a result. The markets are highly volatile and increasingly speculative. They are also extremely expensive. For instance, according to research undertaken in 1987 by Lawrence H. Summers when he was at Harvard, the corporations listed on the New York Stock Exchange had a combined income of $310.4 billion, while the receipts of the firms with membership on the NYSE—the ones that are actually allowed to trade those companies' stocks—totaled $53 billion for the same year. Add to those fees the costs that companies must pay to keep their stocks listed and traded—reporting, presentations to securities analysts, and payments to consultants, accountants, and others to put the companies in legal compliance with the market rules—and the costs of participating in the "official" market increases that sum to $75 billion. According to Summers that means *the markets* today consume about 24.2 percent of total corporate profits. That is only a little less than the $133.8 billion the corporations paid in taxes.

Shrinking Time Horizons

So who is winning in the megabyte economy?

Clearly corporate America—the country's real-economy companies such as GM, Ford, and IBM—are the losers. These companies have had their time horizons shortened, and they have been buffeted unceasingly by the volatility in the stock, bond, and international currency markets.

Since 1971 and the demise of the Bretton Woods system, they have been victimized by rising interest rates, rising commodity prices, and the continued demand from investors for profits that match the expectations of the computer models. They have also been hit hard by rising prices.

Over the years, especially during the 1980s, real-economy companies have been hit by wave after wave of corporate takeovers, with the stock market conspiring in those takeovers by camouflaging rather than revealing true value. These companies have also been handed a big bill from the firms that sell their stocks for the thrill of participating in financial markets that are rigged against real-economy companies. Companies that produce goods but exist in a world dominated by finance have been hurt badly.

Workers have also been hurt. Since 1971 wages have remained flat in real terms because American companies, forced to provide greater profits to satisfy the demands of the markets, have failed to invest in productivity-enhancing machinery.

Old-line financial companies have also lost in the electronic economy. The role of banks, savings and loans, and finance companies are being taken over by smaller, more mobile, and nimbler competitors. Banks continue to have huge overhead costs associated with originating and servicing mortgages and other loans, with those loans now usually bundled together into portfolios that are sold in the markets. Banks and savings and loans, determined to compete, entered markets about which they knew very little and have watched their losses mount. In finance, too, the idea of building and holding a portfolio—loans, in this case—has been replaced by the notion of transacting business. Loan portfolios need to be administered; loans that are sold do not.

The government is also a loser in the electronic economy. The Federal Reserve, though powerful, cannot determine policy if it goes against the wishes and whims of the market. The Fed is a large and important financial factor, but it is only one of many large factors in the world.

The regulators, too, have lost. While trying to maintain distinctions among markets—futures, stock, options, and so on—they have instead created arbitrage opportunities for quick traders. By exploiting the differences among the markets, computers and their masters can amass great fortunes. The regulators, forced to watch powerlessly as they fight their turf wars, are relegated to inconsequential actions such as debating whether one product is an option or a futures contract. While they conduct their debates, market participants continue carrying out their abuses.

America, more than any other country except Britain, is the loser. Our large, open markets have made our real-economy companies especially vulnerable to the ups and downs of the electronic economy. In a world with multiple currencies, where telecommunications has enabled production to be far-flung and global, jobs have migrated offshore. America, the most advanced economy, is the most globally diverse, with more of its profits emanating from abroad. As a consequence, with the majority of trade now for parts instead of products, the trade imbalance has become a structural component of our economy. That means every export contains imports, making it nearly impossible to have balanced trade.

But there are some winners in the megabyte economy. The firms that have a share of the $75 billion or so in fees from trading stocks are big winners. So are the traders. And the firms that design the tools that make the market work—software, telecommunications equipment, and computers—are among the few who have also won big.

ROBERT N. BELLAH *and his fellow sociologists moved American readers with their best-selling book* Habits of the Heart *(1985) in which they showed a profound understanding of the delicate balance between social commitment and individualism.*
"We described a language of individualist achievement and self-fulfillment that often seems to make it difficult for people to sustain their commitments to others, either in intimate relationships or in the public sphere," they wrote in The Good Society *(1991), from which these excerpts are taken. Looking at tomorrow's world, they concluded: "Our institutions are badly functioning and in need of repair or drastic reform, so that if they are to support a pattern of cultivation rather than one of exploitation, we must change them by altering their legal status and the way we think about them. . . ." Bellah and his associates confront us with the understanding of the open choices facing us today: "As this century draws to a close there remain, we believe, vital opportunities—as well as the urgent necessity—for transforming our national and international institutions so as to bring about a new, more democratic, more peaceful world order . . ."*

Robert N. Bellah, Richard Madsen, William M. Sullivan,
Ann Swidler, Steven M. Tipton

Democracy Means Paying Attention

Attending

From the time we were children we were told by our parents and our grammar school teachers to "pay attention!" In more or less peremptory ways we have been receiving the same message ever since. Even though we may have grown inured to this injunction and shrug it off, there are few things in life more important. For paying attention is how we use our psychic energy, and how we use our psychic energy determines the kind of self we are cultivating, the kind of person we are learning to be. When we are giving our full attention to something, when we are really attending, we are calling on all our resources of intelligence, feeling, and moral sensitivity. This can happen at work, at play, in interaction with people we care about. At such moments we are not thinking about ourselves, because we are completely absorbed in what we are doing. Although such moments are enjoyable, we do not seek them out because of pleasure, but because they are things we really want to do in terms of the larger context of our lives. They "make sense." And even though they are moments of minimal self-consciousness and their purpose is not to maximize pleasure, it is in such moments that we are most likely to be genuinely happy.

While paying attention, attending, is very natural for human beings, our attention is frequently disturbed. One of the most obvious features of psychotics is that they suffer from "disorders of attention," in which they have no control over the thoughts and sensations that come flooding into their minds and cannot consciously decide to focus their attention on objects of their concern. But all of us suffer, though less drastically, from such disorders of attention. When we are doing something we "have to do," but our minds and our feelings are somewhere else, our attention is alienated. In such situations of disordered or alienated attention our self-consciousness is apt to be high. We may suffer from anxiety or, today's common complaint, "stress." Working hard at something we care about, giving our full attention to someone we love—these do not cause stress. But studying a subject we're not interested in and worrying about the grade, or doing things at work that we find meaningless but that the boss requires and we must do if we don't want to lose our job, or just being overwhelmed by more than we can cope with to the point where we feel fragmented and exhausted—these cause stress, these are examples of alienated attention. We attend but fitfully—inattentively, so to speak—and therefore we are not cultivating our selves or our relationships with others. Rather, we may be building up strong desires to seek distraction when we have free time.

Unfortunately, many of the distractions we hope will "deaden the pain"—alcohol; restless, channel-flipping TV watching; compulsive promiscuity—do not really help, for such distractions too are forms of alienated attention that leave us mildly, or sometimes severely, depressed. We have not exercised the potentialities of our selves and our relationships, and so we have not reaffirmed our selves in the larger contexts that give our lives meaning. If, after a stressful day, we can turn our attention to something that is mildly demanding but inherently meaningful—reading a good book, repairing the car, talking to someone we love, or even cooking the family meal—we are more apt to find that we are "relaxed."

Attention is, interestingly enough, a religious idea in more than one tradition. Zen Buddhism, for example, enjoins a state of mindfulness, an open attention to whatever is at hand; but Zen practitioners know this is always threatened by distraction. Mindfulness is valued because it is a kind of foretaste of religious enlightenment, which in turn is a full waking up from the darkness of illusion and a full recognition of reality as it is. This idea, common enough in Eastern religions, has analogies in biblical religion as well. God revealed himself to Moses from out of the burning bush as "I am that I am" (Exodus 3:14), and Moses had a hard time getting the children of Israel, distracted by their golden calf, to see the radical truth that had been revealed to him at Sinai. Jesus preached a new reality, a Kingdom of God which he declared was at hand, though most of his hearers could not make it out. Jesus said, "Having eyes do you not see, and having ears do you not hear?" (Mark 8:18) but many were too distracted to see or hear.

This is not the place to attempt to develop a full-scale phenomenology of attention; but, as in the religious examples, we mean to use attention normatively, in the sense of "mindfulness," as the Buddhists put it, or openness to the leadings of God, as the Quakers say. On the face of it, it may seem hard to tell the difference between attention and obsession. But as we shall use the term here, attention implies an openness to experience, a willingness to widen the lens of apperception when that is appropriate, and this obsession is incapable of doing. Obsessive "attention" is in this normative sense not attention at all but distraction, an unwillingness to be genuinely attentive to surrounding reality. The genius or the saint who seems to be obsessive may be attending to a reality whose significance escapes the rest of us.

So far we have considered the issues of attention, of disordered or alienated attention, and of distraction from the point of view of the individual. Self-control and self-discipline have a lot to do with whether we can engage with life or simply attempt to escape it. But people do not deal with these questions all by themselves, as we have already noted in the area of religion, nor can one alone develop a self able to sustain attention. As we have insisted throughout this book, we live in and through institutions. The nature of the institutions we both inhabit and transform has much to do with our capacity to sustain attention. We could even say that institutions are socially organized forms of paying attention or attending, although they can also, unfortunately, be socially organized forms of distraction.

Attention in the Family

Americans place a high valuation on family life. But if the family is only "a haven in a heartless world," a place that provides distraction from the harshness of the rest of our lives, we are certain to be disappointed; for families require a great deal of attention to function successfully. Despite romantic fantasies, marital love is not a narcotic that soothes all wounds. Attending to each other, expressing our deepest concerns and aspirations and listening to those of the other, is fundamental in a good marriage and crucial to the satisfaction it provides. But if we only expect to be attended to and we don't attend to the other, because we've had too hard a day or whatever (and this is more apt to be a male than a female failing), we sow the seeds of marital discord and deprive ourselves of the real rewards of marriage. The fact that married people live longer than single people suggests that marriage provides a kind of attention that is very important for human beings.

Attention is important between marriage partners, but it is fundamental for children. Infants who do not get attention, in the sense of psychic interaction and love, simply cannot survive, even if they are fed and clothed. And the quality of attention that children get has a great deal to do with how they turn out. In a study in Chicago that was concerned exactly with this issue, the psychologist Mihaly Csikszentmihalyi and the sociologist Eugene Rochberg-Halton found that the children of "warm families" (families where high levels of attention were given to each member) were significantly different from children of "cool families" (families where parents were distracted and inattentive and did not relate well to each other): "Children of warm homes are more sympathetic, helpful, caring, and supporting. The next difference is Affiliation: the relevant traits here are loyal, warm, friendly, sociable, co-operative. Warm homes also breed children who are less denying, defensive, and unsure of their worth." [*The Meaning of Things*, 1981.] In short, attentive homes breed attentive children.

It is significant for our purposes that the attentive homes were not "havens" to which the family retreated, avoiding civic and other outside involvements. It was the members of the cool families who had few outside associations; members of warm families tended to participate in voluntary groups outside the home. The capacity to sustain attention was being generalized beyond the family.

There was one worrisome finding in the study. The authors found that a heavy responsibility for the "warmth"—that is, the high level of attention—rested on one person: the wife and mother, who typically devoted her life to her family and children. The study was done in 1977 among families with children ten years of age or older, so it does not necessarily describe how things are now. There were some indications that many of these women, however loving and outgoing (and active in local voluntary associations), felt that they were paying a price for this accomplishment—namely, their own fuller participation in the larger world, in creative and fulfilling work—and were not entirely happy about it. It was not that the fathers were not involved in family life. They were significantly more involved than the fathers in cool families, but often in stereotypically male forms that did not do much to relieve the burden on the mothers; indeed, it may have increased it by amplifying the intensity of family life.

The picture of warm, attentive and cool, inattentive families that the Chicago study draws was taken in a moment during a continuous transition. It would be foolish to imagine that Americans could simply reconstitute such warm, attentive families today. It would be equally foolish to dismiss such families as "patriarchal," lumping them in with all the historic forms of the family since the heroic age of Homer; nor would it be any better to call them "bourgeois." As Csikszentmihalyi and Rochberg-Halton point out:

> For one thing, the classical bourgeois family is held together by the heavy weight of social traditions. Economic advantages, status considerations, social controls, and expectations maintain it; they provide the constricting goals that channel the psychic energy of its members. Thus it might be a closely knit unit, but it is not necessarily a warm one because the meanings that maintain it are rigid creations of social forces. By contrast, the warm families in our midst are practically *invented* by their members. Outside constraints are relatively light; the meanings that keep these families together are woven and mended by the constant attention of those who comprise them.

Now that a considerably higher percentage of the mothers of small children are part of the work force than was the case in the 1970s, many of them full-time, our family capacities for continued institutional invention are strained, even as evidence is growing of the negative consequences for children of not having an intense family life.

The psychiatric social worker Judith Wallerstein has found in a sample she studied of children of divorced parents, ten years after their parents' divorce, between the ages of nineteen and twenty-nine, that many "are drifting through life with no set goals, limited educations, and a sense of helplessness. . . . Although only a few have dropped out of high school, most have not seriously pursued higher education. . . . They don't make long-term plans and are aiming below the intellectual and educational achievements of their fathers and mothers." [*Second Chances*, 1989.] These people suffer among other things from what they perceive as lack of attention; and their own capacity for sustained attention is weak, their capacity for building a coherent life impaired.

If an intense family life is essential both for the satisfaction of adults and for the raising of responsible children who can nurture themselves and the world they live in, then part of the solution to the dilemma is surely that family responsibilities must be shared equitably between the parents. In most cases the new situation of having both parents work has resulted in an unequal and unfair division of labor in the home. The sociologist Arlie Hochschild argues that working women come home to care for house and children at what she calls a "second shift" (in a year it adds up to one month of twenty-four-hour days of work more than their husbands), even when they hold down a full-time job [*Second Shift*, 1989]. The degree of inequality in the household is a major threat to the stability of the family:

In one . . . study, Joan Huber and Glenna Spitze asked 1,360 husbands and wives: "Has the thought of getting a divorce from your husband (or wife) ever crossed your mind?" They found that more wives than husbands had thought about divorce . . . and that wives thought about it more often. How much each one earned had no effect on a spouse's thoughts of divorce. Nor did attitudes about the roles of men and women. But the more housework a wife saw her husband do, the less likely she was to think of divorce. As the researchers noted: "For each of the five daily household tasks which the husband performs at least half the time, the wife is about 3 percent less likely to have thoughts of divorce." (The five tasks defined as taking the most time in housework were meal preparation, food shopping, childcare, daily housework, and meal cleanup.)

Hochschild draws the conclusion:

Happy marriage is supported by a couple's being economically secure, by their enjoying a supportive community, and by their having compatible needs and values. But these days it may also depend more on sharing a value on the work it takes to nurture others. As the role of the homemaker is being vacated by many women, the homemaker's work has been devalued and passed on to low-paid housekeepers, babysitters, and daycare workers. Like an ethnic culture in danger of being swallowed up by the culture of the dominant group, the contribution of the traditional homemaker has been devalued first by men and now by more women.

. . . One way to reverse this devaluation is for men to share in that devalued work, and thereby help to revalue it. Many working mothers are already doing all they can at home. Now it's time for men to make the move. In an age of divorce, marriage itself can be at stake.

To put Hochschild's findings in our terms, there is a crisis with respect to giving and receiving attention in the family. The care of everything and everyone, especially children, is suffering because there is not enough time. Although the solution to this problem involves changes in the larger society, in the short term there is the immediate obligation on the part of everyone in the family to restore the centrality of attention and care. Here Hochschild is surely right that the primary need at the moment is a greater participation of men, of husbands and fathers, in the care that is essential to family life.

We may note here that attention and celebration are related, an issue we shall consider further below. Many of the most time-consuming family tasks have to do with meals: food shopping, preparing, and cleaning up. But the family meal is the chief family celebration, even a family sacrament. What happens when no one has time to prepare a meal, when for days on end the family has no common meal? If everyone joins in the common tasks, husband as well as wife, and children, too, as much as they are able, then the family can enjoy at least several common meals a week, celebrate the pleasure they have in each other's presence and the good things they have mutually helped to prepare. Mealtime, as anyone who has ever had children knows, can also produce conflicts; but learning how to resolve them, to listen and be listened to, is part of the indispensable educational function of the common meal. We can be sure that having a common meal, and one to which all contribute, results in a warmer family and an enhancement of everyone's capacity for attention.

Just as we do not want to romanticize the "warm" families of the past, of any period when family life was allegedly better, so we do not want to advocate any single form of family life. The two-parent family with children has special significance because it is the family form that has carried primary responsibility for raising children and because it has become harder and harder to sustain. But recognizing the symbolic as well as practical centrality of this family form in no way means a derogation of other family forms.

Many children who are raised in single-parent households become strong, self-reliant, and loving adults. Single parents need support from the larger community (as do couples), and the dignity of their task needs to be affirmed. Similarly, committed relationships between two members of the same sex, with or without children, can contribute to a general atmosphere of love and loyalty between couples and should not be seen as a threat to something considered a "normal" family. It is a historical illusion to imagine that there has ever been only a single family form. What is important is the quality of family life, not the diversity of its forms.

But the tasks of restoring family life, whatever form the family may take, cannot be the family's alone. As we noted Hochschild saying, a "job culture" has expanded at the expense of a "family culture." Only a major shift in the organization of work and in American public policy with respect to it will enable us to regain a balance between job and family. It might appear at the moment, when economic competitiveness is such an obsession, that Americans "can't afford" to think about the family if it will in any way hinder our economic efficiency. Nothing could be more shortsighted. In the long run our economic life, like every other aspect of our common existence, depends on the quality of people. How effective will our economy be if it depends on a generation of listless, anxious people unable to concentrate on anything very long and unconcerned about planning a coherent life for themselves? There is literally nothing more important than the quality of our young people, yet American public policy consistently refuses to *pay attention* to this fact. . . .

The Promise of Attention: A Sustainable Life

What the metropolis of the American Century lacked above all was sufficient attention to the whole. Its legacy is environmental damage, social neglect of the least advantaged, and restricted possibilities for all. What is needed for the twenty-first century is not only more and different infrastructure but the sort of "focal structure" that government, the "third sector," and public-private partnerships of business and not-for-profit institutions together can provide. The task of these focal structures is to enhance the capacity of metropolitan citizens and institutions to promote the quality of life for all citizens.

The popularity of urban neighborhood development in the 1970s was strengthened in the 1980s by public-private partnerships, which helped to revive many core cities, though we cannot forget that most of these initiatives benefited the well-to-do and that the position of the urban poor has substantially declined. Today, environmental politics offers an inclusive rallying point that brings together concerns for social justice, economic viability, and environmental integrity. Ecological sustainability as a purpose converges with the desire for safe, diverse, and economically viable communities. As the case of Los Angeles shows, these purposes join in the effort to reverse the indiscriminate sprawl of the postwar decades and aim instead toward more bounded metropolitan environments. The enlargement of our capacity for this will be the office of the democratic public. The public lives through those institutions that cultivate a constituency of conscience and vision. This constituency is the creative matrix from which city, state, and national leaders can arise; its task: to make the interdependency of modern life locally comprehensible so that responsible action is possible.

Americans have pushed the logic of exploitation about as far as it can go. It seems to lead not only to failure at the highest levels, where the pressure for short-term payoff in business and government destroys the capacity for thinking ahead, whether in the nation or in the metropolis, but also to personal and familial breakdown in the lives of our citizens. In this book we have repeatedly suggested the need for a new paradigm, which we can now call the pattern of cultivation. This pattern would not mean a return to the settlement forms of the early nineteenth century, but it would be the attempt to find, in today's circumstances, a social and environmental balance, a recovery of meaning and purpose in our lives together, giving attention to the natural and cultural endowment we want to hand down to our children and grandchildren, and avoiding the distractions that have confused us in the past. Again, what has for a long time been dismissed as idealism seems to be the only realism possible today.

But how can we pay attention to all of the problems that beset us? Even the experts feel more comfortable if they can distract themselves by holding on to simple measures of the situation like GNP or comparative military strength. Fortunately, military dangers have lessened—we can expect continuing conflict in the Third World, but hardly of the magnitude of the Soviet military threat. But it would be foolish to replace a military-political fear of the Soviet Union with an economic fear. Indeed, an obsession with competitiveness against Japan or Western Europe can be just as great a distraction from reality as an obsession with communism. The whole argument about whether the United States is in decline or is as strong as ever is also beside the point and fundamentally distracting. Clearly we are headed toward a future in which a number of highly successful national or regional economies will coexist; rather than worrying about where the United States is in the hierarchy, we should be worrying about creating a humane economy that is adequate to our real purposes, and a healthy international economy that operates for the good of all peoples. As Václav Havel has been saying, we need to replace a politics of fear with a politics of trust. Trust gives us space for attention, even when what we have to attend to seems baffling, whereas fear drives us to seek distraction, the kind of reassurance that only big numbers can provide.

Money and power are necessary as means, but they are not the proper measures of a good society and a good world. We need to talk about our problems and our future with a richer vocabulary than the indices that measure markets and defense systems alone. Words like "attention" and "distraction," "cultivation" and "exploitation" may begin to encourage conversations in which we can define our priorities, our needs to strengthen existing institutions, and our needs to create new ones.

We need experts and expert opinions, and experts can certainly help us to think about the important issues. But democracy is not the rule of experts. It is basic to the education of citizens that they learn how to evaluate expert opinion. Much of high-school and college education actually does give students help in this matter, but more could be done if it was acknowledged as a central task of education. In any event, evaluating the opinions of experts is only the beginning and not finally the most important problem. Weighing the moral implications of different options is what is fundamental. Here the citizen who has learned to pay attention in the family and the local community can generalize to larger issues. When the family is a school of democracy and the school is a democratic community, then the beginnings of such wisdom have already been learned.

Our institutions are badly functioning and in need of repair or drastic reform, so that if they are to support a pattern of cultivation rather than one of exploitation, we must change them by altering their legal status and the way we think about them, for institutional change involves both laws and mores. More than money and power, these need to be at the center of our attention . . . .

Attention and Distraction

. . . By focusing on our immediate well-being (are you better off now than you were four years ago?), and by being obsessively concerned with improving our relative income and consumption, we have forgotten that the meaning of life derives not so much from what we have as from what kind of person we are and how we have shaped our lives toward future ends that are good in themselves.

The end of the cold war, and of what may come to be called the Seventy-five Years' War of the Twentieth Century, of which the cold war was the final phase, gives us a chance to step back from these obsessions and think about the future which, perhaps, we unconsciously doubted we had. Now that the threat of the mushroom cloud is receding, we may see that many things we have been ignoring for too long need our attention.

The major problems that come to light require the virtue of generativity to solve—indeed, a politics of generativity. The most obvious problem is the perilous neglect of our own children in America: levels of infant mortality, child poverty, and inadequate schooling put us at or near the bottom in these respects among industrial nations. We fight a "war on drugs," but we do little to fight the despair that leads to the desire for drugs. It might be obvious that meaning is the best antidote to drugs and that there is no meaning if there is no future; but in our theatrical, macho politics more police, more prisons, more military interdiction are more obvious answers. . . .

The Politics of Generativity

At many points we have observed how shortsighted our mechanisms for decision are. Priority in both American economics and American politics has been given to immediate return. Advertising and public rhetoric focus on the individual income, the individual house, the individual car, the individual gun. Except for invoking the ever-present term "freedom" (even when our actual future freedom is being constantly diminished by short-term decisions), our leaders show little concern for the world we are moving into or that our children and grandchildren will have to live in.

In the face of a mass culture and politics dominated by distraction, which offers not only temporary narcotics for anxiety but also a cover for those whose interests are threatened by serious change, there is an urgent need for a new politics of generativity. In recent years the Democratic party has been only half an opposition party, shifting uneasily between trying to outbid the Republicans in offering individual distractions and offering specific policies (such as legislation mandating unpaid parental leave, or national health care, or aid to education) that are at least part of a politics of generativity. But in the absence of an overall philosophy of generative interdependence (as opposed to narrowly self-interested individualism), this liberal laundry list can be taken apart and discarded at will.

The last two decades have been a time of neglect of America's material and social resources, whatever the verdict may finally be on our economic performance of those years. The breakdown during the 1970s of the informal cooperation among government, business, and labor, which had been typical of the "pluralist" politics of the years 1945–68, set in motion a general erosion of social trust. The material consequences of this regression have been profound. Investment in private and public infrastructure has slowed, especially in the public sector, with manifest consequences for our economic life. And the simultaneous disinvestment in "human resources" has already shown itself in the social decay of crime, addiction, cynicism, eroded civility, weakened education, and most shockingly, perhaps, in the pervasive indifference of youth to the world around them.

This withdrawal of responsible attention has spread throughout American society, weakening our economic competitiveness as compared with that of nations such as Germany and Japan, and sapping the energies for social and political attention as well. The pattern of self-seeking indifference was begun and, as the political analyst Kevin Phillips has pointed out, promulgated by many of the wealthiest and most powerful segments of the nation, which defended and partially masked the socially regressive consequences of this generalization of distrust and self-seeking by sponsoring a revival of the nineteenth-century economic ideology of the free market [*The Politics of Rich and Poor*, 1990]. In the current context of multinational finance, of course, this economic vision cannot mean a return to a world of individual entrepreneurs, however attractive this mirage has proven to some voters: it is simply a carte blanche to the owners and managers of capital to skim profits with even fewer entangling social responsibilities. At the end of the cold war, the great irony is that the Lockean United States may turn out to be more ideologically rigid than the USSR.

We know that the interdependence of modern societies is both complex and fragile. Thus, viability depends, far more than it did in the past, upon the mutual trust and goodwill of all citizens, and notably of the essential functional groups—business, labor, government, the professions, and the "third sector." Viable interdependence, as we have argued repeatedly, requires that participants integrate a cognitive understanding of their interdependence with the practical enactment of goodwill demanded in each institutional context. All-out pursuit of individual or group advantage, which is one consequence of institutional failure in the polity, quickly becomes not only pathological but threatening to the survival of all. Under modern conditions a society's economic and social development hinges essentially on ability to sustain institutions that mediate mutual trust and civic responsibility. Focusing collective attention on this capacity, developing it, and nurturing institutional reforms to promote it is the central theme of the politics of generativity.

In a postindustrial, global economic order, the old categories of (material) "base" and (institutional) "superstructure" are rapidly losing their meaning. Economic development today is the result of a ratio of "inputs" in which raw materials count for less as technological and institutional innovations count for more. It is no longer a matter of mineral deposits and low wages, as in the nineteenth-century model. Not only physical infrastructure but education, socially and environmentally sustainable communities, and managerial and political capacities are the keys to growth and prosperity.

The politics of generativity takes social inclusion and participation as a key theme—for economic no less than for moral and social reasons. Institutions of international cooperation and regulation are necessary for economic growth, even for sustainable competition, within as well as among nations. And it is the real competition among nations to develop capacities for this kind of political learning that the United States, obsessed by an obsolescent economic ideology, is in danger of losing. The Hayek-Friedman ideology of pristine, Darwinian market competition is practiced nowhere—not in international commerce and least of all by the successful trading and exporting nations, though it may serve the short-term political interests of business and investment bankers. It justifies keeping wages low as it protects the banks' disastrously imprudent international investments, but it will be catastrophic for the United States, and finally for business as well, and in the not so very long run. . . .

Even more important, such a politics is premised on active citizen involvement and discussion—with issues of long-term purpose and consequence taking precedence over the simpler indices upon which current policy analysis focuses—public participation in administrative decisions, constituency involvement in corporate decisions, and a closer public monitoring of legislative action, through review commissions and public debates. The emphasis would be on regulation, setting limits beyond which market and monetary forces are inappropriate and administrative action without review cannot go, and on long-term planning.

The structural changes that a generative politics can produce will anchor our economic and political institutions firmly in the moral discourse of citizens concerned about the common good and the long run. This would make it harder for them to operate over the heads of the people. The achievement of such a generative politics will be to realize Robert Dahl's third democratic transformation. But none of this will happen unless a new moral paradigm—a paradigm of cultivation—replaces the old, outworn Lockean individualist one.

A Place for New Perspectives

Walter Lippmann, in his 1937 book *The Good Society*, from which we have taken our title, discussed the "higher law" that he believed Americans had not properly understood when they interpreted it as only the protection of the individual's absolute rights. The higher law, concerned as it is with human rights, is rooted in a fundamentally social understanding of human beings:

> The development of human rights is simply the expression of the higher law that men not deal arbitrarily with one another. Human rights do not mean, as some confused individualists have supposed, that there are certain sterile areas where men collectively may not deal at all with men individually. We are in truth members of

one another, and a philosophy which seeks to differentiate the community from the persons who belong to it, treating them as if they were distinct sovereignties having only diplomatic relations, is contrary to fact and can lead only to moral bewilderment. The rights of man are not the rights of Robinson Crusoe before his man Friday appeared.

The higher law that provides the basis for human rights is not a truth complete in itself already known to select philosophers: "To those who ask where this higher law is to be found, the answer is that it is a progressive discovery of men striving to civilize themselves, and that its scope and implications are a gradual revelation that is by no means completed." Nonetheless, classical philosophy and biblical religion give us our best clues as to what the higher law entails. In so arguing, Lippmann for the first time in his work married his own deeply liberal respect for individuality to older Western traditions.

In a closing section entitled "On Designing a New Society," Lippmann argued that we should be moving toward not a single homogeneous system but a society that respects and encourages diversity and attempts to "reconcile the conflicts that sprang from this diversity." Such a society will indeed require virtue:

It requires much virtue to do that well. There must be a strong desire to be just. There must be a growing capacity to be just. There must be discernment and sympathy in estimating the particular claims of divergent interests. There must be moral standards which discourage the quest of privilege and the exercise of arbitrary power. There must be resolution and valor to resist oppression and tyranny. There must be patience and tolerance and kindness in hearing claims, in argument, in negotiation, and in reconciliation.

But these are human virtues; though they are high, they are within the attainable limits of human nature as we know it. They actually exist. Men do have these virtues, all but the most hopelessly degenerate, in some degree. We know that they can be increased. When we talk about them we are talking about virtues that have affected the course of actual history, about virtues that some men have practised more than other men, and no man sufficiently, but enough men in great enough degree to have given mankind here and there and for varying periods of time the intimations of a Good Society.

That Lippmann turned to biblical religion and classical philosophy for elements of the new vision he thought necessary is relevant in our present situation. Recent events in Eastern Europe, as well as past experiences in our own history, suggest that the churches, synagogues, and other religious associations might be one place open to genuinely new possibilities, where cultivation and generativity have clear priority over exploitation and distraction. As an example of fresh thinking about our situation, we call to mind the American Catholic bishops' 1986 letter on the U.S. economy, which argued eloquently that "the dignity of the human person" provides the moral cornerstone for social and economic life. But for the bishops the human person is not an abstract individual but one whose dignity is realized only in community. The commandments to love God with all one's heart and to love one's neighbor as oneself lay the foundations of human community. All persons have rights, but they arise from a mutual bond to care for one another as members of one creation and are rooted in "reverence for God as Creator and fidelity to the covenant." Justice begins with recognition of the need of all persons to take part in the life of a community in order to be fully human, by being united with one another in mutual activity and, finally, mutual love.

The distinctive contribution that the bishops' letter makes to public debate cuts across partisan lines and challenges the conventional bipartisan wisdom that economic well-being is defined in terms of individual levels of material subsistence and consumption, that the economy's success is measured by the aggregate and average amounts of wealth it produces and its efficiency in doing so. Most fundamentally, the bishops challenge the premise that the economy's activities, rules, and relations lie in a social sphere separate from politics and morality. Instead they propose a thick, organic connection in our moral understanding of economic, political, and spiritual life, centered around the necessity of communal solidarity and realizing the dignity and sacredness of all persons. Economic institutions should be judged not by the amount of wealth they produce but by how they produce and distribute it: in doing so do they enable everyone in the community to take part in productive work, learning, and public affairs? Human rights in general, and in particular the rights of once excluded people to take part in a good society, are rooted in a moral matrix of communal solidarity springing from creation and bound by covenant; they do not arise prudentially from the essential self-interest of individuals and their contractual exchange.

In making this argument the bishops recognize that the renewal of a shared vision of a good society must come through critically interrelating the distinctive moral traditions of American culture instead of trying to flatten them into a uniform consensus. So the church seeks to give its own members moral guidance in terms of biblical narrative, theology, and church tradition. But it also seeks to add its voice to public debate through reasoned argument persuasive to those who do not share its own tradition of faith. The confidence that social cooperation can be sustained in public affairs, and that culturally distinctive moral efforts can be carried out compatibly, is itself an expression of faith: "The common bond of humanity that links all persons is the source of our belief that the country can attain a renewed public moral vision."

Like the Protestant Social Gospel, Catholic social teachings in the past century affirm the traditional emphasis on the need to become good persons through the love of God and neighbor and also a commitment to reorder society's institutional arrangements so that people, flawed as they are by "original sin," may live more justly and humanely with one another. A just social system is impossible without people being just. Justice is first and foremost a virtue, and it inheres in individuals and institutions that carry out God's commandment to care for one another—to feed the hungry, heal the sick, and enable the able-bodied to work and contribute to the commonweal.

In defining the institutional conditions that permit genuine communities to flourish, Catholic social thought underlines three principles: (1) that institutions must protect the dignity and inherent sacredness of persons as God's creatures; (2) that social organizations should be ordered in interdependent and cooperative forms, with attention to the natural subsidiarity by which larger and more powerful political and economic institutions sustain smaller communities instead of dominating them; and (3) the necessary existence of social structures, such as the family, church, professional and civic associations, that mediate between the state and its citizens without being controlled by either the will of the state or the interests of individuals. The purpose of the state, then, is to serve this articulated social order by furthering the cooperation and well-being of all these groupings and institutions.

The principle of subsidiarity favors social cooperation and decentralized power in forms that encourage "a new experiment in participatory democracy" in the American workplace and polity (proposed in Chapter 4 of the bishops' letter). Its notion of government ordered to aid the flourishing of human beings in community harks back to America's founding ideals as a democratic republic. The principle of subsidiarity offers neither progressives nor neoconservatives a partisan blueprint for political economy. Indeed, one crucial subsidiary function of the state in this understanding is that of encouraging and heeding a moral argument in public life that moves beyond ideological stereotypes.

No political party and few political organizations have put forward so comprehensive a vision, a vision remarkably like Lippmann's analysis in *The Good Society*. In a period when one or another version of savage capitalism is pushed as the answer to our quandary about competitiveness, it is a healthy sign that the bishops' letter generated discussion of the fundamental issues of modern economic life.

Responsibility, Trust, and the Good Society

Another key term in our moral vocabulary that is closely related to attention, and indeed to all the issues involved in the effort to create a good society, is "responsibility."

Responsibility must begin with attention. To act responsibly we must ask: What is happening? What is calling us to respond? The theologian H. Richard Niebuhr in his book *The Responsible Self* [1963] argued that all our action is a *response* to action upon us, for we are caught in an inescapable web of relationship with other human beings, with the natural world, and with the ultimate reality that includes and transcends all things—what Jews and Christians call God. In many situations we either passively accept what is happening to us or try to evade the implications of what is occurring around us. But, says Niebuhr, we must *interpret* what is happening; especially, we must interpret the intentions of the people we deal with. A third element in responsibility has to do with the effect on others of what we do, a matter that Niebuhr calls "accountability." But our actions usually are not isolated encounters with persons or things with whom we have no continuing relation but, rather, occur in contexts that are already patterned and partake of an element of *social solidarity*. Summing up, Niebuhr wrote: "The idea or pattern of responsibility, then, may summarily and abstractly be defined as the idea of an agent's action as response to an action upon him in accordance with his interpretation of the latter action and with his expectation of response to his response; and all of this is in a continuing community of agents."

So far Niebuhr is being a good sociologist, for sociologists have understood human action in just such a relational context. Indeed, for sociologists, institutions are defined as those patterns which human agents create to regulate action in a "continuing community of agents." But for Niebuhr the idea of the moral life as the responsible life is not just sociologically descriptive but a key to what he calls the "biblical ethos which represents the historic norm of the Christian life." Two aspects of responsibility go beyond purely sociological description: one is trust, and the other is the scope of the responsible action to which we are called.

Trust—and here Niebuhr is being both sociologically realistic and religiously perceptive—is never to be taken for granted. In our relation to the world, trust is always in conflict with mistrust. Because of previous experiences a degree of mistrust is usually realistic; yet if we are dominated by mistrust we cannot attend or interpret adequately, we cannot act accountably, and we will rupture, not strengthen, the solidarity of the community or communities we live in. But how can we trust? Erik Erikson locates what he calls "basic trust" in the child's earliest experience with the mother (perhaps today we would better say "parent") and suggests that if trust has not been warranted then, it is doubtful that it ever will be adequately established in the personality. Theologians such as Niebuhr suggest that behind parental love, essential as that is, lies a deeper question: Is reality, is Being itself, trustworthy? To argue that trust or faith is justified, that God as the very principle of reality is good, is not obvious—not obvious to Christians and Jews, who down through the centuries have been supposed to believe it, and not obvious to anyone who has to live in the world as it is. Trust or faith, like parental love, is a gift. It comes to individuals and groups in particular experiences at particular times and places. Niebuhr did not say that it comes only to Jews and Christians, or that it comes only to people who think of themselves as religious, but that to whomever it comes, it comes as a gift. And when it does come, it brings a great joy and enables us to live responsibly with our fellow beings.

Because so much of the time we are overwhelmed with mistrust, because it is so difficult to believe that Being is good, that, as Christians say, God is love, yet also because to live without trust altogether would be to be close to paranoid schizophrenia, most people try to limit the scope of their trust. They will trust in this person or this occupation or this ethnic group or this religion or this nation, but not in the others. Yet every such limitation impairs the possibility of responsible action. Since we can only attend to those we trust, we cannot interpret accurately, we cannot be accountable to, we cannot grow in solidarity with those we have put outside the circle of our trust. This is no abstract argument. On it hinges the very possibility of whether or not we can create something even partially resembling a good society. When we care only about what Tocqueville called "the little circle of our family and friends" or only about people with skin the same color as ours, we are certainly not acting responsibly to create a good national society. When we care only about our own nation, we do not contribute much to a good world society. When we care only about human beings, we do not treat the natural world with the respect it deserves. If reality itself is for us empty and meaningless, it is hard to see how our lesser commitments can be anything but brittle and transient. But as H. Richard Niebuhr put it:

> In the critical moments we do ask about the ultimate causes . . . and are led to see that our life in response to action upon us, our life in anticipation of response to our reactions, takes place within a society whose boundaries cannot be drawn in space, or time, or extent of interaction, short of a whole in which we live and move and have our being.
>
> The responsible self is driven as it were by the movement of the social process to respond and be accountable in nothing less than a universal community.

Yet for none of us is it easy to override our mistrust and act responsibly in the universal community. Such a possibility is a gift; and when it comes, our response should be gratitude and celebration.

We can indeed try genuinely to attend to the world around us and to the meanings we discover as we interact with that world, and hope to realize in our own experience that we are part of a universal community, making sense of our lives as deeply connected to each other. As we enlarge our attention to include the natural universe and the ultimate ground that it expresses and from which it comes, we are sometimes swept with a feeling of thankfulness, of grace, to be able to participate in a world that is both terrifying and exquisitely beautiful. At such moments we feel like celebrating the joy and mystery we participate in. Religions at their best help us focus that urge to celebrate so that it will include all the meanings we can encompass. The impulse toward larger meaning, thankfulness, and celebration has to have an institutional form, like all the other central organizing tendencies in our lives, so that we do not dissipate it in purely private sentiment.

Institutionalization is always problematic. Socially organized ways of paying attention can become socially organized ways of distraction. Nowhere is the dilemma of institutionalization more poignant than in the realm of religion. Members of biblical religions are under the obligation to listen to what God is saying in the most mundane events of everyday life as well as in the great events of world history, and to respond as conscientiously as they can to the ethical demands raised by those events. Yet it is easier to repeat old formulas, to comfort oneself with the community's familiar practices, than to risk trusting a new response to new conditions.

Yet if we are fortunate enough to have the gift of faith through which we see ourselves as members of the universal community of all being, then we bear a special responsibility to bring whatever insights we have to the common discussion of new problems, not because we have any superior wisdom but because we can be, as Václav Havel defines his role, ambassadors of trust in a fearful world. When enough of us have sufficient trust to act responsibly, there is a chance to achieve, at least in part, a good society. In the meantime, even in the world as it is, there are grounds for thankfulness and celebration. Meaning is the living fabric that holds us together with all things. To participate in it is to know something of what human happiness really is.

NELSON MANDELA, *the world's most respected statesman, was awarded the Nobel Peace Prize in 1993, and elected President of South Africa in 1994. He had been released from 27 years of imprisonment in 1990. This excerpt is from a speech that he delivered to the United Nations Assembly in 1994 in which he stressed that human reconciliation was one of the most important factors in building a better future.*

Nelson Mandela

Address by the President of the Republic of South Africa to the United Nations General Assembly in New York, 3 October 1994

. . . We have embarked on the road to the remaking of our country, basing ourselves both on the democratic Constitution which came into force on 27 April this year and the Reconstruction and Development Programme which has become the property of all our people.

Clearly, these documents would have no life unless the people gave them life. The words printed in them must inspire common ownership by all our people and their common allegiance to the process and the results which these documents intend. For this to happen, as we propagate the vision these documents contain, we must, at the same time, engage in an historic effort of redefinition of ourselves as a new nation.

Our watchwords must be justice, peace, reconciliation and nation-building in the pursuit of a democratic, non-racial and non-sexist country. In all that we do we have to ensure the healing of the wounds inflicted on all our people across the great dividing line imposed on our society by centuries of colonialism and apartheid.

We must ensure that colour, race and gender become only a God-given gift to each one of us and not an indelible mark or attribute that accords a special status to any.

We must work for the day when we as South Africans see one another and interact with one another as equal human beings and as part of one nation united, rather than torn asunder, by its diversity.

The road we shall have to travel to reach this destination will by no means be easy. All of us know how stubbornly racism can cling to the mind and how deeply it can infect the human soul. Where it is sustained by the racial ordering of the material world, as is the case in our country, that stubbornness can multiply a hundredfold.

And yet, however hard this battle may be, we will not surrender. Whatever the time it may take, we will not tire. The very fact that racism degrades both the perpetrator and the victim commands that, if we are true to our commitment to protect human dignity, we fight on until victory is achieved.

We firmly believe that we who have particular experience of the destructive and anti-human force of racism owe it to ourselves to centre our transformation on the creation of a truly non-racial society. Because we know racism so intimately, we must stand a good chance of developing and nurturing its opposite.

It will perhaps come to be that we who have harboured in our country the worst example of racism since the defeat of nazism will make a contribution to human civilization by ordering our affairs in such a manner that we strike an effective and lasting blow against racism everywhere.

Some of the steps that we have already taken – including the establishment of a Government of National Unity, the orderly transformation of the institutions of state and the cultivation of a national consensus on the major issues of the day – have started us off on a correct footing with regard to continuing the processes leading to the creation of the just society we have been speaking of.

Our political emancipation has also brought into sharp focus the urgent need to engage in the struggle to secure our people's freedom from want, from hunger and from ignorance. We have written this on our banners: that the society we seek to create must be a people-centred society; all its institutions and its resources must be dedicated to the pursuit of a better life for all our citizens. That better life must mean an end to poverty, joblessness, homelessness and the despair that comes of deprivation. This is an end in itself because the happiness of the human being must, in any society, be an end in itself.

At the same time, we are intensely conscious of the fact that the stability of the democratic settlement itself and the possibility actually to create a non-racial and non-sexist society, depend on our ability to change the material conditions of life of our people so that they not only have the vote but have bread and work as well.

We therefore return to the United Nations to make the commitment that, as we undertook never to rest until the system of apartheid was defeated, so do we now undertake that we cannot rest while millions of our people suffer the pain and indignity of poverty in all its forms.

At the same time, we turn once more to this world body to say – "We are going to need your continued support to achieve the goal of the betterment of the conditions of life of the people." We are pleased and inspired that both the Secretary-General and the specialized agencies of the United Nations have taken up the development challenge in South Africa with the enthusiasm that they have shown.

We believe that it is in the common interest that we sustain the common victory that we have scored in South Africa, and take it further by achieving success not only in politics but also in the socio-economic sphere.

It is perhaps common cause among us that everywhere on our globe there is an unmistakable process leading to the entrenchment of democratic systems of government. The empowerment of the ordinary people of our world freely to determine their destiny, unhindered by tyrants and dictators, is at the very heart of the reason for the existence of this Organization.

But it is equally true that hundreds of millions of these politically empowered masses are caught in the deathly trap of poverty, unable to live life in its fullness.

Out of all this are born social conflicts which produce insecurity and instability, civil and other wars that claim many lives, millions of desperate refugees and the destruction of the little wealth that poor countries are able to accumulate. Out of this cauldron are also born tyrants, dictators and demagogues who not only take away or restrict the rights of the people but also make it impossible to do the things that must be done to bring lasting prosperity to the people.

At the same time, the reality can no longer be ignored that we live in an interdependent world which is bound together to a common destiny. The very response of the international community to the challenge of apartheid confirmed this very point that we all understood – that so long as apartheid existed in South Africa, so long would the whole of humanity feel demeaned and degraded.

The United Nations understood very well that racism in our country could not but feed racism in other parts of the world as well. The universal struggle against apartheid was therefore not an act of charity arising out of pity for our people, but an affirmation of our common humanity. We believe that that act of affirmation requires that this Organization should once more turn its focused and sustained attention to the basics of everything that makes for a better world for all humanity.

The elaboration of a new world order must, of necessity, centre on this world body. In it we should find the appropriate forum in which we can all participate to help determine the shape of the new world.

The four elements that will need to be knit together in fashioning that new universal reality are the issues of democracy, peace, prosperity and interdependence.

The great challenge of our age to the United Nations is to answer the question – "Given the interdependence of the nations of the world, what is it that we can and must do to ensure that democracy, peace and prosperity prevail everywhere?"

We are aware of the fact that the United Nations is addressing these questions in many ways; yet there can be no gainsaying the fact that such progress as we have made has been made more by stealth than in the bold and determined fashion that the world crisis demands today.

Perhaps a new and forceful initiative is required. Such an initiative should inspire all of humanity because of the seriousness of its intent. It should also have a chance to succeed because it will have been underwritten by the commitment of the masses of the people in each member country to join hands with other nations, to address together the related issues of democracy, peace and prosperity in an interdependent world.

We are aware of the fact that the dictates of *realpolitik* militate against the speedy realization of such an initiative. But we do believe that the reality of life and the realism of policy will, at some point, bring to the fore the fact that the delay we impose on ourselves today will serve only to increase the pressure on all of us to incorporate, within what we consider possible, a sustainable vision of a common world that will rise or fall together.

Undoubtedly, to inspire greater confidence in itself among all the member nations and to reflect better the impulse towards the democratization of international relations, the United Nations will have to continue looking at itself to determine what restructuring of itself it should effect. This process must naturally affect, among others, the structure and functioning of the Security Council and the peacemaking and peace-keeping issues raised by the Secretary-General in "An Agenda for Peace".

Democratic South Africa rejoins the world community of nations determined to play its role in helping to strengthen the United Nations and to contribute what it can to the furtherance of its purposes. Among other things, we have this morning acceded to the covenants and conventions adopted by this Organization, which address various matters such as economic, social and cultural rights, civil and political rights, and the elimination of all forms of racial discrimination, to say nothing of our irrevocable commitment to the realization of the objectives contained in the Universal Declaration of Human Rights.

We are determined to play our full part in all processes that address the important question of the non-proliferation and elimination of weapons of mass destruction. Our Government has also decided to become a signatory to the Convention on prohibition and restrictions on the use of certain conventional weapons.

In a similar vein, we shall not be found wanting in the quest for sustainable development that is in keeping with the Rio de Janeiro Declaration on Environment and Development as well as with Agenda 21.

Equally, our own national interest dictates that we join forces with the United Nations and all its Member States in the common struggle to contain and end the traffic in narcotics.

Even in constitutional terms, we are committed to the advancement of the objective of the emancipation of women through the creation of a non-sexist society. Apart from anything else, we are therefore actively engaged in the preparations for what we are convinced will be a successful Beijing Conference.

We are part of the region of southern Africa and the continent of Africa. As members of the Southern African Development Community and the Organization of African Unity (OAU), and an equal partner with other Member States, we will play our role in the struggles of these organizations to build a continent and a region that will help to create for themselves and all humanity a common world of peace and prosperity.

Ours must become a continent free of such tragedies as those that have afflicted our own country as well as Rwanda, Somalia, Angola, Mozambique, the Sudan and Liberia. Happily, the OAU is actively addressing the issues of peace and stability on our continent.

We are greatly encouraged that the countries of our region, faced with a crisis in Lesotho, acted together speedily and, with the cooperation of the Government and the people of that country, succeeded in demonstrating that together we have the will to defend democracy, peace and national reconciliation.

Furthermore, as members of the Non-Aligned Movement and the Group of 77, we are committed especially to the promotion of South–South cooperation and the strengthening of the voice of the poor and disadvantaged in the ordering of world affairs. . . .

The millions across our globe who stand expectant at the gates of hope look to this Organization to bring them peace, to bring them life, to bring them a life worth living.

We pray that the new South Africa, which the General Assembly helped bring into being and so warmly welcomed among the community of nations, will, in its own and in the wider interest, make its own contribution, however small, to the realization of those hopes.

Our common humanity and the urgency of the knock on the door of this great edifice demand that we must attempt even the impossible.

OWEN PAEPKE *was trained as a research chemist and is now an attorney in Arizona, specializing in intellectual property rights. This excerpt is the Introduction to his wide-ranging book,* The Evolution of Progress: The End of Economic Growth and the Beginning of Human Transformation *(1993). It is his view that economic advance is coming to an end and human progress is poised to replace it. "Only an amateur, who can search with a floodlight rather than a laser beam, has any hope of discovering phenomena that spread across a vast intellectual, historical, and factual terrain." Paepke is convinced that we are on the awesome threshold of transforming people through advances in genetic engineering, neurobiology, chemistry, and food technology.*

"Within a generation, machine intelligence will be making significant, independent contributions to several fields," predicts Paepke. It is not that tomorrow's machines will be so markedly different from today's, but that human beings themselves will be revolutionized. Introducing startling prospects, Paepke suggests: "Indeed, even using the word 'people' to denote these beings is an anachronism. Within a century or two, genetic engineering will likely have changed our descendants so fundamentally as to prevent them from mating with humans in their present form, making them biologically a separate species."

C. Owen Paepke

The Evolution of Progress
Introduction

This book is about the end and the beginning of progress. The end of one kind of progress, material progress, lies at the heart of the many puzzling changes that are contributing to a growing undercurrent of surliness and despair. The new kind of progress, which makes human traits and abilities the subject rather than just the source of change, will dominate the agenda of the next century, perhaps even the next decade. But these watershed events have somehow escaped notice. The purpose of this book is to bare them for public examination.

Material progress is a comparative newcomer on the historical scene. Economic historian Joel Mokyr concluded *The Lever of Riches*, his recent survey of economic growth and technological advance from antiquity to 1914, by observing that "we are living in an exception. . . . Our age is unique: only in the last two centuries has Western society succeeded in raising the standard of living of the bulk of the population beyond the minimum of subsistence." From the beginning of the Roman Empire until the eighteenth century, a period of almost two millennia, the conditions of life scarcely improved. Napoleon's subjects ate food, wore clothes, and lived in houses that were about the same as those of Caesar. The sick still received more sympathy than cures. Manure remained the state-of-the-art fertilizer. Horses were the fastest form of transportation, and of communication, since information traveled as freight. Water and windmills supplied energy in a few areas. Elsewhere, it was extracted, bit by painful bit, from draft animals and men. The ancient Roman could easily have adapted to the work, the technology, and the lifestyles in eighteenth-century France. The present, by contrast, would seem like a scene from Mount Olympus.

With the beginning of the Industrial Revolution, material progress quickly began to make up for lost time. It has virtually defined the era. Nations wax and wane; creeds and philosophies gain and lose favor; political and social structures evolve; but progress itself continues. Despite the wars, natural disasters, political detours, economic dislocations, and other temporary setbacks that dominate the history texts, every generation has surpassed its predecessor, even in nations in relative decline. Famine, never more than two bad harvests away before the nineteenth century, has been buried by moun-

tains of surplus food in every advanced economy, with even India occasionally exporting grain. The typical supermarket daily offers a wider selection
than people of just a few generations past ate in a lifetime. Houses with
running water, refrigerators, more bedrooms than people, and other commonplace miracles have replaced dirt-floored hovels shared by three or more
generations. Improved health care has stretched life expectancies from less
than fifty years in 1900 to more than seventy today. Before railroads, people
rarely left their home counties. Many thousands now cross continents and
oceans each day. In 1900, not one student in ten earned a high school
diploma, the presumptive minimum for entry into the workplace since
World War II. Telecommunication makes knowledge of events, still the dearest of commodities through the early nineteenth century, available worldwide, instantly, at little or no cost. Progress has been the only true status quo
of the modern era.

This progress has transformed daily life not once, but repeatedly. The
much-pitied industrial worker of late-Victorian England had already pro-
gressed far beyond the nobleman of the preceding century in many of the
material aspects of life. The nineteenth-century robber baron could only envy
the diet, mobility, medical care, and general comforts and amenities available
to the average American worker of the 1950s. The present middle-class
American, so often portrayed as a victim of the 1980s, lives better than even
the wealthiest plutocrat of the 1920s. These long-term improvements owe
little to the clamor for reform and everything to the expanded output that
progress has routinely delivered. The productivity and technology of the
nineteenth century deliver only nineteenth-century squalor whenever and
wherever they occur and however humanely their output is divided.

Two centuries of material progress in many nations with sharply differing
governments and cultures through countless economic cycles have etched an
improving standard of living in the public's mind as one of the few eternal
verities. Rising incomes, larger houses, and more and better things, all
obtained with less effort, are the normal state of affairs, the baseline against
which an economy's actual performance is judged.

That complacency is unwarranted. The current era of progress is over.
It will not return.

Prophecies like this one tend to evoke an immediate and profound skepticism. Past progress occurred in defiance of the many prophets who proved
that it could not happen. Maximilien de Béthune, Duc de Sully, may claim the
dubious distinction of being the first: in 1638, he opined that living standards
would fall because of an irreversibly worsening scarcity of firewood. Thomas
Malthus honed this pessimism to a science with his *Essay on the Principle of
Population*. Malthus argued that the natural fecundity of the species would

quickly transform any excess food supply into a larger population, leaving society always at the edge of famine. Population would tend to grow geometrically (1, 2, 4, 8), while food output would, at best, grow linearly (1, 2, 3, 4), an equation that only starvation would balance. (In the event, of course, precisely the opposite occurred. The output of food and almost everything else expanded geometrically, while rising affluence restrained the birthrate.) More recently, the Club of Rome sought to endow the same thesis with mathematical certitude by using computer models encompassing a range of natural resources and environmental constraints to prove that continued economic growth assured global catastrophe. The oil shock and gas lines even gave gloom some fleeting political prominence in the 1970s, when an earlier incarnation of Jerry Brown tried to ride an "era of limits" theme into the White House. The common element of such prophecies is a threatened shortage of one or more resources, with food, energy, clean air, and minerals among the common candidates.

Intervening events have refuted all such predictions. The fatal flaw has always been the same: progress not only creates shortages, it also provides the means to negate or circumvent them. Technology expands the planet's ability to provide for human needs at a dizzying pace. Natural resources steadily become less, not more, important. Until recently, communication required either copper or the electromagnetic spectrum, both finite resources. With fiber optics, sand replaces copper, and one California beach would supply enough to carry all the messages of the planet for centuries to come. A pound of plutonium provides more energy than a forest of trees. Hybrid seeds triple the amount of grain that each acre of land produces. Even in such grubby areas as metallic ores and fossil fuels, recoverable reserves now satisfy projected usage for longer than they did a generation ago. In practical terms, the planet's resources have become not scarcer, but more plentiful. During the same period, and despite the impression conveyed by activists and the media, environmental quality has generally improved in the developed nations. Resource limitations have never caused more than fleeting inconvenience in the past, nor will they do so in the future.

But limits of a very different kind have virtually halted material progress in the leading economies. Living standards in the United States have barely budged since 1973. People react like heirs deprived of their birthright and begin looking for the culprit. Japan seems to be the leading suspect. Polls identify it as the principal threat to the United States. A supposedly free-market president mouths imprecations over its refusal to buy cars that Americans have shunned in droves and that suffer from the minor additional shortcoming of having their steering wheels on the wrong side. *Rising Sun* topped the best-seller lists not for its undeniable virtues as a mystery, but for its Geraldo-like exposé of Japan's plan to dominate the world. But the facts strike a discordant note in this chorus. Japan's bubble economy has popped, its banks are tottering, its multinationals' profits have nearly vanished, and a tide of retrenchment is in full flood. To the Japanese, of course, the villains are on this side of the Pacific.

There are no villains, here or there. Material progress began when four forces coincided in late-eighteenth-century England. Their continuing presence, alternating in leading and supporting roles, explains its persistence during the intervening two hundred years. Progress in its accustomed form will not survive their passing.

1. Growth of Knowledge

Technology was, both figuratively and literally; the motive force behind the Industrial Revolution. Watt's engine and Crompton's "mule" started the overthrow of traditional handicraft production. Iron began to supplant wood in machinery, heavy construction, and transportation as large coal-fired blast furnaces made the metal available in quantity. Germany and the United States followed England's lead, pioneering in nitrogen fertilizers, internal combustion engines, automobiles and airplanes, electric power systems, the telegraph and telephone assembly lines, synthetic materials, and antibiotics. Improved communications and transportation assured the spread and permanence of these advances. The gains in every field have been immense. Technology has been the proverbial free lunch, delivering more and better for less.

But technology, however ingenious, must obey physical laws, and those laws limit the tangible benefits to be realized from further advances. Consider transportation. Crossing the United States in a Conestoga required considerable grit, some luck, and six months. It now occupies a few hours spent sitting in an easy chair. The next century could shave another hour or two from the transit time, but that improvement would be negligible compared to what technology has already accomplished. Satellites and fiber optics communicate information in all forms worldwide at the speed of light, an absolute physical limit. Energy flows freely from fossil, hydroelectric, and nuclear sources. Contrary to the common perception, it has become not scarce and expensive but abundant and cheap. Vaccines and antibiotics have nearly eliminated the threat from contagious disease in the developed world, allowing all but a small minority to live full life spans. Labor-saving mechanization and rising yields have reduced the number of farmers, once a majority of the population, to negligible levels. Manufacturing productivity increases—more than tenfold in this century alone— are doing the same for blue-collar labor. In these and other fields, future progress will be confined to ever smaller increments between the state of the art and the limits of the possible.

2. Free Markets

Commercial freedom provided the incentives and the framework for progress. The prosperity of the Italian city-states and Holland suggested an alternative to the slavery and feudalism that gripped most of Europe through the sixteenth and into the seventeenth century. The tiny middle class began to grow and to encroach upon the powers and privileges on the hereditary nobility. England's tradition of private property rights, dating back to the Magna Carta, accelerated its progress toward free markets. By the eighteenth century, myriad personal freedoms, originally exceptions carved out of despotic and arbitrary rule, had coalesced to produce the twin concepts of limited government and the rule of law. People came to regard travel, exchange, and voluntary employment as matters of right, not privilege. They could work, spend, and invest by their own lights. Freight moved with little regulation, money circulated freely, and entrepreneurs defied and defeated the restrictive sanctions of trade guilds. By 1776, Adam Smith had observed enough of the emerging commercial freedom to become its original theoretician, philosopher, and chronicler. Born even a century earlier, he would have had little to chronicle.

In the intervening two centuries, free markets spread across most of the world. Their superiority in promoting progress has become too obvious to require discussion. Eastern Europeans and others who have not yet tasted their fruits have become their most zealous and committed advocates. But the very completeness of capitalism's triumph shows that the freeing of markets has already made its major contribution. The restrictions that remain in the developed economies are more irritants than serious impediments. The gains remaining to be realized from this source will necessarily be minor compared to those enjoyed in the past.

3. Market Expansion

Advances in transportation technology widened markets, the third source of progress in the modern era. A few miles surrounding a village once defined the limits of the accessible marketplace. Food rarely traveled more than ten miles from the farm, cloth no more than forty miles from the loom. When longer haulage could not be avoided, it often cost more than the goods themselves. People were scarcely more mobile than freight, with employment prospects effectively restricted to the dimensions of a county. Seasonal market and hiring fairs provided only sporadic commercial intercourse between otherwise isolated regions. Virtual self-sufficiency remained the norm through the eighteenth century.

Canals, railroads, and improvements in shipping broke this multi-millennial tyranny of distance, opening the way for large-scale industry as business expanded to serve customers over a wider area. Rapid communications made control of these farther-flung enterprises possible. The pace of change quickened as innovators were able to deploy advances over larger markets. The overseas explorations of the sixteenth and seventeenth centuries brought even foreign lands into the market. England led in all these developments. Textile mills in Manchester turned raw cotton from the American South into clothing for much of the Western world, while Russian royalty dined on Wedgwood china. The rest of the world soon learned and followed. Regions and nations began to specialize in their fields of comparative advantage. The United States was a particular beneficiary because of its continental expanse. Iowans no longer had to raise cattle or Texans grow corn. Coal from the Appalachians and iron ore from the Mesabi became steel in Pittsburgh. The resulting efficiencies have been incalculable.

But market expansion has reached an obvious and absolute limit. All the advanced nations are integrated into a single worldwide economy. Americans drive European cars burning Arabian oil on roads paved with Mexican cement. Pakistani-born engineers design chips for American companies to fabricate in the United States, following the trail of foreign direct investment blazed by England and the United States. Political impediments continue to restrict international trade in some highly visible products, but the restrictions have less long-term impact than is commonly hoped or feared. With worldwide markets already the norm, any further gains from this source will be inconsequential compared to those of the past.

4. Accumulation of Capital

Stable financial institutions and joint-stock companies began the process of concentrating capital for commercial purposes in late-eighteenth-century England. Before that time, only the state, through its ability to tax, could collect funds widely enough to support large projects. This produced military might and some impressive public works, but no comparable undertakings in the private sector. The few merchant houses that accumulated sizable wealth devoted it to trading, not production. As a result, most private enterprise was based on the use of relatively abundant labor, not scarce capital. But labor without sufficient capital produces little surplus, perpetuating the capital shortage while leaving workers on the edge of subsistence.

Private investment combined with labor-saving technology to break this vicious cycle. Gross capital investment nearly doubled in a single generation.

It flowed into poetry and textile production, roads and canals, and manufactories of all kinds. This capital lifted incomes above subsistence, further increasing private saving and producing an accumulating, self-generating surplus that enabled the economy to expand further. This virtuous cycle has continued (almost) to the present, producing the vast aggregation of factories, machinery, transportation equipment, health care facilities, public infrastructure, and communication networks that characterize every advanced economy.

Everyday observation suggests the importance of this accumulation. Orange juice costs more than gasoline, even though growing an orange tree is much simpler than drilling for oil and refining it. The explanation lies in the disparate use of capital: orange growers employ many workers and little capital, while oil wells, refineries, and pipe-lines are vast concentrations of capital that require little labor. This is not an isolated example: filet mignon costs more per pound than a Hyundai, and theater tickets cost more than a dozen videotape rentals. The principal difference in each instance is the use of capital to achieve efficient mass production.

But capital expansion is reaching effective limits in the developed world. Capital is the accumulated saving of prior generations. Rising incomes have always added to capital by enhancing the *ability* to save. At some point, however, they also diminish the *incentive* to do so. Hardship, not ease, is the mother of frugality. Households with enough assets and earnings to satisfy their wants, and an expectation that those earnings will continue, lack the motivation to accumulate more capital in order to expand their incomes further. Material progress pushes an ever increasing percentage of households into this group. These are, of course, the very households that have the greatest ability and historical propensity to save. Government programs and private insurance and pension plans reinforce this income effect by cushioning against many of the risks that formerly motivated rainy-day savings. (The same factors play havoc with the work ethic, as the stubbornly high unemployment rate throughout the long economic expansion of the 1980s demonstrates.)

These limits are not absolute, but their impact is already evident. Savings rates in the United States declined sharply in the 1970s and through most of the 1980s, despite lower marginal tax rates and higher real interest rates that should have encouraged more savings. In the 1980s, this trend spread to *every* developed nation, including the saving machine that is Japan.

The forces of progress are spent. Without them, living standards are stagnating. President Carter's much-derided "malaise" was a harbinger of this shift. The return to economic vitality that began in 1983, while temporarily masking the transition, was largely a reshuffling of resources. Millions of immigrants and women entered the work force, accounting for most of the resurgence. The rising number of families with two wage earners barely maintained household incomes, and only at the expense of parental child care and involvement in schools, housekeeping, volunteer work, and other services not measured by the economic statistics. Immigration provided the United States with some of its best workers, while depriving other nations of the same workers. Expanding the work force in this way raises measured output, just as a return to sixty-hour work weeks or child labor would, but only on a one-time, irreproducible basis. Untapped reservoirs of labor like nonworking wives of the 1950s and 1960s no longer exist.

The growth of the 1980s, welcome as it was, did not mark a sustainable return to progress. Productivity in the United States has been virtually unchanged since 1973. Output has increased not because of improved *efficiency* of labor or capital, but because of increased *amounts* of capital and, particularly, labor. This contributes little to the standard of living. Indeed, average weekly earnings in constant dollars have actually fallen slightly since 1973. These trends are utterly without precedent since these statistics have been compiled. Not even the Depression produced such a prolonged loss of economic momentum.

This measurable decline is both a symptom and a cause of an immeasurable but significant change in attitude. Americans are becoming less interested in progressing (i.e., producing more and better at lower cost) than in perpetuating the status quo or securing a larger slice of the existing pie. Businesses increasingly seek competitive advantage through legislation and litigation rather than investment and innovation: paid Senate lobbyists rose from a few hundred in 1960 to over 33,000 in 1990, and the number of attorneys nearly doubled in the 1980s alone. The EPA, FDA, and various other federal agencies pursue an objective of zero risk with little regard for the costs they impose on society. The explosion of the *Challenger*, after twenty-four consecutive successful shuttle flights, grounded all manned space missions by the United States for more than two years. The delay barely evoked comment; it was simple prudence, a matter of course given the tragedy. But contrast the early history of aviation, when thirty-one of the first forty pilots hired by the Post Office died in crashes within six years, with no suspension of service. Playing it safe has replaced the pioneering, enterprising, and risk-taking spirit traditionally associated with America.

The economic trends, having persisted through two decades, cannot be dismissed as transitory or cyclical phenomena or as statistical flukes. The sharply differing domestic policies of the Ford, Carter, Reagan, and Bush administrations virtually foreclose attempts to assign the blame to any particular political agenda. Indeed, international data preclude any uniquely American explanation. Every member nation of the Organization for Economic Cooperation and Development (OECD), including Japan, experienced declines in productivity gains in the 1980s compared to the 1970s, a fact conveniently omitted from lamentations over the supposed loss of U.S. competitiveness. No satisfactory explanation has been advanced. Experts, blinkered by their intense specialization, lack the multidisciplinary perspective needed to grasp these trends. Even with better understanding, the standard political and economic nostrums would scarcely alter the present direction. Policies designed to regain past glory only succeed in further sapping the forces of long-term progress: stimulating consumer demand discourages capital accumulation; trade measures disintegrate the world market. The current decline of material progress cannot be reversed.

Some social critics and environmental activists will initially rejoice at this news. Events will disappoint them. They identify progress with smog, traffic jams, and crass materialism, emphasizing the discomforts and dislocations inherent in all change to belittle the practical benefits and question even the idea of progress. The common thread in such criticisms is an intense sensitivity to the costs of economic growth coupled with a virtual disregard of its value. Progress cossets these critics, providing a life-style that enables them to take such a lofty, detached, and contemptuous attitude toward the mere means of existence. But the reality of slow growth will prove less pleasing than the prospect. The end of progress will create a zero-sum game, sharply narrowing the range of society's options. The preferences of privileged elites will not long hold sway when those preferences entail real sacrifice: loggers deprived of their livelihoods will reassert their priority over owls, and drivers with static incomes will refuse to spend more for cleaner vehicles. Grab and hold could become a prevalent attitude. The future will not conform to the "small is beautiful" world that some critics may envision.

The end of material progress will thus produce few winners. But as one form of progress ends, another begins that may more than compensate for the stagnation in living standards. Beginning early in the next century, people will enjoy vastly expanded intelligence and other abilities, finally escaping the natural limitations under which the species has labored since it first appeared.

Such predictions, commonly encountered only in the realm of science fiction, also provoke a skeptical response borne of long experience. Two centuries of otherwise pervasive progress have left intrinsic human traits and abilities almost untouched. Machines add strength and speed, houses and clothing provide warmth and protection, telephones extend the range of communication, civilization cushions and enriches life, but the species itself remains unchanged. Even medicine, the most intimate of technologies, merely strives to restore the body to its natural condition, not to change that condition. But current research establishes the feasibility of improving on innate human characteristics.

One such improvement will be to lengthen the life span. Scientists can "evolve" longer-lived animal strains in the laboratory by killing the offspring of all short-lived parents in each generation. They have also stretched the life spans of dozens of species 50 percent or more by restricting their food intake. These animals do not linger on in decrepit old age; they actually age less quickly. Underfed rats, for example, play, mate, resist disease, and learn new mazes long after their fully fed siblings have lapsed into rodent senescence. Tests on spider monkeys are now under way, and the preliminary results appear promising. The physiological and genetic findings from this research will allow direct intervention in the human aging process within a generation. Even children born during the next few years may reasonably expect to live decades longer than their parents.

This may be the least of the changes they will experience. The Human Genome Project is mapping and sequencing human chromosomes. That monumental compilation will begin a process leading to discovery of the genetic sources of exceptional mental abilities and other favorable traits. The DNA of acknowledged geniuses, both living and dead, will supply researchers with desired patterns. Genetic engineering techniques developed for research and conventional medical purposes promise the ability to select and ultimately to substitute and modify genes with precision at the finest level of detail. Genetic libraries for (re)producing desired and even superhuman traits on demand will follow automatically from these technologies.

Advances in neuroscience may provide an alternative route to extraordinary abilities. New tools are enabling researchers to identify some biological indicators of intelligence. For example, smart brains use less energy and conduct nerve signals faster and more uniformly than average brains. These correlations may prove to be effects rather than causes, but they open the prospect of medical treatments to enhance ability. Meanwhile, neurobiologists are painstakingly teasing out the details of brain cell function and the intricate networks that the cells form. Scientists have learned to culture brain cells using a newly discovered class of neurochemicals (nerve growth factors). Direct administration of such chemicals and nerve cell implants have enhanced learning and memory in monkeys and in human patients suffering from degenerative conditions of the brain. From an anatomical perspective, new radiological techniques and microscopic electrodes are providing detailed maps of brain activity and circuitry. Theories of memory formation and other higher mental functions are being actively investigated, although a synthesis remains elusive. As understanding of the processes grows, the ability to enhance them is likely to follow.

Biology is not the only option for exceeding natural human abilities. Chips with a million transistors and switching times measured in billionths of a second have vastly increased the power of computers. But they remain dependent and servile tools, precisely following detailed instructions provided by people to perform tasks assigned by people. Recent hardware, software, and design advances promise the ability to simulate ever larger reams of intelligence. The next chess champion of the world will be a computer. An experimental neural network system creates its own "rules" of English pronunciation simply from hearing a list of words spoken, while neural nets diagnose heart attacks better than trained emergency room physicians. The Microelectronics and Computer Consortium is now more than midway through its CYC project, which should allow computers to read and understand natural language and to add to their information bases with little or no human assistance. Ever-larger-scale semiconductor integration, optical computing, refinement of expert system designs, and other more familiar kinds of progress continue apace. Each of these developments will slightly enhance performance in some traditional computing tasks. Together, they promise something much more important—systems that will be capable of self-improvement, leading ineluctably to useful machine intelligence in diverse fields.

All this research is far more advanced than is widely appreciated. Machines will be unquestioned leaders in some fields within a generation. Children born in this decade may be receiving treatments to augment their intelligence by middle age. Their children will almost certainly be genetically or biologically engineered for improved brain function. This process will continue and accelerate in future generations, as enhanced minds and intelligent machines shun the well-worked and decreasingly fertile fields of material progress in favor of the fresh challenge of improving human abilities.

These developments will predictably generate opposition, which, just as predictably, the advancing tide will sweep away. The prevention of disease and other uncontroversial objectives will justify the basic research. After it is completed, the resulting knowledge will not be prohibitively expensive or difficult to use. The demand will be irresistible. Consider, for example, the current spending on cosmetics, clothing, and health clubs, which deliver just the *appearance* of youth. The appeal of real youth and longer life will be infinitely greater. An effective ban on any of these technologies is utterly fanciful, as the widespread illegal use of steroids by athletes convincingly demonstrates. Their known availability will trigger a cascade. Even assuming that most parents would prefer a world without genetic or biological enhancement, few would knowingly disadvantage their own children in order to exercise that preference. Any country even considering the possibility of outlawing these technologies would quickly be discouraged by the near certainty that other countries would press ahead. The instability of such a situation is evident. The existence of the knowledge will create a technological imperative, assuring its widespread use. Those nations (and individuals) that embrace this future will fare better than those that attempt to renounce it.

Both the end of material progress and the transformation of human abilities are thus inevitable. Public awareness and political leadership would ease what promises to be a difficult passage. Despite occasional Luddite opposition, ordinary material progress has become a comfortable form of change for most people. Indeed, it provides hope to those unhappy with their immediate circumstances and minimizes class tension and other economic, social, and political frictions. The erosion of that bulwark against despair threatens a rise in factionalism. And the ability to remake and surpass the species will be anything but a soothing prospect to many people; the Frankenstein myth has been a recurrent plot among mankind's worst nightmares.

The current terms of public discourse provide scant grounds for optimism. Like generals always fighting the last war, politicians are planning for a future that is past. The immediate objective is to return to "normal" economic growth, which the United States has not experienced in twenty years and which is, in reality, forever lost. Any speculation about the longer-term potential of technology resembles a scene out of *Star Trek*, where sleek machines do wondrous things, many of which conveniently defy physical law, but the people have not changed. Even the token android is little more than a human with enhanced data storage and retrieval.

The real future will be a mirror image of that picture. The machines will surely differ from those of the present, but what they do, and how well they do it, will not have changed nearly to the same extent as in recent centuries. The people, on the other hand, will be so vastly improved as to defeat current understanding and probably imagination as well. Indeed, even using the word "people" to denote these beings is an anachronism. Within a century or two, genetic engineering will likely have changed our descendants so greatly as to prevent them from mating with humans in their present form, making them biologically a separate species.

The ancient Chinese had a curse: "May you live in interesting times." This cusp in the evolution of progress makes for very interesting times. Recognizing what these trends portend will not cause the problems to vanish. But it is the only option worth contemplating.

Rosabeth Moss Kanter, *Professor of Business Administration at Harvard Business School, studied idealistic communities for her Ph.D. in sociology. "In 1964, before the commune movement had taken new hold in America, I wrote my first paper on utopian communities, and that initial interest in alternatives to established society has changed my life. It focused my thought, research, teaching, and leisure time on the possibilities for social and personal reconstruction, as well as on exploring new models for human relations and social institutions." These excerpts are taken from her book* Commitment and Community: Communes and Utopias in Sociological Perspective *(1972).*

ROSABETH MOSS KANTER

A REFUGE AND A HOPE

Nothing short of everything will really do.
Aldous Huxley, *Island*
O God . . . our refuge and our hope.
Union Prayer Book

Utopia is the imaginary society in which humankind's deepest yearnings, noblest dreams, and highest aspirations come to fulfillment, where all physical, social, and spiritual forces work together, in harmony, to permit the attainment of everything people find necessry and desirable. In the imagined utopia, people work and live together closely and cooperatively, in a social order that is self-created and self-chosen rather than externally imposed, yet one that also operates according to a higher order of natural and spiritual laws. Utopia is held together by commitment rather than coercion, for in utopia what people want to do is the same as what they have to do; the interests of the individuals are congruent with the interests of the group; and personal growth and freedom entail responsibility for others. Underlying the vision of utopia is the assumption that harmony, cooperation, and mutuality of interests are natural to human existence, rather than conflict, competition, and exploitation, which arise only in imperfect societies. By providing material and psychological safety and security, the utopian social order eliminates the need for divisive competition or self-serving actions which elevate some people to the disadvantage of others; it ensures instead the flowering of mutual responsibility and trust, to the advantage of all.

Utopia, then, represents an ideal of the good, to contrast with the evils and ills of existing societies. The idea of utopia suggests a refuge from the troubles of this world as well as a hope for a better one. Utopian plans are partly an escape, as critics maintain, and partly a new creation, partly a flight *from* and partly a seeking *for*; they criticize, challenge, and reject the established order, then depart from it to seek the perfect human existence.

At a number of times in history, groups of people have decided that the ideal can become reality, and they have banded together in communities to bring about the fulfillment of their own utopian aspirations. Generally the idea of utopia has involved a way of life shared with others—and shared in such a way that the benefit of all is ensured. For the most part, the vision of utopia has been a vision of community, as captured in an old Hebrew song: "How good it is for brethren to dwell together in unity."

The ideal of social unity has led to the formation of numerous communes and utopian communities. These are voluntary, value-based, communal social orders. Because members choose to join and choose to remain, conformity within the community is based on commitment—on the individual's own desire to obey its rules—rather than on force or coercion. Members are controlled by the entire membership or by individuals they respect within the community rather than by outside agents or political forces. A commune seeks self-determination, often making its own laws and refusing to obey some of those set by the larger society. It is identifiable as an entity, having both physical and social boundaries, for it has a physical location and a way of distinguishing between members and nonmembers. It intentionally implements a set of values, having been planned in order to bring about the attainment of certain ideals, and its operating decisions are made in terms of those values. Its primary end is an existence that matches the ideals. All other goals are secondary and related to ends involving harmony, brotherhood, mutual support, and value expression. These ideals give rise to the key communal arrangement, the sharing of resources and finances.

The utopian community may also be a centralized, coordinating organization, often combining all of life's functions under one roof. Economic, political, social, and family life may all occur within the community and be coordinated by it. The community may be at the same time a domestic unit (large, extended family), a production unit (farm or business), a political order (village or town), and a religious institution. Unlike the larger society, all these functions are concentrated in one visible entity. And unlike monastic orders, which may serve the interests of a wider church community, or businesses, which are concerned with the interests of the market or of absentee owners such as stockholders, the commune operates to serve first and foremost its own members; any benefits it provides for the outside are generally secondary and based on the need to support its own. Finally, relations among members of the community are more important than are relations of members or the community to the outside world. For example, in the typical nonutopian, noncommunal organization, such as a business, the nature of the work may determine who becomes a member, whereas in the utopian community the nature of the people who are already members may determine what kind of work is performed. Maintaining the sense of group solidarity is as important as meeting specific goals.

From this definition it appears that a utopian community may have something in common with a family or primary group, with an organization, with geographically-defined community, and with a complete society, even though it differs from all of these. It can be as small as a family of six or seven members, like many contemporary communes, or as large as a village of a thousand or more, like some utopian communities of the past. . . .

THE LIMITS OF UTOPIA

Among the communes that are functioning today, each following its separate star, it's extremely doubtful if any will survive. But if any one of these, or any other that may come afterward, proves a single new thing to the remainder of civilization, then the entire communal movement will have shown itself a valid alternative approach to enhancing the essential humanness of man within a society.

William Hedgepeth, *The Alternative:*
Communal Life in New America

The utopian vision of the harmonious, integrated, loving community—the communal enclave of warm, close, supportive relationships—does not always occur according to scenario. Reality modifies the dream. But whether or not communes become permanent entities, legitimate and institutionalized "families" and settlements, they are important to examine and experience. The assumptions they make about what is possible and desirable in social life challenge the assumptions made by other sectors of American society. As experimental groups, they innovate with new forms of social organization, they imaginatively construct their own kind of collective being, and they strive for different and closer forms of human relationships. They attempt to repersonalize a society that they regard as depersonalizing and impersonal, making person-to-person relations the core of their existence. Regardless of what kind of reconstruction of macroinstitutions they envisage, communal utopians put their emphasis on the small, face-to-face primary group.

Utopian communities are not without their limitations. Historically it has taken particular kinds of social arrangements to sustain them—arrangements not considered equally desirable by everyone. The experience of nineteenth century communes as well as the forms and variety of contemporary utopian movements raise questions not only about the possibilities for utopia but also about its limits and costs.

Today communes are often the subject of heated discussion, for the idea of collective living arouses a wide range of strong emotions. In the process, many criticisms have been leveled at utopian communities, some more valid and deserved than others. The questions raised will increasingly trouble the inventors and innovators, theorists and researchers of the communal movement as they face the realities of life in America's complex, urban society.

Short-Lived or Sterile?

One major criticism reflects a belief that, despite evidence to the contrary, vital utopian communities are impossible. Critics argue that communes do not last over long periods of time, with most of them failing after only a short time, or that if they do survive, they immediately lose their vitality, institutionalizing static routines that become even less meaningful to later generations than they were to the first. This viewpoint involves a skepticism about the ability of communal orders to offer any solutions to the problems of society, suggested by its two somewhat contradictory premises: that communes cannot operate at all successfully over time, but that if they do work, they are sterile, unchanging, and by implication unsatisfactory. This is related to the argument that communes are only movements of withdrawal, which do not promote social change in the society at large.

The temporary quality of many communal ventures cannot be denied. In the past a large number dissolved while young. Some communes today deliberately form as temporary systems. Of these, some limit not only their projections for length of life but also their institutional scope; that is, members can maintain ties with other institutions while still belonging to the commune. One example is the small urban "family" commune living together while working outside. Harvey Cox [in *The Feast of Fools*, 1969] described this possibility for flexible, segmented involvement as an advantage of urban life, permitting some people to enter completely into a comprehensive community, while others can innovate and implement communal ideals in just one or two spheres.

Whether or not the group still constitutes a utopian community if it seeks to limit its scope both temporally and institutionally, given the fact that one utopian value is integration rather than fragmentation, some utopian thinkers would contend that the temporary quality of many communes is an advantage. It has been argued that the healthy community is one that can contemplate its own death when it no longer fulfills its members. According to this view, the very dissolution of a commune is a sign of its strength. A young woman in a political group in Washington once remarked, "Of course communes work—I'm in my fourth."

But the high mortality rate of American communes may indicate something other than a desire for mobile, dissolvable groups. It may indicate the difficulty of building viable communities that are sufficiently satisfying for members to be willing to invest themselves fully in support of the continued existence of the group. Some communes and utopian communities are temporary out of choice; others are short-lived because they do not organize in a way that builds commitment and fulfillment.

Even among those groups that officially claim to reject strong commitment and longevity, members' expectations may conflict, with some hoping that the group will continue and others eager to avoid long-range commitment. In a conversation at a New Mexican hippie commune, one member is reported to have said, "What we're doin', I suppose, is mainly just trying to live together and work out our lives." But another said, "I really don't see living here the rest of our lives, though, I don't know quite what exactly I'd like to be doin'." [W. Hedgepeth and D. Stock, *The Alternative*, 1970.] Such discrepancies often reflect the group's own confusion or ambivalence over its goals.

There is still much to be learned about the personal consequences of having a series of temporary relationships and a constant turnover in one's social network. Does it add variety and richness and enhance the ability to relate meaningfully to many different people, or does it eliminate the depth and sharing that comes from mutual commitment? Does it promote strength or insecurity? One question is whether communes are indeed a solution to the alienation suffered by American society if they do not provide long-term relationships. Bennett Berger pointed out, for example, that even though child care duties may be supposedly shared on a commune, ultimate responsibility still devolves on the mother, so that men find it easier to run off, leaving mother and children behind. The effects of this possibility on the child and the women are unclear.

Similarly, it is often demoralizing for a group—even the most "hang loose," "do your own thing" group—to face a continual turnover by losing members or to contemplate dissolution. It is too easy for those left behind to feel like failures, as I observed on one California commune, in that they failed to do whatever it might have taken to have kept the lost one. A member of Sunrise Hill also reported difficult feelings after many people had left at the end of the commune's first summer: "For those that remained, a fearful moment of truth came when we stood in that thinned group and recognized that it was, after all, just we few." [G. Yaswen, *Sunrise Hill*, mimeograph]. With a high turnover of members or rapid change of groups, the question occurs whether feelings of failure may be generated. This is an important area for investigation—how groups cope with the loss of members or with their own death, and how these situations affect the individuals in them. It is also important to learn about the consequences for intimacy, a major goal of many communes, when there is rapid turnover of relationships.

Another unresolved question is whether a group is still a utopian community, fulfilling utopian dreams, if it has a shifting membership, changing composition and even reshuffling or merging with other groups. Warren Bennis and Philip Slater argued that temporary relationships will probably be even more true of America of the future than they are today [*The Temporary Society*, 1968]. If this proves to be the case, then the chances for a group of people to constitute themselves as a utopian community and stay together for a substantial period of time may decline. But the decreased chance for endurance does not mean that some communal ventures, though temporary and short-lived, are not an important way to alleviate the loneliness and alienation symptomatic of the society or to redress economic imbalances through cooperative or socialist enterprises. At the very least, certain communes, like encounter groups, may help to educate people in the possibilities for alternative modes of living and relating. At most, a network of communes allowing for exchange of members may develop and survive.

Though many communes are short-lived, there have been a number of utopian communities in the past that lasted considerable periods of time with a relatively stable membership, and there are groups today, such as the Bruderhof, the Hutterites, Cedar Grove [New Mexico], and Koinonia Farm [Georgia], that have maintained themselves successfully over time. There are over 220 Israeli kibbutzim, the first founded in 1910. Synanon [California], too, is growing and flourishing, with a stable core of people for whom the community is both permanent home and career, as well as a number of people who come for a short period just to participate in the program of re-education. These communities, being far from temporary, prove that viable utopian communities are indeed possible. Any assessment of such communities thus depends on what the observer chooses to observe—the "failures" or the "successes."

But other critics maintain that the very success of a commune means that it loses vitality. They contend that life in a stable utopian community requires settling down to a challenge-free, boring, and placid existence. If a commune does manage to develop a viable social organization, the costs of such a victory, according to these critics, are sterility and a loss of excitement. The "perfection" of utopia means an end to change and struggle. Once utopia is attained, one has nothing more for which to strive. Even Margaret Mead, otherwise a supporter of utopia and communal life, commented that descriptions of heaven are always much less interesting than descriptions of hell ["Towards More Vivid Utopias," *Science*, 8 Nov. 1957]. And Wilbert Moore reported as the most frequent criticisms of utopias that they are unconscionably peaceable, millennialist, and static, missing the utility of conflict ["The Utility of Utopias," *American Sociological Review*, Dec. 1966].

The most vitriolic critic of utopian communities on these grounds was George Kateb in *Utopia and Its Enemies* [1963]. Condemning the nineteenth century communes as "depressing," he argued that any "perfect society" is ultimately unsatisfying. People need change, tension, and stimulation, conflict and war, to make life meaningful, he contended. People prefer not to be happy all the time. What Kateb pictured in the communes was a gray, lifeless, austere existence:

> Truly, what could be more depressing than the series of attempts to set up utopian communities in America in the nineteenth century? The coexistence of a community dedicated to an ideal of perfection and the great outside world could lead to nothing but a sense of isolation and strain in that community. Even to those living in the community, the quality of life inside had to be marked by artificiality and a feeling of *confinement*. The noble experiment had to conclude in a corrupting spiritual pride. The retreat from reality could not help becoming havens for neurotics; the life lived could not help being meager in texture and lacking in complexity. For all these reasons, these utopian communities can excite contempt.

Such contempt, however, is not supported by the evidence. It has not been shown that the levels of strain, artificiality, corruption, eccentricity, neurosis, or meagerness of life in nineteenth-century utopias were any greater than those in the outside world. There is, in fact, some evidence to support the opposite conclusion—that utopian communities may reduce some of the traumatic consequences of life in America. Joseph Eaton and Robert Weil found in their study of mental health among the Hutterites [*Culture and Mental Disorders*, 1955] that in many respects the Hutterites demonstrated fewer symptoms of pathology. Their reputation among physicians was one of relatively low manifestations of neurosis. Whereas Eaton and Weil found that their rate of psychosis was not lower than that of American society, the Hutterite communal organization offered an environment in which psychotics could be cared for without hospitalization. There is also impressionistic evidence that Oneida's systems of genetic mating (stirpiculture) and group child-rearing were at the least, not harmful to the adaptive growth to maturity of Oneida children, and at the most, they nurtured a group of people who later returned to Oneida after its dissolution as a commune to run it as a highly successful, well-managed business. Similarly, from research on the kibbutz comes evidence that kibbutz members have been leaders in Israeli society out of proportion to their numbers and that kibbutz children often became leaders in their army service.

The consequences of life in utopian communities for mental health, then, are far from negative, if indeed mental health criteria and labels such as "neurotic" and "eccentric" can even be applied to groups that challenge other definitions and criteria of the wider society. In fact, it is the commune's avoidance of pain rather than its experience of it that Kateb considered most artificial, stressful, confining, and spiritually corrupting. He championed the point of view that people can find fulfillment only in misery and conflict. This idea is underscored in Aldous Huxley's antiutopian novel *Brave New World* [1932] in a bit of dialogue in which the Savage, an outsider, refuses to become part of the utopian society in which all needs are met and gratification is only a drug away. He chooses pain over perfection:

> "In fact," said Mustapha Mond, "you're claiming the right to be unhappy."
>
> "All right then," said the Savage defiantly, "I'm claiming the right to be unhappy. Not to mention the right to grow old and ugly and impotent; the right to have syphilis and cancer; the right to have too little to eat; the right to be lousy; the right to live in constant apprehension of what may happen tomorrow; the right to catch typhoid; the right to be tortured by unspeakable pains of every kind."
>
> There was a long silence.
>
> "I claim them all," said the Savage at last.

The fact is, though literary utopias may pretend to eliminate pain or conflict, actual utopian communities have never succeeded in this respect. Some, both in the past and the present, have come together for ends compatible with the Savage's critique of the brave new world, that is, to be entitled to their own unhappiness, as much or as little as they chose; to protest, as many of today's communes do, someone else's definition of what is "good" for them; and to share collectively whatever suffering must be suffered and thereby reduce its impact.

The long-lasting communes of the past remained together through famines, floods, and fires; through successive migrations to new territories and the building of new communities; through persecution by their neighbors and agents of the wider society's morality (including a mob invasion of the Shakers); and through participation in social reform movements of the time. Creating a utopian group that is highly fulfilling and provides for all of a person's needs is not incompatible with that same group seeking adventure, challenge, or even struggle. The fixed or permanent social organization that is decried by critics of utopia—if any empirical group ever indeed becomes so internally rigid—still may interact as a unit with its environment in such a way as to promote or maintain challenge.

This helps to answer the question that many people ask about motivation in communal societies: why should anyone work in utopia? If one's welfare is ensured, why work? Kateb, for example, argued that utopias result in lowered exertion since they provide the blessings of life as one's due. The fact is that people work for causes and challenges beyond making sure they will eat or be paid. In a commune, they work to sustain the transcendent meaning of the community; they work because the effort may be intrinsically satisfying, may be chosen work; or they work because they are committed to the other people in the group and want, positively, to do their share to ensure the collective welfare and, negatively, to avoid the disapproval of people they love. Such a system does not operate perfectly, of course, and communal history is full of shirkers, idlers, and hangers-on. Contemporary communes in particular have this problem. But it would be interesting to undertake a study of the comparative rates of idleness and shirking and behind-the-scenes subversion in big bureaucracies versus utopian communities. To use one example where research has been done, the productivity of the Israeli kibbutzim has often been disproportionately higher than that of other kinds of agricultural ventures in Israel [Kateb, *Utopia*].

Even if there can be external challenges and higher purposes, the question remains whether life inside a utopian community necessitates settling for a stable, placid, boring, austere, and lifeless existence, isolated from the rest of society. Need a commune be, as Kateb suggested, "a closed world forever without change"? Given the large number and variety of communal ventures, the answer depends both on the characteristics of the commune in question and on the point of view of the observer, for what is boring and lifeless to one person may be invigorating to another. Some communes, such as the more austere religious communities of the past, essentially cut themselves off from the changes and developments of the society around them. Partly from choice on religious grounds, partly of necessity in order to survive, such communities sometimes form tight little islands in the midst of society. Their children often leave to seek freedom and opportunity elsewhere. Even some of the new generation of hippie communes wish to disengage themselves from progress, change, and complexity in a similar way, by moving on to farms or into the woods and creating a simple survival culture. But other utopian communities have tried to find ways to incorporate change and create dynamic, exciting environments in which new elements can be introduced while maintaining the sense of a warm, loving community. Oneida was decidedly experimental in this sense. Neither the kubbutzim nor Synanon nor Twin Oaks today cut themselves off from the rest of society; rather, they search for ways to adopt new ideas and new technology to their communal ethics.

The issue of austerity and sterility is even more complicated, for just a simple look at a commune can be deceptive. A group providing no outlets for the release or expression of tension and strong emotion could not survive for long. All continuing human groups strike a balance between asceticism and ecstacy, and their social practices swing between the two, just as commitment involves both giving up and getting [P. Rieff, *The Triumph of the Therapeutic*, 1968]. Groups whose most novel or striking characteristics are their asceticism may have ecstacy lurking close behind, and vice versa. The Shakers and Oneida, two nineteenth-century communes whose life styles superficially appear quite different and seem to represent the two opposite ends of the continuum, are cases in point. The celibate Shakers, who worked in silence all day long and gave up such vestiges of worldliness as art, burst out in ecstatic fervor every evening in their ritual, rivaling any modern encounter group in both imagined and realized sensuality. The free-loving Oneidans, accused by the surrounding society of "wanton licentious-ness," in some respects led a life of rigorous self-control, exemplified by male continence in which men refrained from ejaculating. In today's communes are also seen swings between asceticism and ecstacy—the asceticism of with-drawal from the evil city to an untouched piece of nature, perhaps giving up meat, cars, television, electricity, or other creature comforts, and taking on difficult physical labor, combined with the ecstacy of freer sexual contact, nudity, and drugs.

To the extent that communities move back and forth between asceticism and ecstacy—as the Shakers did by working hard one moment, and the next abandoning themselves to frenzy—they may be generating cycles of renewal for themselves rather than boring routines. Members of one contemporary urban commune agree that their exhausting work during the day and their joyful encounters at night provide a rhythm and a renewing cycle to their lives. This issue, too, requires further investigation.

The argument about sterility and a lack of vitality in communes is related to another criticism—that utopian communities are anti-intellectual, often having a bias against art, reason, science, and technology. Many critics regard utopias as opposing technological development in particular, which they equate with progress and forward motion. Although communes often promise to reintegrate parts of a person, to use all of his capacities, and to cre-ate a group of "whole persons" relating to "whole persons," there has in fact been a tendency for communal groups to value the body more than the mind. The return to the land characteristic of many full-scale communities has meant that physical labor assumes a more legitimate place than intellectual effort. The farmer-intellectuals of Brook Farm in the last century found that the life of the mind and of art did not blend well with the demands of agriculture for sweat and toil. The asceticism and artistic endeavors. [In *Coop-erative Communities at Work*, 1947] Henrik Infield wrote of the Hutterites:

"[They] want to live a simple life wherein all intellectual sophistication is pro-hibited. They show little or no interest in the fine arts. They read no fiction, see no shows, hear no orchestras, draw no pictures. Even history must not be studied, for it might bring the martial sounds of the outside world into this peaceful, purposely colourless society." But this kind of austerity is unusual, and more commonly communes incorporate art, music, and entertainment.

Utopian groups have more often been characterized by a bias against science or intellect rather than one against art. Many small, rural hippie communes today reject modern science and technology as well as intel-lectual effort. Encounter groups, too, stress the expression of feelings over reason or analysis, to the extent that they have been accused of being anti-intellectual. The American "counterculture" in general has promoted a return to mysticism and spiritualism through adopting such systems as astrology. It is natural, however, that many communal groups have devalued the intellectual, for groups tend to value what they need the most. Hence, land-based ventures subsisting at a simple level, organized around the soil and requiring constant physical effort, will value physical labor. Communes dependent on a suspension of disbelief and on ideological commitment, whose members must adopt wholeheartedly a set of not-always-rational or scientific principles, will value faith and unquestioning acceptance. Thera-peutic groups attempting to make people open and vulnerable and sensitive to one another will value direct expressions of emotion. All groups concerned with struggling for their creation and survival will value doers more than thinkers. Creativity in such groups often has a practical cast, as in Shaker artistry that was channeled into making sturdy, simple furniture. The intel-lectual who sees several sides to every issue may also be out of place in a utopian community. Generally, the only "philosopher" permitted is the charismatic leader, who enunciates the guiding principles that give the group its focus. He is the modern equivalent of the "philosopher-king" described in Plato's Republic.

Though scientific and intellectual analysis have often had little place in utopian communities, and though the body and soul have often been devel-oped to the exclusion of the mind, this condition has been for the most part a reaction to a society characterized by the opposite extreme. Moreover, there have been notable exceptions. Oneida stressed education and intellectual life and sent many of its children to universities. The life of the mind need not be incompatible with communal existence if it is well integrated into the fabric of the community. The wider issue of the effect of utopian communities on intellectuality and creativity is still largely uninvestigated.

Life in communal groups need not be unchanging or incompatible with social change. As planned or predicted societies, utopian communities are not necessarily unsuited to existence in a rapidly changing society, for what is planned may be a process that can remain despite shifting content. The process of discussion, of reflection, of criticism and feedback, and of decision-making can enable a group to incorporate new elements and engage in continual renewal. This is a challenge for the future—to build commitment to process rather than structure.

The Issue of Relevance

Another major criticism of communes deals with their social significance and relevance. The issue concerns the relevance of utopian communities to the rest of society, and the number of people for whom they actually provide an alternative. Historically, most communal groups have maintained strong boundaries and have been concerned almost exclusively with life inside the community rather than with the outer world. For this reason many people consider utopias to be escapist or withdrawal movements, and many even accuse commune members of evading their social responsibilities. By retiring from established society, they are doing nothing to correct the problems which afflict that society.

Although this tendency may have been true of communities of the past, it is probably less true of present-day attempts. Synanon manifests great social concern, and in fact, by virtue of establishing a strongly bounded community, a "monastic" enclave within the urban jungle, it may be serving a very vital function for America by helping large numbers of drug addicts who are not helped elsewhere. The Shakers have always provided a home for orphans. Other utopian communities address themselves to important social problems as well. Camp Hill Village cares for the mentally retarded; Koinonia, New Communities, Inc., in Southwest Georgia, and other rural cooperative communities devote themselves to problems of rural poverty. In many ways the intense love and care, the close coordination of production and consumption, the participation in and sharing of power, the integration of home and work, and the elimination of private property often characteristic of fully developed utopian communities make them well suited to attacking problems of therapy, of integration and incorporation of minority groups and women, and of poverty. The stress on cooperation and self-help makes the communal venture a good setting for grass-roots social change—change from the bottom of society up, change that operates by people organizing themselves.

Menachem Rosner pointed out [*Communitarian Experiments*, mimeograph, 1970] that one of the differences between the Israeli kibbutzim and many utopian communities in the United States is that the kibbutz movement does not remain isolated from the rest of Israeli society. Martin Buber considered this one of the great strengths of the kibbutz movement, and in his book on utopia [*Paths in Utopia*, 1958] he referred to the kibbutz as "an experiment that did not fail." The fact that over two hundred kibbutzim, though of varying ideological persuasions, have joined together in the Kibbutz Federation gives the movement the power of numbers and organization, which increases its significance as an alternative institution in a way not possible for isolated communal ventures. At one time about a third of the members of Knesset, the Israeli parliament, came from kibbutzim, so that the movement also had political significance. It is possible, therefore, that if communal ventures can combine into politically and socially significant units, they may have the potential to bring about social reform and to perform valuable change functions for the rest of society.

Yet it is still true that up to the present, American communes have not done much to change the society at large. For their members they may provide an intensely participatory group in which power is equitably shared, but they do not affect the power structure of the surrounding society. Internally they may become totally cooperative or socialist, effecting a truly equitable distribution of goods, but still do nothing to change the inequitable resource allocation and income distribution in American society. They may offer intensely loving relationships within a small group, but they do not erase the hatred, violence, and conflict between peoples that exist outside their boundaries. They have contributed to culture (the Shaker songs, dances, and crafts) but not to politics. Like Koinonia, communes are generally isolated havens of peace and cooperation. Utopians would argue that their usefulness is as a model for others, and that by building the kinds of relations they value among a small number of people, they prove to the rest of the world that utopia is possible. When the rest of society comes to recognize the worth of the communal model and begins to adopt its practices, utopians argue, the macroinstitutions of society will indeed change.

This dream was held in particular by nineteenth-century utopians like Robert Owen, whose communal village of New Harmony was to be an example for the whole world to follow. Similarly, the Oneidans regarded their community as a "shining example" of the better world to come. Though Oneida survived much longer than New Harmony, which failed dramatically after two years, none of the nineteenth century utopias had significant influence on American society. They were communal curiosities, swimming against the great tide of industrialization and urbanization. Groups today incorporating utopian ideas—from encounter groups to communes to New Towns like Columbia, Maryland—have a greater chance of persuading and changing by example, partly because they are so much more numerous than in the last century, partly because the mass media and instant communication make them more visible, partly because of the stronger need for them, and partly because they exist in so many different forms and varieties, to almost all of which planners and architects of the social environment are giving serious attention. There are nevertheless vast segments of the society still relatively untouched by the search for what, after all, remains primarily a white middle-class utopian vision, pursued mostly by those unfulfilled by affluence who turn to their emotions for salvation.

Involved with the concern that utopian communities are not relevant to social change on a large scale is the issue of size. Viable American utopian communities of the past had a modal size of about two hundred members—large enough to offer some variety, but small enough to manage easily. At one time the Shakers had six thousand members, but these were organized into eighteen villages located in different parts of the country. Kibbutz planners indicate that if a kibbutz becomes larger than a thousand, many problems ensue. The Hutterites have over ten thousand members, but they too are divided into villages of about one hundred each, and when any one village grows too large, another is started. Most extended-family communes in America have about eight to fifteen members, with the largest verging on thirty. Encounter groups and other growth communities typically consist of one to four groups of twelve each.

Some critics assert that it is no longer realistic to place hopes for utopia on the small communal ventures that, as self-contained societies, encompass only the tiniest fraction of the world's population and often turn their collective backs on the global village. Even at the turn of the century, utopian thinkers criticized the communitarians as isolationist, arguing that utopia lay in large- rather than small-scale social reconstruction, which aimed at total societies rather than villages, or even, as H.G. Wells wrote, at the planet itself: "No less than a planet will serve the purpose of a modern utopia." By the 1960s, Robert Boguslaw [*The New Utopian*, 1965] was referring to the systems engineers engaged in large-scale, computerized social planning as "the new utopians." Whereas such concern for macrosocial reconstruction is appropriate in an urban age of large and complexly interrelated populations, its relevance to the utopian community is questionable. Its aims and ideals may not be translatable from groups of twenty or two hundred people to new cities or towns of upwards of ten thousand. The utopian community—never very large at most—may not be able to survive the transition from small group to urban community, from isolated retreat to complex society. Perhaps it cannot serve the greater numbers that new towns and other value-oriented community ventures are called upon to serve.

If the commune gets much larger than a few hundred members, its organization must change. Georg Simmel pointed out [*The Sociology of Georg*

Simmel, ed. K.H. Wolff, 1964] that pure socialistic societies have been possible only in very small groups, having failed in larger ones. In writing on the significance of numbers for social life, he stated: "The principle of socialism—justice in the distribution of production and reward—can easily be realized in a small group and . . . can be safeguarded there by its members. The contribution of each to the whole and the group's reward to him are visible at close range; comparison and compensation are easy. In the large group they are difficult, especially because of the inevitable differentiation of its members, of their functions and claims." In other words, as a group, even a utopian group, gets larger, it increases in complexity, differentiation, distance between members, and potential for inequality. Only the division of labor, according to Simmel and other theorists, can provide the interdependence to integrate a large group; but such a division of labor may give rise to the specialization and separation that are antithetical to communal ideals. Other social scientists argue that these same communal ideals, even if they could survive in a complex, highly-differentiated urban community, may not be particularly desirable over large populations. Homogeneity may be a commitment-building asset in a small commune, but heterogeneity and diversity are exciting components of urban life. Full participation and close contact are laudatory in a communal group; these same practices may be unwieldy, inefficient, and sometimes frustrating in very large communities, or they may not provide the same sense of political ownership, involvement, closeness, and emotional support that they do in small groups. It is clear, in any event, that communes cannot be built on the scale of urban communities, or even of component parts of such communities, such as neighborhoods, merely by retaining the communitarian social institutions viable for populations of two hundred and simply increasing the number of people. Larger size necessitates differences in social organization that may violate utopian ideals.

Perhaps utopian communities are relevant for very large urban populations if that large number is divided into rather small units, each of which becomes the communal enclave. But then questions arise of intergroup coordination and cooperation that have never been addressed in the prior history of utopian experiments, and which are today being addressed by the Kibbutz Federation in only a limited way, as compared to the vast and complex American urban existence. There are no answers in the experience of utopian communities of the past or present to the problem of building large and complex structures out of very small ones—especially when the small ones may need their distinctiveness and identity in order to survive as close communities. In fact, history suggests that the process by which large social systems are constructed out of small, intimate ones is the very process by which Gesellschaften (societies or complex organizations or cities) are created out of Gemeinschaften (close, family-like communities). How communal and utopian ideals can be translated to large-sized units is therefore a difficult question, one that will be faced often by social planners of the future.

One answer to the question of size may be the same as that for acquiring political significance—a federation of small communes. Many communes in union have the potential to create cooperative facilities and organizations that are suitable to urban life, such as schools, day care centers, food cooperatives, or shared enterprises that employ commune members, while at the same time preserving the small size of each "family." Several such federations have been begun: in northern California an attempt was made by several communes to build a free school; in Vermont a health collective services area communes; in Boston a federation of twenty communes has operated a food cooperative and a commune-matching service. Still another Boston group has an arrangement with New Hampshire farm communes to produce organic food for urban communes. There is much promise in these cooperative ventures, but also some difficulty. The Israel kibbutzim could federate because of the many shared values among them, and because they always saw themselves as part of a larger movement; but even so, there are four separate kibbutz movements of varying ideological persuasions. Commune federations creating viable alternative institutions will have to work on the problems of developing common values and goals among communes and of dealing with possible conflicts. How to build intergroup cooperation without bureaucratization or centralized control by a federation will be a major issue for the future.

Finally, critics assert that utopian communities are insulated from many of the realities of life in the wider society, while at the same time being highly dependent on the existence of that society. They contend that utopian communities can exist only as a counterculture within a society organized on very different principles, but which can make available to the commune goods and services it cannot provide for itself. Many communes today reject technology but benefit from its products. Personal growth groups can create close, warm, loving relations just because they avoid dealing with power relations or with decision-making issues that create strain in relations outside encounter groups. There is also some truth to the argument that utopian groups need to have the larger society to fight against or complain about, in order to coalesce around a shared rejection. It is a social psychological canon that extra-group conflict heightens intragroup cohesiveness, that having an external enemy gives a group added strength. It is unknown how many utopian communities have survived in fact because they were persecuted, but enmity of some kind with the outside society has been a fact of life for practically every utopian community on record.

Some of these criticisms of utopian communities today stem from the perceived limitations of utopian experiments. Others reflect skepticism that the small, close, homogeneous, loving community can have anything but a deviant place in a highly technological, diverse urban society. Paul Goodman has argued, however, that utopian dreams should be retained, with a new community model, more similar to the kibbutz than to American communities, substituted:

> In our era, to combat the emptiness of technological life, we have to think of a new form, the conflictful community. Historically, close community has provided warmth and security, but it has been tyrannical, antiliberal, and static (conformist small towns). We, however, have to do with already thoroughly urbanized individuals with a national culture and a scientific technology. The Israeli kibbutzim offer the closest approximation. Some of them have been fanatically dogmatic according to various ideologies, and often tyrannical; nevertheless, their urban Jewish members, rather well educated on the average, have inevitably run into fundamental conflict. Their atmosphere has therefore been sometimes unhappy but never deadening, and they have produced basic social inventions and new character-types. Is such a model improvable and adaptable to cities and industrial complexes? Can widely differing communities be accommodated in a larger federation? How can they be encouraged in modern societies? These are utopian questions.
>
> [*Utopian Essays and Practical Proposals*, 1964]

The utopian questions Goodman raised cannot yet be answered, because despite all the debates on communes and utopias, there has been little systematic research addressed to these critical issues. . . .

The Importance of Utopias and Communes

Some of the criticisms directed against utopian communities are concerned with valid social, political, and philosophical issues in the life of communal orders. Others, however, stem from the American ideology rooted in a Puritan conscience, which values pain over gratification and regards deprivation and suffering as prime human motivators; which prefers "progress" and linear movement forward to cyclical activity; which values change for its own sake; which considers movements that lack immediate or apparent social utility to the wider society as "escapist"; and which views the separateness and isolation of the individual as superior to close group relationships. Not only does communal life challenge many of these assumptions, but the current movement may have some impact on reshaping them.

In any human group there is a gap between what works or has functional or organizational value, and what is desirable or has personal or social value. Utopian communities attempt to narrow this gap between the practical and the ideal, but they are not always successful. Measures that some communes have found to be practical, their critics do not feel are ideal. Methods that other communes chose as ideal were pragmatically impossible. The life of communes, therefore, like other groups, has its limits and costs as well as its benefits and advantages. Utopian communities are not the answer to everything. They are difficult to create, even more difficult to sustain. They exact a dedication and an involvement that many people find unappealing. They sometimes have shortcomings that make them fail of the perfection they promise. But as thoughtful, concerned people have discovered, they do supply partial answers. Erich Fromm, for example, [in *The Sane Society*, 1955] described communal orders as one of the roads to sanity that will reassert the dignity of humanity.

Utopian communities are in fact possible, within limits. Even though they may provide less than they promise, communes and alternative communities are increasing in number today as more and more Americans seek more fulfilling social relations. Most of these new ventures will probably not last very long, but as rapidly as some communes dissolve, others spring up. The impact of communes and new communities on American society cannot be predicted, but it is no longer possible to regard them merely as interesting aberrations. As an independent movement, they may be difficult to sustain in this society, but they will undoubtedly affect the future organization of the family, of religion, of work, and of therapy. Their existence has raised a new set of options for Americans, which may influence expectations about the quality of life. For example, children reared in communal ventures, even for part of their lives, may grow up desiring different life styles and social institutions than do those raised in isolated nuclear families [in, for example, B.M. Berger and B. Hackett "Child-Rearing Practices of the Communal Family," report to NIMH, 1970].

Utopian communities are important not only as social ventures in and of themselves but also as challenges to the assumptions on which current institutions are organized. The work organization of nineteenth-century groups, for example, with its job rotation, communal work efforts, mutual criticism, shared ownership, equality of compensation, participatory decision-making, infusion with spiritual values, and integration with domestic life, may provide alternative models for contemporary work organizations. Nineteenth-century communes are also a rich source of ideas for developing decentralized communities in which production and consumption as well as domestic and economic life are closely linked. Synanon and other communes dealing with societal outcasts offer one alternative to mental hospitals and prisons. Koinonia represents an alternative model for dealing with rural poverty and racial tension. The Shakers, Oneida, Amana, and the kibbutzim in Israel offer models for the alternative organization of highly efficient but cooperative agricultural or industrial enterprise. Small communes are alternatives to the isolated nuclear family. Therapeutic communities based on utopian notions are alternatives to traditional one-to-one, pathology-oriented therapies. The utopian community itself represents a model for a different kind of community organization, one from which community planners can derive a useful set of options.

The importance of considering the potential for utopias thus transcends the more limited issue of whether or not individual communes work. Utopian visions of social reconstruction supply an antidote to the pervasive assumption that "sick" or deviant individuals are both the source and the symptom of social problems, and that the individual must therefore be changed. Utopian thinking and experimentation are aimed at structural reform, at the creation of new social worlds or communities where the old problems no longer arise. Social problems, according to this view, are a function of structural defects in society and can be solved only by constructing a new society or by reshaping social institutions. Although some utopian experiments are more successful than others, and some succeed in eliminating particular problems only to introduce others, the mode of thinking that goes into the invention of a utopian community should be encouraged. It strives to implement ideals of a better way of living and relating, to consider options and alternatives, to become structurally inventive, and to experiment with the creation of wholly new social worlds. Utopian communities are society's dreams.

Regardless of their form or stability, today's communes, like those of the past, tend to reflect, by their very formation, a romantic, optimistic, utopian vision of human potential. They believe that by living together, people can overcome loneliness; by generating and respecting shared dreams, life can become more meaningful; by creating small, cooperative, group-run communities, individuals can gain a sense of personal control; and by returning to the simple, uncomplicated, "organic" sources of sustenance, basic human satisfactions can be achieved. A communal vision assumes the best of people: that they are willing to sacrifice and share, and that they can work out their differences so as to live together in harmony, peace, and love. As John Leonard expressed it in 1971: "The romantic notion of the perfectibility of man is really all we have to sustain us, no matter how illusory it may prove to be. . . . The rest is rhetoric, and the romantics have the best rhetoric."

Tom Athanasiou *runs an electronic publishing group in California and has been active in environmental politics for more than two decades. In* Divided Planet, 1996 *(published as* Slow Reckoning *in the UK), he declared that only radical economic and social changes could alter the planetary divide between rich and poor, between developed and developing nations. Unless the balance was righted, disaster was inevitable. These excerpts are taken from two chapters in that book. While Athanasiou feels great personal empathy towards the "Greens," he believes they are reaching the end of their "alert function." The global agenda he advocates is a truly daunting one.*

TOM ATHANASIOU

APOCALYPTICS

"Radical Environmentalism"

> *Two Legs Bad! Four Legs Good!*
> *Two Legs Bad! Four Legs Good!*
> *Two Legs Bad! Four Legs Good!*
> Rally chant, Redwood Summer, Fort Bragg, California, 1991.
> (And, of course, Orwell's *Animal Farm*.)
> Ironic intent unclear.

During the 1980s, with the environmental mainstream visibly stalled, a new "radical environmentalist" opposition turned away from legislative maneuvering to invent a new kind of *very* direct action—"monkeywrenching" bulldozers and "spiking" trees, camping high in ancient redwoods threatened with clear-cutting, and even shooting "slow elk" (cows) caught grazing in national parks. Earth First! stands out in the history of those times, for through its media-savvy irreverence it was able to put the corrupt management of the U.S. Forest Service, and the imperative of preserving biodiversity, into political play in a way that the environmental establishment had never dreamed to do. Like the early Greenpeace and Sea Shepherd before it, Earth First!, motivated by a rough-and-ready realism and a desire to value nature above all compromise, put a powerful new green activism into motion.

Unfortunately, Earth First! was in all ways a product of its times. Brave enough to face truths that most people shrank from, it was also—with its weakness for Malthusian horror stories and its knee-jerk reaction of the left tradition—squarely in the main line of ecoapocalypticism. Its turn toward deep ecology, and its desire (as Dr. Seuss put it in *The Lorax*) to "speak for the trees," came packaged with a frustration that deepened into green fundamentalism and flirted (and more) with self-hatred and misanthropy. Its fate, and the fate of the ideas it came to be associated with, thus make important cautionary tales.

Earth First!'s unraveling was announced to the world on May 1, 1987, when "Population and AIDS"—an article written by one Christopher Manes, right-wing deep ecologist extraordinaire, under the pseudonym "Miss Ann Thropy"—appeared in the *Earth First! Journal*. The article argued the classical

Malthusian line that human population growth is the root cause of the ecological crisis, but this, obviously, was not news. That came when, with a stunning, self-satisfied consistency, Manes asserted that "if radical environmentalists were to invent a disease to bring human population back to ecological sanity, it would probably be something like AIDS." Seeing no other way to stop the "biological meltdown" than by sharply reducing the human population, Manes observed that AIDS was ideal for the job because "it only affects humans," and that, "[as] radical environmentalists, we can see AIDS not as a problem, but as a necessary solution." [See S. Zakin, *Coyotes and Town Dogs*, 1993.]

There was, not surprisingly, a storm of protest. But Manes soon returned to justify himself. On December 22, in the same journal, he wrote that a die-off in human population was inevitable, one way or another, and while it would inevitably cause terrible suffering, it was still to be welcomed because it "will mean the end to the industrial tyranny which controls every aspect of our lives, which determines how we work and where we live and even what we think."

This is a dark apocalypticism, as brutal and arrogant as Christian millenarianism. Nature stands in for God, but she is as hard as ever was old Jehovah. Her retribution is strong but just. The chosen few will be redeemed by their survival and, as Manes explains in *Green Rage: Radical Environmentalism and the Unmaking of Civilization* [1990] live lives defined by "the simple ecological modesty of primal society." The way forward is back to the garden, "back to the Pleistocene."

Most radical environmentalists objected to Manes's fond words for AIDS, but they were hobbled in their efforts to denounce him by their general sympathy with his posture, if not all his conclusions. Earth First! cofounder Dave Foreman was quick to disavow Manes's excesses, but has made some injudicious statements himself. He once told Bill Devall, coauthor of *Deep Ecology*, that "the worst thing we could do in Ethiopia is to give aid—the best thing would be to just let nature seek its own balance, to let the people there just starve." [Quoted in R. Scarce, *Eco-Warriors*, 1990.] On another occasion, Foreman explained the roots of his pessimism [Manes, *Green Rage*, p. 232]:

> There is no way to take five billion people in the world today, with the worldview they have, and the economic and industrial imperatives they live under, and turn it into a sustainable Earth-harmonious culture. That's just not going to happen. What is going to happen is that the system is going to collapse of its own corruption. The next several decades are not going to be a very pleasant time to be alive.

It must be stressed that these words express not malevolence but despair. In a 1990 open letter of resignation from the Earth First! movement, written with his partner Nancy Morton, Foreman made his beliefs and their pedigree clear [*Earth First! Journal*, Sept. 1990]:

> Yes, we do believe that overpopulation is a fundamental problem. William Catton in *Overshoot* restates Malthus's dictum in ecological terms as "the biotic potential of any species exceeds the carrying capacity of its habitat." We believe that human overpopulation has led to overshooting the carrying capacity of the Earth and will result in a major ecological crash. We do not think that believing this means that one is racist, fascist, imperialist, sexist or misanthropic even if it is politically incorrect for cornucopians of the Left, Right or Middle.

Radical environmentalists are in a fix. Unable to accept the solaces of either techno-optimism or political resistance, they are left with only the mock-heroic posture of the beautiful loser. Thus, while radical environmentalism played a crucial role in the 1980s, it is difficult to believe that it, or anything like it, will again make a decisive difference. There are many reasons for this, but chief among them is that Malthusian pessimism is so debilitating a hobble.

Thus, Earth Firsters, too, are adapting to the new world, either by embracing expansive new social agendas and thus ceasing to be "radical environmentalists" proper [see *Defending the Earth*, 1991], or by digging in their heels and embracing apocalyptics as politics by other means. This second road, by the way, is not without its political theory, though it is rarely articulated. The Australian John Young is an exception. He writes: "The hope is that when the crisis comes . . . there will be enough converts to the role of ecological sanity to take advantage of the situation. This apocalyptic tradition has much in common with the earlier Doomsday tradition of the 1960s, based as it is on the fantasy of standing alone in the smoking ruins, having been right all along." [*Sustaining the Earth*, 1997.]

Malthusianism, the radicalism of those without hope, is always a bad business. It is also, and this is true of other rigid, all-explaining ideologies, an invitation to stupidity. We may not be able to imagine the social reforms that will allow the establishment of a stable, ecological society, but before we define the problem as population and imagine that AIDS will solve it, we might do a bit of research. Worst-case projections have another 100 million people being infected by AIDS by the end of the millennium, but in that same time almost ten times as many children will be born. Paul Kennedy is right to say that, in the more likely future, "Africa's overall population would still be growing rapidly, therefore, but in the midst of an appalling scene in which millions of people were dying of disease." [*Preparing for the Twenty-First Century*.]

In the face of such a world as this, we would like to ask Lenin's old question: What is to be done? Unfortunately, it is difficult, these days, to do so with hope of an answer that is both clear and convincing. Philip Raikes explained why in his study of African famine, *Modernizing Hunger* [1988]. Impending tragedy demands practicality, but, "it becomes increasingly difficult to say what are practical suggestions when one's research tends to show that what is politically feasible is usually too minor to make any difference, while changes significant enough to be worthwhile are often unthinkable in practical political terms."

Thus, despair. Instead of an impossible practicality we dream of deliverance by catastrophe. We reinvent old stories, with plots dominated by necessity and rough justice. William Ophuls, in his 1977 green Hobbesian classic *Ecology and the Politics of Scarcity*, wrote that ecological crisis makes "the individualistic basis of society"—"inalienable rights, the purely self-defined pursuit of happiness," and "liberty as maximúm freedom of action"—all "problematic," and concluded that "democracy as we know it cannot conceivably survive." His solution (of course he has one) depends on a class of "ecological guardians" who would "possess the esoteric knowledge" needed to run a "complex steady-state society." Christopher Manes, for his part, takes a postsixties route and proposes to avoid altogether the need for hard choices by denying complexity and returning to the Stone Age.

These two visions share a tradition of political despair. Their differences are cultural, generational, even aesthetic. Both are dreams, not strategies, and both products of a school of thought that can properly be called Cold War environmentalism. Both tell us that adequate changes in the real historical world, the world of power and politics, are impossible. Both articulate an abstract model that we will all be forced to follow for the good of the ecosystem. In the end, both come to illustrate the wisdom of an old critique of apocalyptic radicalism—easily frustrated, it easily degenerates into a coercive utopianism that cares more for its own prejudices than for sober confrontation with reality.

There's no good reason to expect that we'll soon see a political opening encouraging enough to push pessimism from the stage. Radical environmentalism and its cousins—ecocentric philosophies that allow humanity no place in nature, reductionist technology-bashing, eco-primitivism of all varieties—will likely haunt the green movement for years to come. They are the shadows of its political failure.

Worse, volunteers have stepped forward to blame radical environmentalism for that failure and, by strategic caricature, to imply that in the worst excesses of green fundamentalism they have found the dark secret of the entire movement. Martin W. Lewis, the academic author of *Green Delusions:*

An Environmentalist Critique of Radical Environmentalism (1992), was the pathbreaker, painting it as "an ill-conceived doctrine that has devastating implications for the global ecosystem," and making much of the claim that its "ideas are beginning to lead the environmental movement towards self-defeating political strategies, preventing society from making the reforms it so desperately needs."

This is nonsense, if only because radical environmentalism is old news. The excesses and dangers of deep green culture are obvious. When Father Thomas Berry, in his widely praised *The Dream of the Earth*, tells us, "We are an affliction of the world, its demonic presence. We are a violation of the Earth's most sacred aspects," he hardly encourages clear thinking or bold new political departures [quoted in M. Bookchin's "Will Ecology Become 'the Dismal Science?' " *The Progressive*, Dec. 1991]. And Lewis's particular concern—revealing the much-idealized ecological "purity" or primal societies as a myth—is an ugly job that must be done . . . .

Since *Green Delusions*, the literary marketplace has evolved. Richard Preston, searching for a rousing ending for his bestselling *The Hot Zone* [1994], revived the spirit of Miss Ann Thropy by painting "AIDS, Ebola and any number of other rainforest agents" as evidence that "the earth is mounting an immune response against the human species." Meanwhile, new titles—Paul R. Gross and Norman Levitt's *Higher Superstition* [1994] is a notable example, as is Gregg Easterbrook's momentously sloppy and Panglossian *A Moment on the Earth* [1995]—have stepped forward to attack both green "radicalism" and "pessimism" (which are typically treated as equivalents), and to tell us that realism lies in optimism, rationalism, moderation, science, and the unimpeded logic of the market. Like Lewis, they have their points, but like him they both caricature radicalism and avoid the real problem of "pessimism"—it is more a symptom than a cause. Nicholas Wade, reviewing *Green Delusions* for the *New York Times*, got it just right. "Radical environmentalists are not a potent political movement, nor are they likely to become one as long as the establishment can show that it is responding, however grudgingly, to serious dangers like ozone layer depletion, the destruction of species and the possibility of global warming."

"The establishment," unfortunately, has yet to make any such demonstration.

False Choices

Environmentalists live double lives. As activists and politicians, even as technicians and entrepreneurs, they must think their efforts worthwhile, they must believe that they will win. In these roles energy and initiative are essential, and it is optimism, not any depressive realism, that opens paths to profit and advantage. Yet greens are lost without their darker suspicions. Optimism tilts almost inevitably toward complacency, naïveté, and green-wash. Fortunately, and despite all the comforts of pragmatism, greens know this well. In private moments, even public optimists often profess themselves powerless, and dream of upheavals sudden and wrenching enough to open more adequate spaces.

It is a movement commonplace that political diversity is crucial, that radicals back up pragmatists, stiffening their spines, and that the two groups combine into a stronger force than either could muster alone. Despite all bitterness and friction, this is true. It may be, however, that it is not the whole truth. The rest, I think, is that environmentalism is trapped in a tense, sometimes panicked oscillation between liberal optimism and radical despair, a false choice that has hobbled the movement for decades if not from its beginnings.

The big picture was long easy to ignore. The world's political structures were frozen in place, and viewed from the North, life in the peripheries appeared exotic and inconsequential. Besides, in the early glory days of modern environmentalism, faith in pragmatism and liberal reformism was easy to justify. In the United States the 1960s ended with a spate of almost visionary legislation—the Clean Air Act, the Endangered Species Act, the Occupational Safety and Health Act, the National Environmental Policy Act—and with the first Earth Day. In Europe the green parties began their rise less than a decade later. The rest of the world existed, more or less, only in vague outline. It was easy to imagine a future in which rationality would prevail.

In the 1980s the Cold War reached its final denouement. In the United States, the antienvironmental backlash began in earnest with the election of President Reagan, and this was more than a backlash against the greens. By the late 1980s, a new round of economic globalization—embodied in burgeoning cross-border capital flows and trade deals like NAFTA and GATT—revealed economy, ecology, and human rights as a single inextricable tangle. The illusion of "the environment" as a politically distinct area, one that could be saved alone, passed away. The world was roiling, at once shrinking within a tightening electronic net and dividing into warring camps of rich and poor. By 1992 anxiety set the political tone. Despite "success stories" like South Korea and Taiwan, the South as a whole continued its decline. In the North the middle classes imagined themselves among the poor, and realized that their future held no certain comfort, security, or even opportunity. Ecology was part of the stew, but only part.

Today it is easy to believe that matters will worsen in both North and South. Then, Northern democracies will likely be besieged by anxiety, anger, and a terrifying turn to the strange and volatile mix of fear and nationalism that pundits call nativism. Add a long ecological decline, and it's easy to finally imagine what Murray Bookchin has long called ecofascism. Here pessimism would rule, and ideology would teach that only monumental, centralized initiatives are worthy of support.

Ecofascism is no groundless fear. Despair is everywhere in the green movement, and despair has its own crazy logic. A few more decades of decline could themselves seem to justify a functionally (if not explicitly) ecofascist regime. The biologist Garrett Hardin argued as much years ago, in his famous essay "The Tragedy of the Commons" [*Science*, 13 Dec. 1968]: "Coercion is a dirty word to most liberals now, but it need not forever be so." He met a loud chorus of agreement from the apocalyptic greens of the time. More recently, and anxiously, German green jurist Birgit Laubach has warned that the failure to control the ecological crisis within the "democratic constitutional state" may lead to a time when an "ecological emergency state" will appear as the only remaining alternative [see John Ely, "German Debate on the New Constitution," *Capitalism, Nature, Socialism* 3, No. 1, March 1992].

In the end, we fall easily into the apocalyptic narrative because it is difficult to imagine social changes large and rapid enough to avert catastrophe. Things look particularly bad in the South, where the grounds for pessimism are all too manifest. Martin Khor, a tired and dignified Malay activist who emerged during the run-up to the Earth Summit as a spokesman for the South, drew his conclusions even before the Summit, when it was still possible to hope for major new initiatives to emerge from its tortured but still-unprecedented negotiations. Khor, though, expected nothing. "The fading of the Cold War has left the South much more vulnerable to the power of the North," he wrote, and it was "likely that the governments will keep on haggling for years to come, whilst the global environment continues to be degraded and destroyed." He concluded, with an honesty rare among politicians of any stripe, that "the problems of humanity appear too complex and deeply entrenched for Earth to be saved." [*The Future of North-South Relations*, 1992.]

Such pessimism is not lightly held. In researching this book I found that many of the best-informed green activists have decided not to have children, or have yielded to their desire for children only after protracted ambivalence. I also found that optimism was often, as the Italian Marxist theorist Antonio Gramsci remarked long ago, a matter not of intellect but of will. One person I spoke with [in 1991] comes particularly to mind, a thoughtful economist named Lyuba Zarsky who spent a long hour extolling the virtues of a strategy aimed at "greening" markets through a flexible, adaptive politics.

Then, in reply to a question about her deepest feelings, she burst out:

> I'm afraid it's too late, that we won't be able to turn things around, that the world will be so ugly that we won't feel any joy in living in it, that the things I love most will be gone, that my daughter will never know them. When I say an ugly world, I don't just mean a paved-over and polluted world. Even maintaining compassion will be difficult. Sometimes it seems that all our attempts to get a handle on the destruction will just not be enough.

But she soon recovered:

> I feel I have to cultivate a sense of optimism. We all have to. We have to search for and do what can be done even if we just don't know if it will be enough. . . . We're in for a bumpy ride the next fifty years. The next ten to twenty years is going to be crucial. If the greens can get it together not just to fight but to build, the twenty-first century could look pretty different.

It is traditional when discussing matters such as these to call for hope. Christopher Lasch did so in *The True and Only Heaven* [1991], his history of "progress and its critics," but with a twist. In this almost final book, Lasch spoke for a "more vigorous form of hope, which trusts life without denying its tragic character." This is not hope against dread and pessimism, but just the opposite, hope against cheap confidence. "We can fully appreciate this kind of hope only now that the other kind, better described as optimism, has fully revealed itself as a higher form of wishful thinking."

The apocalyptic mood is no guide to action, and it certainly fails as a "more vigorous form of hope," but at least it breaks with denial. As Lasch wrote: "It is the darker voices especially that speak to us now, not because they speak in tones of despair but because they help us to distinguish 'optimism' from hope and thus give us the courage to confront the mounting difficulties that threaten to overwhelm us."

This comment is just, and well timed. Here we stand, at the end of an almost century-long war against communism, with nature groaning beneath our feet. Obviously, new paths must be pioneered, but who will take them? It is the old paths that still claim the most attention, the old paths that are thick with traffic. With energy and vast impatience, people around the planet seek to emulate our lifestyles, if not our fading democratic traditions. Given the vast power of consumer culture, and given its consequences, what surprise is there in the apocalyptic mood?

REALISM

We have about 50% of the world's wealth, but only 6.3% of its population. . . . In this situation, we cannot fail to be the object of envy and resentment. Our real task in the coming period is to devise a pattern of relationships which will permit us to maintain this position of disparity without positive detriment to our national security. To do so, we will have to dispense with all sentimentality and day-dreaming; and our attention will have to be concentrated everywhere on our immediate national objectives. We need not deceive ourselves that we can afford today the luxury of altruism and world-benefaction. . . . We should cease to talk about vague and . . . unreal objectives such as humans rights, the raising of living standards, and democratization. The day is not far off when we are going to have to deal with straight power concepts. The less we are then hampered by idealistic slogans, the better.

George Kennan, "Policy Planning Study No. 23," 1948
cited in Noam Chomsky, *What Uncle Sam Really Wants*, 1993

In the 1950s American sociologist C. Wright Mills coined the term "crackpot realism" to name the peculiar self-delusions of a "power elite" that, looking forward, could see only the indefinite prolonging of its privileged circumstances of life. Now, years later, at the brink of truly dark possibilities, it is a term worthy of revival.

Crackpot realism is realism gone mad, and crackpot realists are those who "in the name of practicality have projected a utopian image of capitalism." They have information in abundance, but "have replaced a responsible interpretation of events with the disguise of events by a maze of public relations." They have the power to move both money and machines, but have confused "the capacity to elaborate alternatives and gauge their consequences with the executive stance" [*The Power Elite*, 1956]. In a world torn between affluence and poverty, the crackpot realists tell the poor, who must live from day to day, that all will be well in the long run. Amidst deepening ecological crisis, they rush to embrace small, cosmetic adaptations.

Yet Mills called them "realists," for thus they flatter themselves. His sarcasm reveals an important problem—"realism" rings with ironic and cynical overtones. It names a violently contested terrain. Engineers, dictators, and politicians of all kinds have long thought themselves to be the true realists, as, from time to time, have radicals. My claim is simply that, in an age of global ecological crisis, realism must presume a break with denial.

In 1987 the Brundtland Commission announced that ecology and economy had merged "into a seamless net of cause and effect" [*Our Common Future*, 1987], and in so doing had demanded a new global bargain between rich and poor. Despite the subsequent collapse of communism and a long series of well-publicized, high-level planetary conclaves—the Earth Summit, the Population Summit, the Social Summit, the Women's Summit, and all the rest—what real progress toward such a bargain have we seen? Almost none. It is time, then, to be blunt about the requirements of a global New Deal, which, if it is to be real, must compel the rich, the major consumers of the planet's resources, to profoundly reform their societies and make room for others. And it must provide the poor with the means to raise their living standards without embarking on a futile effort to copy the Northern model of affluence and development. Above all, it must make "sustainable development" into something more than a cruel slogan.

Condoms, recycling, and energy efficiency can buy time, but they will not ultimately do. A global New Deal must include, according to Robert Goodland, Herman Daly, and Salah El Serafy, a trio of maverick geo-ecologists then writing from within the World Bank, both "population stability" and "income redistribution." Markets, now the defining institutions of public society, must also "learn to function without expansion," and "without wars"; and "economic policy will have to suppress certain activities in order to allow others to expand, so that the sum total remains within the biophysical budget." [*Population, Technology and Lifestyle*, 1992.]

It's a tough brief but an honest one. Visions of a better world come hard these days. The world's division into rich and poor is too obvious and too obviously a wellspring of ecological crisis, to be effectively waved away. As Yale historian Paul Kennedy pointed out in *Preparing for the Twenty-First Century* [1993], the great divide between the rich and the poor is the key to decoding the perpetual sterile pseudodebate between "optimists" and "pessimists." In the end, "the optimists are excited about the world's 'winners' whereas the pessimists worry about the fate of the 'losers.'"

A transition to an ecological society must involve a vast increase in justice and democracy; unfortunately, this does not seem to be the direction of history. Around the world, the welfare state is in deep trouble, and there are many who even say that the dream of equality died in the rubble of the Soviet bloc. Capitalism is triumphant. It has its many variations, but few glorify equity or justice, and few are kind to "the losers." Even this could change, but what good purpose is served by pretending, as today's vogue for optimism demands, such change will be easy?

In 1960, during the heart of the Cold War, Daniel Bell published *The End of Ideology*, a milestone of right-wing society that argued that the failure of communism, its collapse into a Leninist-Stalinist dictatorship, marked not only the end of the dream of socialism but the end of the whole "age of ideology," an age hospitable to large, deterministic social theories, and specifically to "Marxist . . . dogmatism about the inevitability of a deepening economic crisis and polarized class conflict under capitalism." Capitalist society, according to Bell, was far more adaptable than Marx imagined, and far too adaptable to allow any safe pronouncements about its limits.

The greens think otherwise. Though they seldom name this society as "capitalist," their insistence that "growth" must end is the core of the green challenge to capitalism, and though it is often ignored, it is never effectively refuted. Capitalist economies must expand, but the ecosystem that is their host is finite by nature. It cannot tolerate the indefinite growth of any human economy, least of all one as blindly dynamic as modern capitalism. Murray Bookchin has long argued that capitalism is unreformable, that it must "grow or die." His judgment if correct, portends almost inconceivable suffering, and so far there are few data to dispute it.

The core question of ecological politics is, Can this society bend, far and fast and deeply enough, and what strategy will maximize its flexion? It's an uncomfortable question that demands our facing the possibility of failure, of death on an enormous scale, and that asks us to think strategically.

Capitalism has shocked its critics before with its ability to adapt to, and even thrive under, challenging new conditions. It may be that tomorrow holds wave after wave of green technological breakthroughs, a planetary New Deal, a revolution of values, massive ecological restorations, enlightened and effective forms of global government. It may even be that "development" can be unlinked from primitive physical "growth," that capitalism can somehow find a steady state that avoids both war and economic collapse. We do not know. What we do know, or should, is that none of this will happen by itself.

Another Realism

We may all be riding on "spaceship Earth," but as German essayist Hans Magnus Enzensberger pointed out decades ago, some of us ride first class and some in steerage ["A Critique of Political Ecology," *Dreamers of the Absolute*, 1988]. Traditional realists see this as a fact of life, and even extoll the virtues of poverty. In the business section of the daily newspaper, if not on the editorial page, unemployment is necessary, for it keeps inflation down and bond prices up, just as low environmental and labor standards in the Third

World keep prices down. As American policy analyst George Kennan explained back in 1948, in days less sensitive to the demands of liberal rhetoric, "Our real task in the coming period is to devise a pattern of relationships which will permit us to maintain this position of disparity without positive detriment to our national security."

Such postures have lost any claim to the name of realism. Not all future Third World regimes, Robert Heilbroner has noted, will "view the vast difference between first class and cattle class with the forgiving eyes of their predecessors," [quoted in Homer-Dixon, *On the Threshold*], and the same can be said about the losers in general. Moreover, since weapons proliferation is at all levels unimpeded by any serious efforts at control, we must assume that the poor of the future will be armed to the teeth. They will be bound to the rich by the global economy and by planetary TV, but it will be a loose and unstable coupling. Barring new departures, competition and violence will only increase, as the ecological plunder will continue.

Though it is not a pleasant thought, it seems that we, and our children, will live to see a prematurely discarded theory of 1960s political apocalypticism finally tested. That theory is that things must get worse before they can get better. It posits an ugly futurism, and it has dispiriting consequences, but look hard at the emerging world and say that its day is not coming round at last.

What, then, is realism? Worldwatch's Lester Brown says that we must either "turn things around quickly or the self-reinforcing internal dynamic of the deterioration-and-decline scenario will take over," [*State of the World*, 1992], and then argues for an "Environmental Revolution" as the best hope. His strategy is to say much that is chilling and yet to remain upbeat and, when it comes to politics, abstract. We have "underestimated what it will take" to reverse the trends now threatening to overcome us, and "can no longer separate the future habitability of the planet from the current international distribution of wealth." Large statements, both of these, but they are left to float in warm generality. "Stabilizing the climate," will require "restructuring the world's economy to phase out fossil fuels," but when it comes to how this can be done there is only anticlimax: vague talk of gradually shifting investments, reforming technologies, and changing values. [*Worldwatch*, May/June 1992].

Here, too, there is implicit a political theory—large change will come exclusively by small degrees. No need to solve problems like regulating the planetary corporations, halting the spread of nuclear arms, or substantially redistributing land and wealth. We will wake one day to find that incremental reforms have made all the difference. Brown first tells us the environmental revolution is not political, but rather a cousin to the industrial and agricultural revolutions. He then explains that we do not have the kind of time that they required but even this does not inspire him to discomforting conclusions. If there must be changes that will not come politely, they are best left unremarked.

There is a method here. Worldwatch regales us with fact-laden overviews of ecological deterioration, then leavens its message with a large measure of bright possibilities, from green taxes to windmills. It makes good reading, for it balances pessimism with optimism, and there is nothing to offend. Change makes good rational sense, and change is necessary, so change will come. Even land reform, which once rang throughout the world in calls for "land and liberty" and heroic, bloody peasant uprisings, will come, perhaps easily. First necessity must be established, and this isn't too diffi-cult—the facts are compelling enough. Worldwatch's Holly Brough can therefore review a grim situation and conclude, "If the Earth is to survive and its people prosper, land reform is indispensable." Then comes the optimism: "Donors and developing states now may be less likely to per-ceive radical land reform as a Communist conspiracy and more as a policy capable of addressing the needs of both the environment and the people." [*Worldwatch*, Jan./Feb. 1991.]

These are reassuring words, but they contain an optimism that quite overwhelms realism. Meaningful land reform will *not* come easily. Elites have long used anticommunist ideology as an excuse to oppose the re-distribution of land, and now they must do without it. But they will find new excuses easily enough. In both the United States and Mexico, "effi-ciency" is the favorite justification for the destruction of both peasant and family farming.

Herman Daly, in his 1994 farewell lecture to World Bank staff, addressed this crucial problem of narrow self-interest and the refusal to change. Arguing that chronic high unemployment, coupled with the ecological crisis, makes it imperative to shift to policies that promote employment and penalize pollution and the depletion of resources, he invited his listeners to consider the role that a greatly reformed future version of the Bank could play in forcing such policies on the North. "The shift," he suggested, "should be a key part of structural adjustment, but should be pioneered in the North. . . . It is absurd to expect any sacrifice for sustainability in the South if similar measures have not first been taken in the North."

If this is a dream as wild as revolution, if the World Bank, the IMF, and the whole global institutional apparatus must be deeply reformed before a clear path to change can emerge, this at least gives us a metric by which to measure the halting progress of the eco-diplomats, a sieve with which to separate rhetoric and good intentions from meaningful reforms.

The story, of course, does not end here. There are good reasons to believe that change is possible, reasons that range from the green movement itself, to the technological and economic reforms we hear so much about from policy activists, to the obvious fact that greens are hardly alone in seeing the state of the world as intolerable. To see hope in concrete form, one need only pick a subject, from water pollution to family planning to democracy. A few hours of research will generally reveal ideas in profusion, and demonstrate that it is politics, and not any lack of technological or policy alternatives, that holds us in this stasis.

The strongest grounds for hope is this—that time and resources both remain. If, fifty years hence, our children find themselves so in thrall to necessity that they cannot even imagine a better world, it will not be because they met their inexorable fate, but because we failed now, when the broad shape of the future is still open to dispute. Realism lies in acknowledging that change is a practical necessity, that contrived optimism must be rejected, that we cannot always be circumspect about the realities of power. It lies, most of all, in admitting that there is no easy path to a green transition, and perhaps no path at all—for powerful minorities everywhere do not want change.

Last Words

Environmentalism has a peculiar history. As a modern movement, it arose in a century shaped by war, and in particular by the long war—not always cold— against the "reds." Greens have generally remained apart from that war, for real socialism was a pretty unattractive proposition, and it cast a long, dim shadow. No wonder that greens, seeking a new politics, have long claimed to be neither left nor right.

The time for such political innocence is over. This has been a dark century, but the planet is wavering at the edge of even darker possibilities. Given the key role they are fated to play in the politics of an ever-shrinking world, it is past time for environmentalists to face their own history, in which they have too often stood not for justice and freedom, or even for realism, but merely for the comforts and aesthetics of affluent nature lovers. They have no choice. History will judge greens by whether they stand with the world's poor.

Environmentalism emerged in a world where left and even liberal radicalism were lost in the cold corridors of Soviet-style communism. Whatever price the greens paid for their independence from the left tradition, it allowed them to face the world anew, to claim dozens of crucial cultural, political, and technological domains—from safe energy systems to greener cities—for their evolving and fluid agenda. Before environmentalism's rebirth in the late 1960s, even visionary reformers rarely saw such things as transportation systems or diet as intimately linked to the prospect for freedom and dignity. Today millions take it for granted that this is so.

The green movement is reeling under an antienvironmental assault, but there are grounds for hope about its future. Even its long tradition of apolitical, technological pragmatism, its concerns with nuts and bolts, has a bright side. Pragmatism can yield results. Greens, often enemies of "free markets," have generally come to their position less by ideologically colored analysis than by observing what most economists still will not admit—that left to their own devices, markets shift ecological and social costs into the "commons," and destroy both nature and human communities in the process.

We find ourselves just now in a strange, strained lull. Our real conditions of life are increasingly visible. There is a pervasive sense that broad change is necessary, and even that it is imminent. Brush aside the charge that ecology is merely a form of nostalgia, and ecology's real lesson is apparent. The past is no guide, the future must be different. Always, other matters force ecology from the front pages, but always it returns, each time more insistently.

The official UNCED treaties prove the point, for there is, in them, little talk of global poverty, of the dark sides of the new economy, of the corporations, of militarism, of democracy. Yet these are the decisive matters, those that will determine our fate. If there was hope in Rio, it was because these subjects, the true agenda of the future, were nevertheless present. They were there in the "alternative treaties" hammered out by thousands of activists from around the world, in excited, staccato conversation, and, most important of all, in the globally shared sense of an emerging common agenda, common movement, common project.

We may be forgiven for being unfamiliar with the alternative treaties. The *New York Times*, in all its reams of Earth Summit coverage, did not mention them at all, while the *Los Angeles Times* graced them with a single snide report, "Strong Treaties Elude Even Activists at Earth Summit," that seemed to delight in the fact of friction, and the necessity of compromise, between Northern and Southern activists.

Whatever the Earth Summit's failures, it broadcast waves of lucid, radical realism around the world. Here is a fragment found soon after Rio on Econet, the North American node of the green movement's semiofficial global computer network. It was entitled "Celebrating the Failure of UNCED" [*Peace News*, London, July 1992], and it captured a mood that has not been altogether forgotten.

What is needed now is the mobilization of ever larger and more vocal social movements rather than more conversation for conservation. Mainstream Northern

NGOs are happy to speak of such movements (and, to a very much lesser degree, support them) when, and only when, the movements are in the South. None of them are building or even supporting true people's movements in the North. They have a membership, usually drawn from liberal professionals, which they encourage to give money, buy T-shirts, and send in lobby cards—but which they actively discourage from taking their own initiative and expressing their rage, horror, or fear over what we are doing to ourselves.

It may be difficult for us to understand that this is not an isolated voice. Change did not come at Rio, but it did announce itself, and the announcement demands blunt repetition—it is long past time to see that the future does not lie with the "already over-emphasized and over-funded national compromise branch of our movement," as it was so precisely called by the grassroots People's Alliance for the Earth Summit.

As awareness of biophysical limits increases, it will become difficult to keep faith with small remedies. It is not impossible that soon ecological deterioration will routinely inspire echoes of William James's call for a "moral equivalent of war," [*Essays on Faith and Morals*, 1949], only this time as a war of cooperation, a war to save the earth. That is what it will take.

Somehow, we must open the future, yet we are haunted by the past, by ghosts of old ideologies, old canards, old dichotomies that obscure the real conditions of our lives. And what are those conditions? That we do not all share the same interests; that it is late—too late for purity, too late for simple utopias, too late for the dream of retreating to "the land," too late for the eco-politician's fantasy of an altogether polite, rationally negotiated global transition. It is *not* too late to act, or to recall the old imperative to "educate, agitate, and organize," or to remember that the deepest springs of hope lie in engagement, in making the choice to make a difference.

We inhabit a paradox. Our age is tragic, and catastrophe does threaten, but though the future is obscure, it does not come to us inexorable and inescapable. Our tragedy lies in the richness of the available alternatives, and in the fact that so few of them are ever seriously explored. It lies in the rigidity of war machines, the legacies of colonialism, the inflexibilities of the industrial tradition, the solaces of consumerism, the cynicism born of long disappointment, the habits of power. No wonder, given all this, that our age seems not merely tragic but tragic in the classical sense, that despite all possibility, we seem trapped in just that remorseless "working of things" that the Greeks saw as the core of tragedy.

STEVEN WEINBERG *capped a lifetime dedication to the exploration of elementary particle physics with a Nobel Prize in 1979 for his theoretical work in explaining the unifying factors of the electromagnetic and the weak nuclear force. His many books and publications include* Dreams of a Final Theory: The Search for the Fundamental Laws of Nature *(1992). His article, "What Can We Know About the Universe?" looks far beyond our present confines into a distant future in which Weinberg asks whether there are limits to man's explanation of the origins of life and matter. "What Can We Know About the Universe?" is adapted from an article entitled "The Limits of Knowledge," published as "Life in the Universe" in the* Scientific American *of October 1994, and reprinted in* Life in the Universe *(1995).*

STEVEN WEINBERG

WHAT CAN WE KNOW ABOUT THE UNIVERSE?

In Walt Whitman's often quoted poem "When I Heard the Learn'd Astronomer," the poet tells how, being shown the astronomer's charts and diagrams, he became tired and sick and wandered off by himself to look up "in perfect silence at the stars." Generations of scientists have been annoyed by these lines. The sense of beauty and wonder does not become atrophied through the work of science, as Whitman implies. The night sky is as beautiful as ever, to astronomers as well as to poets. And as we understand more and more about nature, the scientist's sense of wonder has not diminished but has rather become sharper, more narrowly focused on the mysteries that still remain.

The nearby stars that Whitman could see without a telescope are now not so mysterious. Massive computer codes simulate the nuclear reactions at the stars' cores and follow the flow of energy by convection and radiation to their visible surfaces, explaining both their present appearance and how they have evolved. The observation in 1987 of gamma rays and neutrinos from the supernova in the Large Magellanic Cloud provided dramatic confirmation of the theory of stellar structure and evolution. These theories are themselves beautiful to us, and knowing why Betelgeuse is red may even add to the pleasure of looking at the winter sky.

But there are plenty of mysteries left. Of what sort of matter are galaxies and galaxy clusters made? How did the stars and planets and galaxies form? How widespread in the universe are habitats suitable for life? How did the earth's oceans and atmosphere form? How did life start? How does the brain think?

We may be very far from the solution of some of these problems. Still, we can guess what kinds of solutions they will have in a way that was not possible 150 years ago. New ideas and insights will be needed, which we can expect to find within the boundaries of science as we know it.

Then there are mysteries at the outer boundaries of our science, matters that we cannot hope to explain in terms of what we already know. When we explain anything we observe, it is in terms of scientific principles that are themselves explained in terms of deeper principles. Following this chain of explanations, we are led at last to laws of nature that cannot be explained within the boundaries of contemporary science. And in dealing with life and many other aspects of nature, our explanations have a historical component. Some historical facts are accidents that can never be explained, except perhaps statistically: we can never explain precisely why life on the earth takes the form it does, although we can hope to show that some forms are more likely than others. We can explain a great deal, even where history plays a role, in terms of the conditions with which the universe began, as well as the laws of nature. But how do we explain the initial conditions? A further complex of puzzles overhangs the laws of nature and the initial conditions. It concerns the dual role of intelligent life—as part of the universe we seek to explain, and as the explainer.

The laws of nature as we currently understand them allow us to trace the observed expansion of the universe back to what would be a true beginning, a moment when the universe was infinitely hot and dense, some 10 to 20 billion years [10 to 20 thousand million years] ago. We do not have enough confidence in the applicability of these laws at extreme temperatures and densities to be sure that there really was such a moment, much less to work out all the initial conditions, if there were any. For the present, we cannot do better than to describe the initial conditions of the universe at a time about 10^{-12} second after the nominal moment of infinite temperature.

The temperature of the universe had dropped by then to about 10^{15} degrees, cool enough for us to apply our physical theories. At these temperatures the universe would have been filled with a gas consisting of all the type of particles known to high-energy nuclear physics, together with their anti-particles, continually being annihilated and created in their collisions. As the universe continued to expand and cool, creation became slower than annihilation, and almost all the particles and antiparticles disappeared. If there had not been a small excess of electrons over antielectrons, and quarks over antiquarks, then ordinary particles like electrons and quarks would be virtually absent in the universe today. It is this early excess of matter over antimatter, estimated as one part in about 10^{10}, that survived to form light atomic nuclei three minutes later, then after a million years to form atoms and later to be cooked to heavier elements in stars, ultimately to provide the material out of which life would arise. The one part in 10^{10} excess of matter over antimatter is one of the key initial conditions that determined the future development of the universe.

In addition, there may exist other types of particles, not yet observed in our laboratories, that interact more weakly with one another than do quarks and electrons and that therefore would have annihilated relatively slowly. Large numbers of these exotic particles would have been left over from the early universe, forming the "dark matter" that now apparently makes up much of the mass of the universe.

Finally, although it is generally assumed that when the universe was 10^{-12} second old its contents were pretty nearly the same everywhere, small inhomogeneities must have existed that triggered the formation, millions of years later, of the first galaxies and stars. We cannot directly observe any inhomogeneities at times earlier than about a million years after the beginning, when the universe first became transparent. Astronomers are currently engaged in mapping minute variations in the intensity of the cosmic microwave radiation background that was emitted at that time, using them to infer the primordial distribution of matter. This information can in turn be used to deduce the initial inhomogeneities at 10^{-12} second after the beginning.

From the austere viewpoint of fundamental physics, the history of the universe is just an illustrative example of the laws of nature. At the deepest level to which we have been able to trace our explanations, those laws take the form of quantum field theories. When quantum mechanics is applied to a field such as the electromagnetic field, it is found that the energy and momentum of the field come in bundles, or quanta, that are observed in the laboratory as particles. The modern Standard Model posits an electromagnetic field, whose quanta are photons; an electron field, whose quanta are electrons and antielectrons; and a number of other fields whose quanta are particles called leptons and antileptons. There are various quark fields whose quanta are quarks and antiquarks, and there are 11 other fields whose quanta are the particles that transmit the weak and strong forces that act on the elementary particles.

The Standard Model is certainly not the final law of nature. Even in its simplest form it contains a number of arbitrary features. Some 18 numerical parameters exist whose values have to be taken from experiment, and the multiplicity of types of quarks and leptons is unexplained. Also, one aspect of the model is still uncertain: we are not sure of the details of the mechanism that gives masses to the quarks, electrons and other particles. This is the puzzle that was to have been solved by the now canceled Superconducting Super Collider. We hope it will be unraveled by the Large Hadron Collider being planned at CERN near Geneva. Finally, the model is incomplete; it does not include gravitation. We have a good field theory of gravitation, the General Theory of Relativity, but the quantum version of this theory breaks down at very high energies.

It is possible that all these problems will find their solution in a new kind of theory known as string theory. The point particles of quantum field theory are reinterpreted in string theory as tiny, extended one-dimensional objects called strings. These strings can exist in various modes of vibration, each mode appearing in the laboratory as a different type of particle. String theory not only provides a quantum description of gravitation that makes sense at all energies; one of the modes of vibration of a string would appear as a particle with the properties of the graviton, the quantum of the gravitational field, so string theory even offers an explanation of why gravitation exists. Further, there are versions of string theory that predict something like the menu of fields incorporated in the Standard Model.

But string theory has had no successes yet in explaining or predicting any of the numerical parameters of the Standard Model. Moreover, strings are much too small for us to detect directly the stringy nature of elementary particles; a string is smaller relative to an atomic nucleus than is a nucleus relative to a mountain. The intellectual investment now being made in string theory without the slightest encouragement from experiment is unprecedented in the history of science. Yet for now, it offers our best hope for a deeper understanding of the laws of nature.

The present gaps in our knowledge of the laws of nature stand in the way of explaining the initial conditions of the universe, at 10^{-12} second after the nominal beginning, in terms of the history of the universe at earlier times. Calculations in the past few years have made it seem likely that the tiny excess of quarks and electrons over antiquarks and antielectrons at this time was produced a little earlier, at a temperature of about 10^{16} degrees. At that moment the universe went through a phase transition, something like the freezing of water, in which the known elementary particles for the first time acquired mass. But we cannot explain why the excess produced in this way should be one part in 10^{10}, or calculate its precise value, until we understand the details of the mass-producing mechanism.

The other initial condition, the degree of inhomogeneity in the early universe, may trace back to even earlier times. In our quantum field theories of elementary particles, including the simplest version of the Standard Model, several fields pervade the universe, taking non-zero values even in supposedly empty space. In the present state of the universe, these fields have reached equilibrium values, which minimize the energy density of the vacuum. This vacuum energy density, also known as the cosmological constant, can be measured through the gravitational field that it produces. It is apparently very small.

In some modern theories of the early universe, however, there was a very early time when these fields had not yet reached their equilibrium values, so that the vacuum would have had an enormous energy density. This energy would have produced a rapid expansion of the universe, known as inflation. Tiny inhomogeneities that would have been produced by quantum fluctuations before this inflation would have been magnified in the expansion and could have produced the much larger inhomogeneities that millions of years later triggered the formation of galaxies. It has even been conjectured that the inflation that began the expansion of the visible universe did not occur throughout the cosmos. It may instead have been just one local episode in an eternal succession of local inflations that occur at random throughout an infinite universe. If this is true, then the problem of initial conditions disappears; there was no initial moment.

In this picture, our local expansion may have begun with some special ingredients or inhomogeneities, but like the forms of life on the earth, these could be understood only in a statistical sense. Unfortunately, at the time of inflation gravitation was so strong that quantum gravitational effects were important. So these ideas will remain speculative until we understand the quantum theory of gravitation—perhaps in terms of something like a string theory.

The experience of the past 150 years has shown that life is subject to the same laws of nature as is inanimate matter. Nor is there any evidence of a grand design in the origin or evolution of life. There are well-known problems in the description of consciousness in terms of the working of the brain. They arise because we each have special knowledge of our own consciousness that does not come to us from the senses. In principle, no obstacle stands in the way of explaining the *behavior* of other people in terms of neurology and physiology and, ultimately, in terms of physics and history. When we have succeeded in this endeavour, we should find that part of the explanation is a program of neural activity that we will recognize as corresponding to our own consciousness.

But as much as we would like to take a unified view of nature, we keep encountering a stubborn duality in the role of intelligent life in the universe, as both subject and student. We see this even at the deepest level of modern physics. In quantum mechanics the state of any system is described by a mathematical object known as the wave function. According to the interpretation of quantum mechanics worked out in Copenhagen in the early 1930s, the rules for calculating the wave function are of a very different character from the principles used to interpret it. On one hand, there is the Schrödinger equation, which describes in a perfectly deterministic way how the wave function of any system changes with time. Then, quite separate, there is a set of principles that tells how to use the wave function to calculate the probabilities of various possible outcomes when someone makes a measurement.

The Copenhagen interpretation holds that when we measure any quantity, such as position or momentum, we are intervening in a way that causes an unpredictable change in the wave function, resulting in a wave function for which the measured quantity has some definite value, in a manner that cannot be described by the deterministic Schrödinger equation. For instance, before a measurement the wave function of a spinning electron is generally a sum of terms corresponding to different directions of the electron's spin; in such a state the electron cannot be said to be spinning in any particular direction. If we measure whether the electron is spinning clockwise or counterclockwise around some axis, however, we somehow change the electron's wave function so that it is definitely spinning one way or the other. Measurement is thus regarded as something intrinsically different from anything else in nature. And although opinions differ, it is hard to identify anything special that qualifies some process to be called a measurement, except its effect on a conscious mind.

Among physicists and philosophers one finds at least four different reactions to the Copenhagen interpretation. The first is simply to accept it as it stands. This attitude is mostly limited to those who are attracted to the old, dualistic worldview that puts life and consciousness on a different footing from the rest of nature. The second attitude is to accept the rules of the Copenhagen interpretation for practical purposes, without worrying about their ultimate interpretation. This attitude is by far the most common among working physicists. The third approach is to try to avoid these problems by changing quantum mechanics in some way. So far no such attempt has found much acceptance among physicists.

The final approach is to take the Schrödinger equation seriously, to give up the dualism of the Copenhagen interpretation and to try to explain its successful rules through a description of measurers and their apparatus in terms of the same deterministic evolution of the wave function that governs everything else. When we measure some quantity (like the direction of an electron's spin), we put the system in an environment (for instance, a magnetic field) where its energy (or momentum) has a strong dependence on the value of the measured quantity. According to the Schrödinger equation, the different terms in the wave function that correspond to different energies will oscillate at rates proportional to these energies.

A measurement thus makes the terms of the wave function that correspond to different values of a measured quantity, such as an electron spin, oscillate rapidly at different rates, so they cannot interfere with one another in any future measurement, just as the signals from radio stations broadcasting at widely spaced frequencies do not interfere. In this way, a measurement causes the history of the universe for practical purposes to diverge into different non-interfering tracks, one for each possible value of the measured quantity.

Yet how do we explain the Copenhagen rules for calculating the probabilities for these different "worldtracks" in a world governed by the completely deterministic Schrödinger equation? Progress has recently been made on this problem, but it is not yet definitely solved. (For what it is worth, I prefer this last approach, although the second has much to recommend it.)

It is also difficult to avoid talking about living observers when we ask why our physical principles are what they are. Modern quantum field theory and string theory can be understood as answers to the problem of reconciling quantum mechanics and special relativity in such a way that experiments are guaranteed to give sensible results. We require that the results of our dynamical calculations must satisfy conditions known to field theorists as unitarity, positivity and cluster decomposition. Roughly speaking, these conditions require that probabilities always add up to 100 percent, that they are always positive and that those observed in distant experiments are not related.

This is not so easy. If we try to write down some dynamical equations that will automatically give results consistent with some of these conditions, we usually find that the results violate the other conditions. It seems that any relativistic quantum theory that satisfies all these conditions must appear at sufficiently low energy like a quantum field theory. That is presumably why nature at accessible energies is so well described by the quantum field theory known as the Standard Model.

Also, so far as we can tell, the only mathematically consistent relativistic quantum theories that satisfy these conditions at all energies and that involve gravitation are string theories. Further, the student of string theory who asks why one makes this or that mathematical assumption is told that otherwise one would violate physical principles like unitarity and positivity. But why are these the correct conditions to impose on the results of all imaginable experiments if the laws of nature allow the possibility of a universe that contains no living beings to carry out experiments?

This question does not intrude on much of the actual work of theoretical physics, but it becomes urgent when we seek to apply quantum mechanics to the whole universe. At present, we do not understand even in principle how to calculate or interpret the wave function of the universe, and we cannot resolve these problems by requiring that all experiments should give sensible results, because by definition there is no observer outside the universe who can experiment on it.

These mysteries are heightened when we reflect how surprising it is that the laws of nature and the initial conditions of the universe should allow for the existence of beings who could observe it. Life as we know it would be impossible if any one of several physical quantities had slightly different values. The best known of these quantities is the energy of one of the excited states of the carbon 12 nucleus. There is an essential step in the chain of nuclear reactions that build up heavy elements in stars. In this step, two helium nuclei join together to form the unstable nucleus of beryllium 8, which sometimes before fissioning absorbs another helium nucleus, forming carbon 12 in this excited state. The carbon 12 nucleus then emits a photon and decays into the stable state of lowest energy. In subsequent nuclear reactions carbon is built up into oxygen and nitrogen and the other heavy elements necessary for life. But the capture of helium by beryllium 8 is a resonant process, whose reaction rate is a sharply peaked function of the energies of the nuclei involved. If the energy of the excited state of carbon 12 were just a little higher, the rate of its formation would be much less, so that almost all the beryllium 8 nuclei would fission into helium nuclei before carbon could be formed. The universe would then consist almost entirely of hydrogen and helium, without the ingredients for life.

Opinions differ as to the degree to which the constants of nature must be fine-tuned to make life necessary. There are independent reasons to expect an excited state of carbon 12 near the resonant energy. But one constant does seem to require an incredible fine-tuning: it is the vacuum energy, or cosmological constant, mentioned in connection with inflationary cosmologies.

Although we cannot calculate this quantity, we can calculate some contributions to it (such as the energy of quantum fluctuations in the gravitational field that have wavelengths no shorter than about 10^{-33} centimeter). These contributions come out about 120 orders of magnitude larger than the maximum value allowed by our observations of the present rate of cosmic expansion. If the various contributions to the vacuum energy did not nearly cancel, then, depending on the value of the total vacuum energy, the universe either would go through a complete cycle of expansion and contraction before life could arise or would expand so rapidly that no galaxies or stars could form.

Thus, the existence of life of any kind seems to require a cancellation between different contributions to the vacuum energy, accurate to about 120 decimal places. It is possible that this cancellation will be explained in terms of some future theory. So far, in string theory as well as in quantum field theory, the vacuum energy involves arbitrary constants, which must be carefully adjusted to make the total vacuum energy small enough for life to be possible.

All these problems can be solved without supposing that life or consciousness plays any special role in the fundamental laws of nature or initial conditions. It may be that what we now call the constants of nature actually vary from one part of the universe to another. (Here "different parts of the universe" could be understood in various senses. The phrase could, for example, refer to different local expansions arising from episodes of inflation in which the fields pervading the universe took different values or else to the different quantum-mechanical worldtracks that arise in some versions of quantum cosmology.) If this is the case, then it would not be surprising to find that life is possible in some parts of the universe, though perhaps not in most. Naturally, any living beings who evolve to the point where they can measure the constants of nature will always find that these constants have values that allow life to exist. The constants have other values in other parts of the universe, but there is no one there to measure them. (This is one version of what is sometimes called the anthropic principle.) Still, this presumption would not indicate any special role for life in the fundamental laws, any more than the fact that the sun has a planet on which life is possible indicates that life played a role in the origin of the solar system. The fundamental laws would be those that describe the *distribution* of values of the constants of nature between different parts of the universe, and in these laws life would play no special role.

If the content of science is ultimately impersonal, its conduct is part of human culture, and not the least interesting part. Some philosophers and sociologists have gone so far as to claim that scientific principles are, in whole or in part, social constructions, like the rules of contract law or contract bridge. Most working scientists find this "social constructivist" point of view inconsistent with their own experience. Still, there is no doubt that the social context of science has become increasingly important to scientists, as we need to ask society to provide us with more and more expensive tools: accelerators, space vehicles, neutron sources, genome projects and so on.

It does not help that some politicians and journalists assume the public is interested only in those aspects of science that promise immediate practical benefits to technology or medicine. Some work on the most interesting problems of biological or physical science does have obvious practical value, but some does not, especially research that addresses problems lying at the boundaries of scientific knowledge. To earn society's support, we have to make true what we often claim: that today's basic scientific research is part of the culture of our times.

Whatever barriers now exist to communication between scientists and the public, they are not impermeable. Isaac Newton's *Principia* could at first be understood only by a handful of Europeans. Then the news that we and our universe are governed by precise, knowable laws did eventually diffuse throughout the civilized world. The theory of evolution was strenuously opposed at first; now creationists are an increasingly isolated minority. Today's research at the boundaries of science explores environments of energy and time and distance far removed from those of everyday life and often can be described only in esoteric mathematical language. But in the long run, what we learn about why the world is the way it is will become part of everyone's intellectual heritage.

CONTINUATION OF TEXT ACKNOWLEDGMENTS FROM PAGE 4:

Excerpt from Chapter 18 "The Political Order and Foreseeability" from *The Art of Conjecture* by Bertrand de Jouvenel and translated by Nikita Lary. Copyright © 1967 by Basic Books, Inc. Reprinted by permission of HarperCollins Publishers, Inc.

Excerpts from "Epilogue" from *Futurehype* (1989) by Max Dublin. Copyright © 1989, 1991, by Max Dublin. Used by permission of Max Dublin and Dutton Signet, a division of Penguin Books USA Inc.

'Transitions to a More Sustainable World" from *The Quark and the Jaguar: Adventures in the Simple and the Complex* © 1994 by Murray Gell-Mann. Used with permission of W. H. Freeman and Company.

Excerpt from "Technology, Industrialization, and the Idea of Progress in America," by Merritt Roe Smith, from *Responsible Science* by Kevin Byrne, Editor. Copyright © 1986 by Gustavus Adolphus College. Reprinted by permission of HarperCollins Publishers, Inc.

"Perspectives" (pp. 152–63) from *Dawn of a Millennium: Beyond Evolution and Culture* by Eric Harth (first published USA and Canada by Little, Brown & Co. 1990; UK by Penguin Books, Harmondsworth, 1991). Copyright © by Eric Harth 1990. By permission of Little, Brown and Company; and reproduced by permission of Penguin Books Ltd.

Excerpts from "Studying the Future" from *Embracing the Future: Meeting the Challenge of Our Changing World*, Thomas L. Saaty and Larry W. Boone. Copyright © 1990 Thomas L. Saaty and Larry W. Boone. Reproduced with permission of Greenwood Publishing Group, Inc., Westport, CT.

Extract from *The Next Three Futures* (Adamantine Studies on the 21st Century, vol. no. 4) by W. Warren Wagar reprinted by arrangement with Adamantine Press Limited.

Excerpts from "Conclusions and Recommendations." © The Independent Commission on Population and Quality of Life (1996). Reprinted from *Caring for the Future: Making the Next Decades Provide a Life Worth Living: Report of the Independent Commission on Population and the Quality of Life* (1996) by permission of Oxford University Press.

Excerpts from *The Futurological Congress* by Stanislaw Lem, translated by Michael Kandel, English translation © 1974 by The Continuum Publishing Corporation, reprinted by permission of the Continuum Publishing Company; and by permission of Random House UK Ltd. (published in the UK by Martin Secker & Warburg, 1985).

"January First" by Octavio Paz, translated by Elizabeth Bishop, from *The Complete Poems 1927–1979* by Elizabeth Bishop (and included in *A Draft of Shadows*, ed. and trans. Eliot Weinberger et al, 1979). Copyright © 1979, 1983 by Alice Helen Methfessel. Reprinted

by permission of Farrar, Straus & Giroux, Inc.

"Scientific Humanism and Religion" by Edward O. Wilson, from *Challenges to the Enlightenment: In Defense of Reason and Science*, eds Paul Kurtz and Timothy Madigan, 1994, originally published in *Free Inquiry*, Spring 1991. By kind permission of Free Inquiry.

"After the End of Social Engineering" and "The Spiritualization of Economic Life." Reprinted with the permission of The Free Press, a Division of Simon & Schuster, from *Trust: The Social Virtues and the Creation of Prosperity* by Francis Fukuyama copyright © 1995 by Francis Fukuyama; and by permission of International Creative Management, Inc.; and reproduced by permission of Penguin Books Ltd (published in the UK by Hamish Hamilton, 1995).

"Prospect: On Being Fully Human" from *The End of Economic Man*, Third Edition by George P. Brockway. Copyright © 1995, 1993, 1991 by George P. Brockway. Reprinted by permission of W. W. Norton & Company, Inc.

"The Centerless Whole." Reprinted with the permission of Simon & Schuster from *The Death of Money* by Joel Kurtzman. Copyright © 1993 by Joel Kurtzman.

"Democracy Means Paying Attention" from *The Good Society* by Robert N. Bellah et al. Copyright © 1991 by Robert N. Bellah, Richard Madsen, William M. Sullivan, Ann Swidler and Steven M. Tipton. Reprinted by permission of Alfred A. Knopf Inc.

Excerpt from Nelson Mandela's Address to the United Nations General Assembly, 1994, from the *Provisional Verbatim Records of the General Assembly of the United Nations*, A/49 PV, 14, New York, 1994.

Introduction from *The Evolution of Progress* by Owen Paepke. Copyright © 1992 by Owen Paepke. Reprinted by permission of Random House, Inc.

Excerpts from "A Refuge and a Hope" and "The Limits of Utopia." Reprinted by permission of the publisher from *Commitment and Community: Communes and Utopias in Sociological Perspective* by Rosabeth Moss Kanter, Cambridge, Mass.: Harvard University Press, Copyright © 1972 by the President and Fellows of Harvard College.

Extracts from "Apocalyptics" and "Realism" from *Divided Planet: The Ecology of Rich and Poor* by Tom Athanasiou, Copyright © 1996 by Tom Athanasiou. By permission of Little, Brown and Company; and by permission of Random House UK Ltd. (published in the UK by Martin Secker & Warburg as *Slow Reckoning: The Ecology of a Divided Planet*).

"What Can We Know About the Universe?" by Steven Weinberg adapted from the article originally entitled "The Limits of Knowledge," published as "Life in the Universe," *Scientific American*, 1994, and reprinted in *Life in the Universe*, W.H. Freeman, New York, 1995. Copyright © 1994 Steven Weinberg. By kind permission of Steven Weinberg.